A
PORTRAIT OF BRITAIN
UNDER
TUDORS AND STUARTS
1485–1688

BY

MARY R. PRICE

AND

C. E. L. MATHER

ILLUSTRATED BY

R. S. SHERRIFFS

OXFORD
AT THE CLARENDON PRESS

Oxford University Press

OXFORD LONDON NEW YORK

GLASGOW TORONTO MELBOURNE WELLINGTON

CAPE TOWN IBADAN NAIROBI DAR ES SALAAM LUSAKA ADDIS ABABA

DELHI BOMBAY CALCUTTA MADRAS KARACHI DACCA

KUALA LUMPUR SINGAPORE HONG KONG TOKYO

First edition 1954
Reprinted 1957, 1960, 1964, 1966, 1969
Reprinted as Paperback in 1976

Printed in Great Britain
at the University Press, Oxford
by Vivian Ridler
Printer to the University

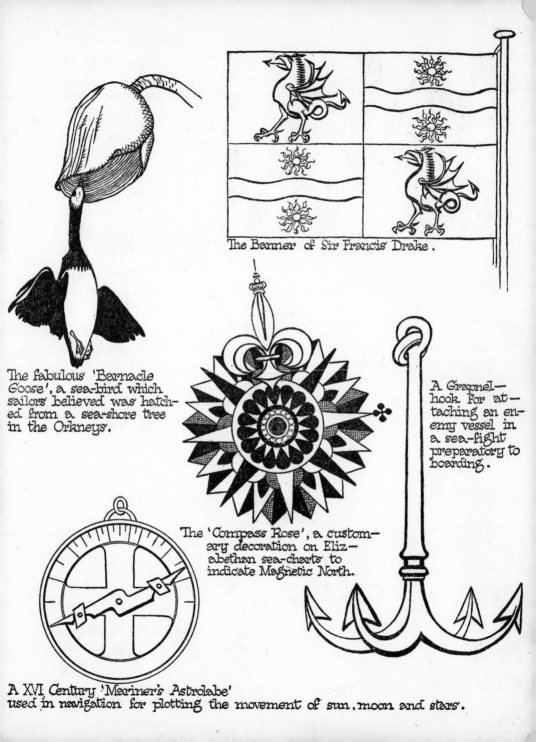

The Banner of Sir Francis Drake.

The fabulous 'Barnacle Goose', a sea-bird which sailors believed was hatched from a sea-shore tree in the Orkneys.

A Grapnel-hook for attaching an enemy vessel in a sea-fight preparatory to boarding.

The 'Compass Rose', a customary decoration on Elizabethan sea-charts to indicate Magnetic North.

A XVI Century 'Mariner's Astrolabe' used in navigation for plotting the movement of sun, moon and stars.

THE OXFORD INTRODUCTION
TO BRITISH HISTORY

General Editor: H. S. DEIGHTON

THE OXFORD INTRODUCTION
TO BRITISH HISTORY

General Editor: H. S. DEIGHTON

GENERAL EDITOR'S PREFACE

THE inspiration of this series has been Mr. G. M. Young's *Victorian England: The Portrait of an Age*. A number of teachers suggested that Mr. Young's technique might usefully be adapted and used in a set of books designed as a History course for pupils from 11 to 15 or 16 in Grammar Schools. We have therefore attempted a double task. The books are intended for use as class textbooks, and we have accepted the responsibility for providing enough information to meet the needs of classes preparing for the General Certificate of Education at Ordinary level. But it has been our purpose to give the children, along with this knowledge of the sequence of events, an understanding of the character of the periods—periods which may later be studied in greater detail in, for example, *The Oxford History of England*. We have thought of historical study as productive, not merely of knowledge, but of understanding. Thus we have regarded the period of four years for which the course is designed as providing, not only a minimum of historical information, but the beginning of the pupil's historical reading—and his introduction to the practice of applying historical knowledge to the understanding of life.

H. S. D.

PEMBROKE COLLEGE, OXFORD

AUTHORS' PREFACE

THE period of History covered by this book is the first included by historians in 'Modern Times'—a definition in itself puzzling to the young. It is a highly complex period too, when society, politics, and religion rested on assumptions which children today find very difficult to understand; for instance, they hear much of political but almost nothing of religious intolerance. The teacher is more than ever faced with the double task of making clear these difficult concepts, and at the same time of keeping before the children, as whole as possible, the portrait of the period. We have tried to do both these things, and those who miss a detail which they feel should have appeared, or an emphasis that they expected to find, may remind themselves that we set out to write a book which is readable as well as instructive, and not to take the place of the teacher.

We should like to record our gratitude to Miss J. D. Brown, Principal of Coventry Training College, for her contribution of most useful material to certain chapters.

M. R. P.

C. E. L. M.

OXFORD

CONTENTS

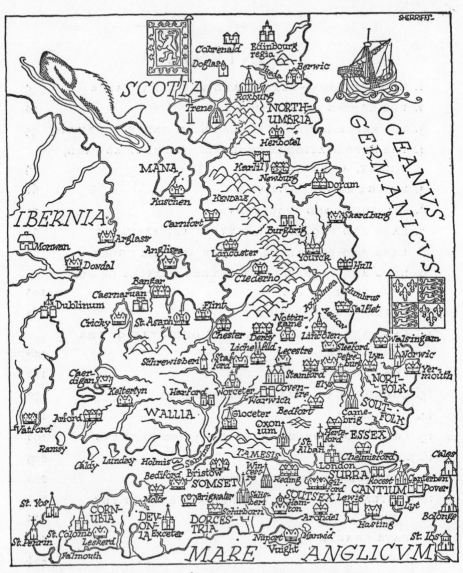

A MAP-MAKER'S IDEA OF BRITAIN IN 1540

1. Introduction: Europe and the Renaissance

IN 1453 the long warfare between France and England, which had begun with the Battle of Sluys (1340) in the reign of Edward III, came at last to an end, leaving only the city of Calais in English hands. Thirty-two years later Henry VII, the first of the Tudors, and, through his mother, the great-great-grandson of Edward, forced his way to the English throne. It is with his reign that this book begins. Those thirty-two years were uneasy ones for England, filled with strife and violence, for during them the great families of York and Lancaster contended grimly for power and for the Crown, and a host of lesser men sided and fought with one or other of the two houses, seeking their own profit and advancement in the struggles of their superiors. Indeed it almost seems as if English history consisted for about fifty years only of battles and the confusing ups and downs of Yorkists and Lancastrians, which are difficult to remember and not very edifying. Yet during this time English

HEADPIECE. William Caxton (left), showing the trade-mark of his press, and (right) Christopher Columbus and one of the many votive banners flown on the *Santa Maria*

9

towns were growing, trade, especially in wool and cloth, increased, and English ships were busy with the work of carrying merchandise to and from the ports of the Continent. Indeed it was while the Wars of the Roses were in full swing that William Caxton set up the first English printing-press in London close to the royal palace of Westminster. Caxton was a wool expert. He had worked for many years in Bruges as agent for the Merchant Adventurers of England, but besides being a very successful business man he had a passion for reading, and rather than go without books he would copy them out by hand until his eyes were strained and weary. He heard of the printing of books, which was first done in Germany about 1460, and eventually built himself a press in Bruges. Then he came home to England and set up a press, and put a printer's sign outside his London house.

This single event was one of the most important in the whole of English history and its date—1476—should be remembered before the dates of any battles of the period. For not only was the invention of printing a great achievement in itself, but it came at a time when more knowledge than ever before was surging into the world, and it is certain that without printing, with only the old laborious method of writing books by hand, much of this knowledge would have been lost. Printing not only helped to preserve it but made it widely known.

The fact was that during the three centuries from 1300 to 1600 a great change came over Europe—a change which affected every side of human life. It was given the name of the Renaissance. It began in Italy and spread gradually to every country in Europe. Indeed its results still affect us today. At the very root of the movement was a new spirit of curiosity which made men eager to inquire and experiment in every side of life, to ask how and why this had come about, how this or that worked, whether one idea was better than another, and what lay beyond the known horizons not of the seas and oceans only but of their own minds and thoughts.

At first this curiosity was chiefly concerned with the past, and Italian scholars of the fourteenth century were the first to be touched by it. This was not at all surprising for in their beautiful country there was much to draw their attention backward in time. All over Italy were to be seen the remains of a great civilization of the past—the civilization of

Rome—and indeed in some places, if the soil were merely turned over, the ruins of temples and theatres and paved highways were laid bare. When people first became sufficiently interested to dig these up they were enthralled by the beauty and majesty of what they found. Their curiosity did not stop at ruins: it led them to search for the writings of the people who had lived and moved among the buildings. Scholars hunted out Latin manuscripts and copied them and studied them, and as they pored over them they found themselves lured still farther back into the past. For beyond Roman civilization lay another and greater still—the civilization of Greece. At the time few people could read and write Greek, but fortunately there were in Italy many rich men who were ready to spend their surplus wealth in employing scholars, not only to dig for statues or search for manuscripts, but to visit Constantinople where much Greek learning was still preserved. They invited Greek scholars to come and live in Italy so that they could teach their language and expound the learning of their race, learning which seemed new to the scholars of Italy and the rest of Europe, but was in fact very old.

Some of this learning actually reached England from Italy in the reign of Edward IV and the first man to bring a Greek manuscript here was William Selling of All Souls College, Oxford. Selling taught Thomas Linacre, and then Linacre visited Italy and studied Greek before becoming Physician to Henry VII and Henry VIII. Another scholar who went to Italy was William Grocyn, the first man to teach Greek literature at Oxford, and he in his turn inspired John Colet, who, as we shall hear later, refounded St. Paul's School, London, to teach the New Learning—as it was called. Linacre, Grocyn, and Colet, and their wise and witty friend Sir Thomas More, became known as the Oxford scholars, and it was their learning and humanity which so attracted the great Dutch scholar Erasmus when he visited England, and made him eager to stay with them. Erasmus once wrote to his friend Robert Fisher, 'Believe me, dear Robert . . . when I hear my Colet I seem to be listening to Plato himself . . . and what has nature ever created more sweet, more endearing, more happy than the genius of Thomas More?'

It did not, however, matter where the scholars lived: in Oxford or Italy or Paris, the study of Greek manuscripts opened up a completely new world of thought to those who read them for the first time. Not only did they discover that the Greeks were a people of truly marvellous knowledge about medicine and mathematics, sculpture, architecture, and science, but they found that their outlook on life—their philosophy —was marvellous too. For the Greeks had delighted in the world they lived in, they had enjoyed the beauty of the human body and the power of the human mind, and above all they had never feared to inquire into everything that interested them and to seek the answers to a multitude of questions. The influence of this outlook upon the men of the Renaissance (of the fourteenth, fifteenth, and sixteenth centuries) was tremendous. It was also revolutionary in the changes that resulted. At first, as we have just seen, people sought answers to questions about the past, about Rome and Greece, but soon their curiosity turned from the old to the new and they began to seek knowledge of every kind which had hitherto been quite unknown or only guessed at, for a spirit of inquiry when once aroused will seek to penetrate into every field of human activity. So it came about that the Renaissance influenced learning and letters, painting, architecture, science, and geography, and most of all perhaps religion. The horizons expanded in every direction.

Most spectacular of all was the vast expansion of the known world which occurred during these three centuries of ferment. In the Middle Ages those who had studied geography seriously realized that the world was round and that it should be possible to travel completely round it, without dropping from its edge somewhere into space. But no one had attempted this—indeed many had feared it would be impossible to travel at all in the region of the equator because they believed that there the sea would probably boil and the land would scorch any man who tried. This belief in the intolerable heat of equatorial regions was very common in spite of the fact that Marco Polo (1254–1324) and many others after him had travelled overland to China and returned safely to Italy by way of the Indian Ocean and the Persian Gulf.

About 200 years after Marco Polo the spirit of curiosity, backed by a desire for trade or plunder, drove men to cast about for better ways to reach the East so that they might tap its riches, the spices, the precious stones, and drugs which they desired, and which in the case of spices and drugs were practical necessities to Europeans. It was then that the Portuguese completely shattered the old idea of the fatal heat of the equatorial regions. Prince Henry of Portugal (1394–1460), nicknamed the Navigator, a great-grandson of Edward III, sent seamen venturers out into the Atlantic Ocean, to the Azores, the Canary Islands, the Cape Verde Islands, and eventually little by little along the coast of Africa. Even when the Prince died these voyages went on, and at last in 1487— twenty-seven years after his death—Bartholomew Diaz rounded the Cape of Good Hope. He was followed in another ten years by Vasco da Gama, who finally reached India by sea and opened for Portugal a new route to the East. The equator had been crossed twice each way without disaster.

But before the Portuguese seamen actually achieved this useful triumph, another great expansion of the known world had occurred, and another step been taken towards the practical proof that the world was round. In 1492 Christopher Columbus, an Italian sea captain, employed, with considerable misgiving, by the Queen of Spain, who profoundly doubted his sanity, set sail westward across the Atlantic—the Sea of Darkness as sailors called it. Columbus undoubtedly knew that the world was round, and he set out in that knowledge, believing that if he sailed west he would reach India, possibly more quickly than by first rounding the enormous land mass of Africa. What he did not know was that the American Continent and the Pacific Ocean lay in between, and his achievement was, not to sail round the globe, but to found for Spain an empire in the New World.

These great discoveries—the sea route to India and the New World— were made in the name of Portugal and Spain, and Spanish too were Balboa, the first European to see the Pacific, and Magellan, the first to organize the circumnavigation of the world (1519–22).

England came far behind them in spite of the fact that her geographical position was every bit as favourable as theirs. But England's interest and her seafaring remained for a long time obstinately European and she was bent only on maintaining against fierce competition her trade in the narrower area of European seas, and not on discovering regions beyond. This trade took her seamen to the ports of the Netherlands, to the Baltic Sea, to France, Spain, Portugal, and to a smaller extent to Italy, and few Englishmen looked farther. It was this limited vision which made them at first slower than Portugal and Spain to

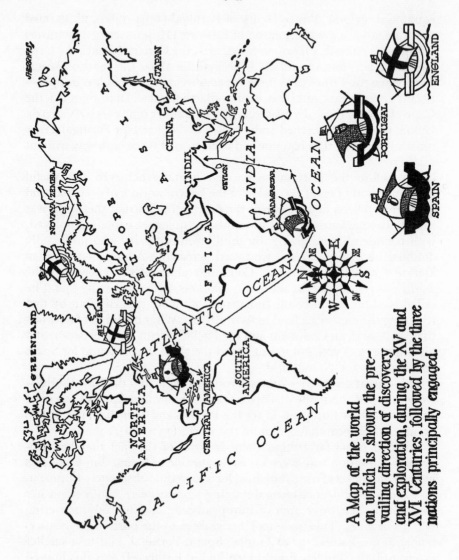

A Map of the world on which is shown the prevailing direction of discovery and exploration, during the XV and XVI Centuries, followed by the three nations principally engaged.

undertake great seafaring enterprises, and caused Henry VII to refuse his help when Bartholomew Columbus begged it for his brother's tremendous schemes.

Yet here and there in English ports there was talk of new voyages to new lands. This was specially true of Bristol whose ships went farther than most on the fish trade route to Iceland, and where Spanish and Portuguese vessels often tied up to the quayside. From Bristol in 1497 sailed John Cabot to land on the unknown shores of Newfoundland. Cabot believed he had reached Cipango (Japan), 'an island where all the spices and all the precious stones in the world originate', and though he was impressed by the quantities of fish he saw he was also disappointed by the absence of more obvious treasure.

Under the early Tudors England was friendly with Spain, and Englishmen, although they were not allowed to sail to Spanish America, had a 'factory' or business house in Seville where they could trade in the goods of the New World. But in Elizabeth's reign England and Spain quarrelled and the 'factory' was closed. At the same time a great economic crisis in Antwerp ruined England's trade with central Europe. For these two reasons English merchants began to look for trade elsewhere, and found that Spain and Portugal between them monopolized the riches of the expanding world and that there were open to themselves only two ways of winning a share of the trade. One was by direct attack on the men already in possession, which was frequently tried but was never likely to be permanently successful, and the other was by discovery of new routes and lands.

So it came about that for many years the English adventurers sought either the north-west or the north-east passage to the lands of the East, in contrast to Spain's south-west and Portugal's south-east routes. In 1509 Sebastian, son of John Cabot, set out to find a north-west passage to India and explored the coast of Labrador. In 1553 Willoughby and Chancellor made an attempt to sail by a north-east route. Willoughby was lost in a storm; Chancellor landed near Archangel and eventually reached Moscow where he was received by the Tsar of Russia, but he never reached India. In 1576 Martin Frobisher believed he had struck the way when he found the mouth of Frobisher Sound, and came back to England in high hopes. The Cathay Company was formed to finance further search, but there was no passage and no gold. In fact none of these English attempts bore the fruit that was desired, and England's footholds in the East and in the New World came in quite different ways, through the East India Company and through the colonies of Virginia and New England set up in Stuart times.

There were many other aspects of the Renaissance, besides the New Learning, and the expansion of the world, and one of these was a mighty outburst of artistic energy and creativeness, especially in painting and, to begin with, especially in Italy. During the Middle Ages painting and sculpture had been, on the whole, very conventional, and the chief purpose of both arts had been to express religious ideas and to illustrate religious stories and lessons. Beautiful though the results were in colour and design they often give us an impression of stiffness and unreality; we notice the flatness of the figures and objects, and the absence of variety in background. Now one of the effects of the Renaissance was to sharpen men's interest in themselves, their minds and bodies, and the world they lived in, and this passionate interest forced artists to experiment and especially to draw from living and actual models and scenes. The results were astonishing. For one thing the range of their subjects widened and although a great number of sacred pictures were still painted, artists no longer confined themselves to religion but depicted pagan gods and goddesses, battles, legends, portraits of successful men and beautiful women, and many other subjects. The figures in their pictures were no longer stiff and formal but lively and rounded, and clearly the result of close observation of the human body, and they were set in a great variety of backgrounds alive with interest in the world of nature, with landscapes and buildings, with flowers and animals. The changes can best be understood by looking at some of the actual pictures themselves, for instance in the National Gallery in London, or in other great collections of paintings both in this country and abroad, especially in Italy. Until you are able to do that you can find excellent reproductions in illustrated books on art and painting.

Of course there were many supremely great artists who lived before the fifteenth century and others who painted after the strongest impulse of the Renaissance had spent itself, but nevertheless the giants of that time, Botticelli and Michelangelo, Raphael and Leonardo da Vinci, still dominate the history of art. Their influence has gone far beyond the boundaries of Italy and their experiments still powerfully affect both painting and sculpture.

It is clear from what has been said that the spirit of inquiry and the new ideas and experiences which surged through Europe as the result of the Renaissance greatly enriched men's lives. But besides adding much they also destroyed a good deal and their destructive force was specially felt in the realm of religion. During the Middle Ages, as you know already, there was one universal (Catholic) Christian Church in Western Europe which ministered to the spiritual needs of all men. Its teachings and its rules of behaviour were supposed to be accepted without question. Its greatest service was the Latin Mass; its Bible was the Vulgate version, revised chiefly by St. Jerome in the fourth century, and because this was in Latin and because copies were not possessed by the uneducated, the contents were passed on to the unlearned by the ordained ministers of the Church.

It was not to be expected that so vast an organization, found in every Christian country, could possibly be perfect and without blemish, and frequently voices had been raised to demand reforms in the Church. Those in Holy Orders, bishops and priests, monks and nuns were by no means blameless and many of them were criticized for living worldly, even evil lives, and for losing sight of their true vocation. In England, John Wycliffe (c. 1320–1384) had been a strong critic. He had attacked the clergy in his sermons, and he had translated the Bible into English so that anyone capable of reading that language could unlock for himself its treasures and teaching, instead of depending entirely on the priests.

As the result of the Renaissance the voices raised against the Church grew in number and in force. Its present state was compared with its past, the truth of some of its teachings was questioned, and the lives of its ministers, from the Pope to the poorest monk or priest, were subjected to fierce criticism. Moreover, criticisms, suggestions, and demands for reforms alike circulated rapidly and to a vastly increased audience because of the printing-presses. Many who were convinced of the need for reform were deeply religious people, devoted to the traditions of the Church and because of their devotion longing to see it purified of evil. Many believed, too, that reform should and could come from within the Church, and one of these was Erasmus of Rotterdam, the friend of More and Colet.

The great Dutch scholar had been brought up in a most indifferent monastery and had hated the wrongs he saw going on there and else-where in the Church, most especially in Rome itself. In 1514 he wrote a book called *In Praise of Folly*. Its title is sarcastic, and it was a sarcastic attack upon the lazy and ignorant among the monks and nuns and priests, in which Erasmus made cruel fun of them. It was his hope that the book might help to awaken the Church to the need and the task of reform, and he wrote it not because he was an enemy of that Church but because he thought that the people he attacked were.

More important still was his next book, published in 1516—a new, careful, and accurate translation of the New Testament, which made it plain to all who read it that there were some serious mistakes of fact in the Vulgate version in use in the Church. These books had the effect, as Erasmus must have expected, of increasing the demands for reform. But he and his friends, particularly the Oxford scholars, ardently hoped that the Church itself would take the matter in hand and carry reforms through in a peaceful way, so that criticism would be silenced and the unity of European Christendom be preserved. Indeed they had no desire for anything else. But this was not to be; instead a violent explosion tore the Church apart, and destroyed that unity.

The man who set off the fuse of this explosion was Martin Luther, a German friar of some learning and great earnestness, who was born in Saxony in 1483. The friary which he entered was a strict one, and Luther was all the more shocked when in 1511 he was sent to Rome on a mission and observed the worldly lives of the Pope and the high officials of the Church. He thought they made sport of true religion and he returned to Germany, deeply disturbed and unhappy. He took up his work again at the University of Wittenberg where he had been made a lecturer in theology, but pondered long upon the state of the Church. Six years later in 1517 the Pope, Leo X, needed money to rebuild the great church of St. Peter in Rome, and it was decided to raise some of it by a sale of indulgences. The Church taught that people who had sinned, being truly sorry, must confess their sin to a priest who could pronounce the forgiveness of God, at the same time ordering a penance or punishment for the sin committed. An indulgence was a remission of the penance due—even of penance due after death, in Purgatory—and the sale of them was a very old custom. But it had grave dangers, one of them being that too little stress was laid on true penitence. The sale of indulgences in Germany in 1517 was in the hands of a Dominican friar called Tetzel, and his methods were scandalous to a degree, for he offered them to any who had money to buy, and said nothing about confession and penitence but only that 'as soon as the coin rang in the chest, the soul for whom the money was paid would go straight way to heaven'. Luther with many others was revolted by this shameless traffic, and he wrote out ninety-five theses, or reasons why the sale was wrong and boldly nailed a copy on the church door in Wittenberg. The effect was tremendous. Luther became a focal point for all protests and all desire for reform, and in a few years, emboldened by what he had done and by the support he had gained, he became more defiant and violent. He now attacked the authority of the Pope, and the teaching of the Church on other matters, and in 1520 Leo X, who at first had rather laughed at him, realized that the defiant friar must be silenced and issued a Bull excommunicating him. This was a dreadful matter in the eyes of all Catholics and likely to ruin Luther completely unless he withdrew all that he had said and written. But far from doing this Luther publicly burnt the Bull in the market-place of Wittenberg. When ordered to appear before the Emperor Charles V at Worms, thereby being given a last chance to recant, he declared that his conscience told him he was acting rightly. 'Here stand I. I can do no other. God help me.' He was thereupon pronounced heretic and outlaw.

Although when he left the Emperor's presence his life was in great danger, Luther was protected by his friend, the Elector of Saxony who, believing in the rightness of the protest, kept him in his own castle, the Wartburg, where he occupied himself by translating the Bible into German and writing hymns—an apparently peaceful occupation. But the effect of his protest had been to divide Germany into two camps, on

the one side the Catholics who held by the old ways, on the other reformers who in time took the name of Protestants—for obvious reasons
—and who set up churches and services of their own. Bitter strife and
hostility, bloodshed, and open robbery of Church property resulted and
went on after Luther himself died (1546). Men had no idea as yet of
tolerating a difference of religious belief—their only thought was to
stamp it out; and thus the effect of the Reformation was to destroy the
unity of the Church and the religious peace of Europe. After nearly ten
years of war between Catholics and Protestants in Germany, the Peace
of Augsburg was made in 1555, by which it was agreed that certain
German rulers might adopt the Protestant religion and renounce the
authority of Rome. The religion of their subjects was simply to be the
same as theirs, which is not a tolerant idea.

When Luther first protested against the sale of indulgences in 1517
he could not even have imagined how far-reaching the results would
be, nor did he dream that a Church quite separate from the Roman
Church would be established by his followers and in his name. Yet not
only was the Lutheran Protestant Church founded in parts of Germany,
but the movement and its influence spread to other European countries.
Moreover at Geneva, in Switzerland, another form of Protestant
Church was established by John Calvin, a Frenchman who had been
forced to leave France to escape persecution for his religious views.
Calvin's Church greatly influenced the religion of France, the Netherlands, England, and, through John Knox, Scotland, and his followers
were often known as Presbyterians, for the control and management of
each congregation was in the hands of 'presbyters' or elders. In England
they were nicknamed Puritans and in France Huguenots. Many
people were aghast at the course the reforming movement had taken,
Erasmus for one, and the Oxford scholars for others. Many books and
pamphlets were written condemning Luther, the Protestants, and all
their works, and among them a particularly strong one, which greatly
pleased the Pope, came from England. It was called *The Golden Book*
written by an author who 'ever since he knew Luther's heresy in Germany, made it his study how to extirpate it'. The author was Henry
VIII and the book was sent to Leo X in 1521. Thirteen years later
Henry, as you will read later in this book, himself excommunicated,

renounced the authority of the Pope, and separated the Church of England from Rome.

And so the old bonds which had bound Christian countries together for centuries were broken, the result of the strong ferment of the Renaissance acting upon the accumulated discontent of generations.

2. The Coming of the Tudors

On 22 August 1485 Richard III, the brother of Edward IV, was killed in battle near Market Bosworth in Leicestershire. This swarthy hunchbacked man was a usurper of the throne; that is he had taken it from the rightful king, for when Edward died in 1483 the real heir was his thirteen-year-old son—also an Edward—who for a few brief weeks had been called king. Most men had realized that a boy king would be a weak king, at least until he grew up, and that this would mean a continuation of the struggle among the great nobles for possession of the throne with the power and wealth it could give. People were so heartily sick of this state of affairs that Richard, being a grown and experienced man, might very well have settled himself successfully on the throne in spite of the suspicious way in which young Edward and his brother Richard dis-

HEADPIECE. The yeoman gaoler of the King's bodyguard at the Tower of London in the mid-sixteenth century. Two of the abundant London kites are shown. (This rank still parades, carrying a similar armament)

appeared from the Tower of London, where their uncle had lodged them. Usurper though he was, Richard was also shrewd and clever. But he had no chance to prove himself able to govern England, for he was killed before he could live down the black deeds which he certainly had committed and the even blacker suspicion with which many of his subjects regarded him.

The battle at Bosworth was not very spectacular except for the death of Richard, and at the time it probably seemed to most men just one more flare-up of the civil wars between the families of Lancaster and York, which had been blazing up and dying down and smouldering away for as long as people could remember—for over thirty years in fact. This time it was the Lancastrians, under Henry Tudor, Earl of Richmond, who were the victors, and it seemed clear that Henry would be made king. People quite expected the usual crop of executions of the defeated leaders and the confiscation of their lands and goods. Many foresaw that after a few years of uneasy peace, as likely as not, the fire of war would blaze up and devour Henry Tudor and bring the Yorkist family back into power. For the moment, however, the defeated captains and their followers scattered from Bosworth and made for their homes or hiding places, hoping that if they lay low they might escape the vengeance of the new king.

Although these civil wars had been going on for so long the majority of people had stuck doggedly to the business of feeding, clothing, and warming themselves and had taken little part in the fighting. Many had never even seen a battle. It had been a war of the nobles and their private armies, that is of the class to whom fighting was an occupation for which they had been carefully trained from childhood, and of the men they kept dressed in their own uniform, or 'livery', to follow them in battle. Humble people were only drawn in when they could not help themselves and when the opposing armies had actually moved into that part of the country where they lived. There was no large-scale devastation, and the war did not destroy great numbers of villages and towns, so that the ordinary life of England was not seriously disturbed. Farming did not stop and trade went on quite steadily. It even increased in some ways, for between 1460 and 1485 more wool was sold abroad in Flanders and more rough woollen cloth was made at home and sent overseas. Wool merchants had money to spare. They built fine churches like the one at Northleach in Gloucestershire, and larger houses with perhaps two front doors instead of a shop entrance that served for everything. But, although a number of such men became richer, there could be no certain security or prosperity for anyone, merchant, farmer, housewife, or priest, as long as the great men and their armies harried each other back and forth throughout the land in a struggle for power and wealth. Very vivid descriptions of the utter lawlessness of powerful men can be found in a collection of letters which were written between 1450 and 1490 by members of the Paston family who lived in Norfolk. One of their neighbours, Lord Molynes, coveted the manor house of Gresham which William Paston had bought and left to his eldest son John. In January 1450, when John was away in London, Molynes sent a force of 1,600 men armed with 'currasse, brigaunders, jakks, salettes, bowes, arrows, etc.' and carrying picks, battering rams, and 'pannys with fier' to seize the place. Mrs. John Paston was there with only a few servants who, of course, were quickly driven out. The invaders battered 'down the wall of the chamber wherein she was and bore her out of the gates'. They stole everything they could and badly damaged the house. John Paston wrote to ask for help from the Sheriff of Norfolk but he was afraid to offend the powerful Lord Molynes and replied that he would help Paston in any other action but this.

Nine years later a certain Sir John Fastolf died leaving his fine house, Caister Castle, to his 'best friend and helper' John Paston, and there was more trouble for John. This time the Duke of Norfolk wanted Caister and he simply seized the place and went to live in it for a time, until the Pastons gained enough influence at Court for him to realize that they were becoming too powerful to be bullied. Such men as the Duke and Lord Molynes were typical of the nobles of the time, dangerous to all their weaker neighbours and defiant even of the King.

They were altogether over-mighty even when they were not actually fighting. They robbed and killed their poorer neighbours, but few dared accuse them in a court of law; and even when this was done it took a very brave judge to pronounce sentence on them, knowing that if he did so the next person to be beaten up and robbed would probably be himself or his relations. He could expect little help from the King, who was often in grave danger of being dethroned by his opponents and was himself afraid to offend his most powerful subjects. Not since the reign of Stephen, 300 years before, had the royal government broken down so completely and been quite unable to control the barons, so that they could attack anyone whose lands and possessions they coveted without any fear of the consequences.

In 1485 Henry Tudor was obviously the most powerful of the English nobles, for he had succeeded in killing King Richard III, beating his army, and taking his place as king, but it must have seemed quite likely that in time exactly the same thing would happen to him, and that the war would start all over again. Happily those who thought this were wrong, for Bosworth was the last serious battle of the Wars of the Roses and Henry VII managed not only to remain on the throne himself but also to establish his family on it for the next 118 years, until in fact the last Tudor, Elizabeth I, died in 1603.

In his portraits Henry appears distinctly unattractive. His face is hard, his mouth a thin line, and his eyes are red-rimmed, narrow, and rather crafty-looking. But all these portraits show him at the end of his reign after years of danger and of striving and scheming to get the better of his enemies and make himself secure. In 1485 he was only twenty-eight years old and although he 'had no great stature but a body lean and spare' he was 'strong and of a fair complexion, his hair like burnished gold and his countenance merry and smiling'. In the months and years after Bosworth Henry was faced with great danger and many difficulties, but he was cool and wary, and he gradually overcame them all.

The one thing above all others that he had to do, if he was not to follow Henry VI and Richard III, was to restore order and the force of law. For this he could count on the support of almost everyone except the great nobles. Most Englishmen wanted to live in peace and carry on with their ordinary everyday affairs without disturbance. All the farmers, small landowners, merchants, and craftsmen would certainly back a king who proved that he could keep order and bring the turbulent nobles under control, and Henry did prove it.

In order to get the support of just these ordinary people, he called Parliament, and when in November 1485 the nobles, the chosen knights from the shires, and the burgesses from the towns arrived at Westminster they, the Lords and Commoners of the realm, declared Henry to be the rightful King of England. They ignored the fact that there were others with a better hereditary right than his, for instance the five young daughters of Edward IV and his two nephews.

They tactfully dated Henry's reign from 21 August 1485, the day before the Battle of Bosworth, thus making a traitor of anyone who had fought against him on the 22nd. Parliament followed this up by an Act of Attainder, and the chief men who had fought for Richard were thereby accused of treason and were arrested and beheaded. This disposed of the most dangerous of Henry's enemies, and when they were gone he pardoned the lesser men, perhaps in order to impress people with a sense of his mercy and, at the same time, of his strength. Parliament then entreated Henry to marry the Princess Elizabeth of York, and to this he graciously agreed. He had determined to do so some time before. It was an excellent way of disposing of her as a rival for the throne, but he was careful not to marry her until after he had been crowned, for he did not want it to seem that he owed his throne in any way to a Yorkist wife.

Although Parliament did all these things, and appeared to settle the matter of the kingship, its members had as yet very little power. There always was a sensible understanding between Henry VII and Parliament, an alliance which went on after his death and through the reign of his son and grandchildren, but even so the plain truth was that the King called it when he wished and dismissed it when he wished. And he generally only called it when he needed extra money and hoped the members would help him to get it, or, as in 1485, when for some reason he wanted their special support. Invitations to attend Parliament were (and still are) called writs, and a separate one was sent to all the earls, bishops, barons, and mitred abbots of the realm. Others were sent to the sheriff of each county, ordering him to see that two knights from the shire and two burgesses from certain towns were chosen and sent to Westminster. Only towns which held a royal charter of rights were asked to send their representatives. In their writs the Lords were invited to 'discuss with us and give us your counsel' but the knights and burgesses (the Commons) were 'to consent and do what shall be decided by the common council'. The Commons were only there to agree to what the

King and the Lords had already decided, not to give advice and certainly not to make suggestions. There were, however, two important things that they could do. They could, if they dared, refuse a request for money, and so the King, if he were wise, tried to get their willing support for such requests. They could also present petitions to the King. Of course such petitions could be ignored or rejected, but as they usually dealt with matters that the Commons felt strongly about they did at least show the King what his subjects were feeling or wanting, and so if he were wise he paid some attention to them. For instance, among the first requests presented to Henry VII in 1485 was one asking that the price of long-bows should not be allowed to rise above 12s. 6d., and another which asked, very sensibly, that the same weights and measures should be used all over England. The members of Parliament did not usually stay very long in Westminster, nor did they meet regularly. For this the Commons at least were extremely thankful: it was an expensive business to ride to London from, say, Truro or York, and to pay for board and lodging on the journey, and for a stay of some weeks in the capital as well. Members were not paid a salary as they are now. In fact a good many respectable knights and citizens did their best to avoid being elected to this costly honour. Henry VII called six Parliaments during his first four years on the throne, but after that only one more before he died in 1509.

After 1485 the Yorkist families were very seriously weakened. Many were executed as traitors, and many more lost their lands, or had to pay such enormous fines to get them back that they became quite poor, while the King became richer and stronger. Then, too, they had now no strong leader to hold them together. The Princess Elizabeth of York, daughter of Edward IV, had the best claim on their loyalty, for she was certainly the true heir to the throne after the murder of her young brothers, but she was now Henry's wife. In any case she was only twenty years old and no one, not even her relatives, seemed to have thought it would be a good plan to have a woman on the throne in those dangerous times. Her four sisters were even younger than she was. Henry prudently arranged for three of them to marry loyal and rather unimportant men. The youngest of them, Bridget, became a nun at Dartford Priory in Kent. Next to the princesses as a possible leader with a good claim came their cousin Edward, Earl of Warwick, but he was also under Henry's eye—a prisoner in the Tower of London. In fact the shortage of really suitable claimants to the throne was so serious that when the Yorkists did rebel they had to rake up impostors and pretend they were royal personages.

Within five months of the Battle of Bosworth Henry had been proclaimed king, crowned king, and married to Elizabeth of York; but he still had much to do. The unruly nobles must be brought to heel, and though they had been weakened they were still a menace. They continued to keep bands of followers, armed and wearing their master's livery, and with these private armies they rioted, robbed, and murdered. They also saw to it that if possible no unfavourable verdicts in the law courts were ever given against themselves or any of their supporters. Some of them still beat up juries, and bribed and terrified judges, and so 'maintained' their causes in the courts. In 1488 an Act of Parliament said that 'for the not punishing of these men (i.e. the nobles and their retainers) the laws of the land take little effect to the increase of murders and robberies and to the great displeasure of Almighty God'. Obviously this was a state of things most dangerous to the peace of the realm. So in 1504 Parliament, at Henry's request, passed an Act of Livery and Maintenance to forbid it. Such laws had been passed before, but without the slightest effect, because no one was strong enough to enforce them. Since the ordinary courts were useless against powerful men Henry used part of his own Royal Council for the job. This Council had no fixed number of members, but usually consisted of the great officials of the Court—the Chancellor, the Treasurer, and so on, and a good many others personally chosen by the sovereign either for their special qualifications or simply because they were friends of the King. Henry VII chose great churchmen like Fox, Bishop of Winchester, and Morton, Archbishop of Canterbury, and also men like Sir Reginald Bray, 'a sage and grave person', who was a very skilful lawyer. Most of them owed their important position to the King and could be dismissed by him when he pleased. Such men carried out the King's will in all the most vital and secret matters of government, and they were much more afraid of him than of the most turbulent nobles.

A group of these counsellors sat at the palace of Westminster in a

IN THE COURT OF THE STAR CHAMBER, 1490

room whose roof was painted with stars, and they came to be called the Court of Star Chamber. Over-mighty nobles were called by the King's written order to appear before this court and they soon developed a very healthy respect for it. It was very powerful, very near the King, and was responsible only to him. It worked in secret, and it could and did use torture to get evidence. All kinds of cases came before it. In 1505 the Archbishop of York and the Earl of Northumberland, who had been quarrelling, were summoned to attend. They were warned not to bring their armed servants to Westminster upon pain of the 'high displeasure' of the King. When they came it was clear that they had allowed these servants to carry on their masters' quarrel by 'great riots and other enormities'. The Archbishop and the Earl swore to keep the peace thereafter or else to pay a fine of £2,000. Again, the Earl of Oxford was once fined £15,000 for keeping 500 retainers in his personal livery, and so breaking the law. These culprits were all great men, and the Star Chamber was used specially to deal with such cases. Gradually, as its judgements and penalties became so well known and feared, the threat of being called before it was more than enough to restrain wrongdoers. In fact Shakespeare, in his play *The Merry Wives of Windsor*, makes one of his characters say that he 'will make a Star Chamber matter of it' because, he goes on, 'You have beaten my men, killed my deer, and broke open my lodge.'

Clearly the Star Chamber was a most useful and necessary instrument, as by its fines the judges were paid, and the surplus went into Henry's pocket. But equally it was an instrument which might become very dangerous and tyrannical if it went on after the real need for it was over. Years later, in the reign of Charles I, it was attacked for that very reason and then abolished.

Year by year the wary Henry worked and watched, knowing well that sooner or later the Yorkists would make some attempts to overthrow him. The first of these came in 1487, when a baker's son, Lambert Simnel by name, was set up as Edward, Earl of Warwick, who was all the while imprisoned in the Tower. Lambert was crowned in Dublin by the Yorkists and brought to England, but Henry easily defeated this puppet and his supporters at Stoke in Nottinghamshire. He took him prisoner and then set him to work in the royal kitchen. No one could

THE KING VISITS LAMBERT SIMNEL IN THE ROYAL KITCHEN

think much of Lambert after that, and when Henry knew he was no longer dangerous he actually promoted him to a better job—as a royal falconer.

The next attempt came in 1497, when the Yorkists found another impostor, a young man called Perkin Warbeck. This attempt was more serious, for they gained help from Henry's enemies abroad. For two years before he actually landed in England, Warbeck had been pretending to be the younger of the two sons of Edward IV; having escaped, as he said, from the clutches of his uncle Richard III; and he was well received both in Paris and in Vienna. He was a man of great charm and beautiful manners, and he convinced many that he was speaking the truth, but soon he too was captured and was shut up in the Tower with the Earl of Warwick. Two years later they both tried to escape, and both were executed. There were no more attempts to dethrone Henry.

As well as restoring order, quelling the nobles, and watching ceaselessly for Yorkist rebellions, Henry knew it was important to make

England—and himself—respected abroad. Since the end of the Hundred Years War, no English king had had the time or the money to interfere much in European affairs. Henry VI, Edward IV, and Richard III had been far too busy with their own troubles at home. European rulers now thought little of English power, and probably regarded Henry himself as a vulgar upstart, who was quite likely to lose his new throne before long.

Yet in spite of this it was in his reign that England began to rank with the great powers of Europe, with France and Spain and the Empire ruled over by the Hapsburg family. Henry's chance of increasing his own and England's influence came because these three powers were deadly rivals. They were all bent on conquering the beautiful land of Italy and each was anxious to have Henry as an ally, or at the least to keep him from helping its opponents. Thus Henry's friendship was sought, and in 1496 the King of Spain proposed that his daughter, Catherine of Aragon, should marry Henry's eldest son, Prince Arthur. Henry, who was a firm believer in useful marriages, was much pleased by the proposal, and after the royal fathers had haggled and bickered over the financial side of the bargain for as long as two years, Catherine came over to England in 1501 and married Arthur in St. Paul's Cathedral on 14 November. She was only sixteen, slender and straight, with grey eyes and russet-gold hair, not quite what the English expected in a Spanish princess. But everyone liked her—indeed she remained popular even when, later on, sore trouble shadowed her life—and she had quite a triumphant progress to London, which lasted for three weeks. Henry himself went to meet her at Dogmersfield and insisted on her removing the veil which she wore for the presentation to her future father-in-law. Catherine's duenna was shocked at this breach of etiquette but Henry was delighted with what he found behind the veil.

After their marriage, and the pageants and tournaments which followed, Catherine and Arthur journeyed to Wales where they were to hold a Court. At Ludlow Castle Arthur was taken ill and he died there in April 1502, only five months after their wedding. Was this tragedy to mean Catherine's return to Spain, the breaking of the new connexion between the two countries, the loss of the cherished dowry? Henry hoped not and he at once proposed that she should marry his second son Henry, now heir to the throne. The chief obstacle to this plan was that Church law forbade marriage between such near relations unless special permission was given by the Pope. However, the Pope gave this permission—or dispensation, as it is called, and the marriage took place. It was to be one of the most fateful in English history.

One other marriage was arranged by Henry VII for the sole purpose of convenience and security. His daughter Margaret became the wife of James IV of Scotland, and Henry hoped to heal the old hostility between the two countries and replace it with friendly alliance. But it was a hundred years before this really came about, and by that time Henry's own direct line had died out.

In 1509 Henry died. He was buried in a beautiful tomb made by Italian craftsmen in his own chapel at Westminster Abbey. He was fifty-two. Many must have thought it impossible that he would weather all the dangers of the first part of his reign and remain upon the throne. He not only did so, but left England much more peaceful, her trade improving, her prestige growing, and his son able to ascend the throne without the slightest difficulty or opposition. The unattractive Henry was 'a wonder for wise men'.

His son, Henry VIII, was just eighteen, and he had everything in his favour. He was rich, he was greatly liked, he was a good sportsman—there is a famous description of him at tennis written by the Venetian Ambassador in 1511, who said it was the 'prettiest sight in the world to see him playing'. Moreover, he was very intelligent and well educated, speaking Latin, French, and Spanish, a friend to some of the most famous scholars of the day, men like Dean Colet, Thomas More, and the Dutchman Erasmus. He was outwardly good-natured and certainly pleasure-loving, and at first 'nothing minded to travail in the busy affairs of the realm'. He added to his personal popularity as soon as he ascended the throne by arresting two of his father's ministers, Empson and Dudley, men who were detested by everyone for the way they unjustly twisted the law so as to extort more and heavier fines from men accused of breaking it. They were both beheaded.

Henry VIII soon found a minister of his own. This was Thomas Wolsey, the son of an Ipswich tradesman, who had entered the Church and gone up to Oxford, where he soon gained a reputation as a very able man. He became chaplain in a nobleman's household, and in this way he came to Court. Henry VII soon found him hard-working, shrewd, and trustworthy, and made him one of his own chaplains. In those days by no means all a chaplain's duties were religious, for as there was no civil service, most of the work of the government was carried on by clergymen, and Wolsey was sent on missions to Scotland and the Netherlands which he carried out very well. But his real rise to power came with the accession of Henry VIII. Henry was at first much too busy enjoying himself to be bothered with the day-to-day routine of governing; he found Wolsey's great industry and ability very useful, and put more and more government business into his hands. In 1515 Wolsey became Chancellor, and one of the greatest men in the land. The Venetian Ambassador wrote, 'He alone transacts the same business as that which occupies all the magistrates and councils of Venice, both civil and criminal, and all the affairs of state are managed by him, let their nature be what it may.'

Wolsey made full use of the Star Chamber to put down riots and retainers, and he did something to help the poor by stopping the enclosure of land, but he used his position also to gain more wealth and power for himself. In the Church he was even more powerful, for Henry rewarded him with many Church appointments. By 1514 he was Archbishop of York, and he later became Bishop of Winchester as well, and also Abbot of St. Albans, the richest monastery in the country. In 1515 the Pope made him a cardinal, and in 1518 he became Papal Legate, or the Pope's personal representative in England. He was now immensely rich, for he had the income from all his Church posts, profits from the Chancery Court, and great sums in presents from those who wanted his favour, both at home and abroad. For seventeen years Wolsey practically ruled England. Much of his time was taken up with foreign politics, for both France and Spain were anxious for England's support and Wolsey was able to hold a balance between them, but his real ambition was to become Pope himself, and in much of his dealing with foreign powers he had this in mind. But in spite of all his power, dignity, and wealth, Wolsey owed his whole position to the King, and when at last Henry turned against him nothing could prevent his downfall.

SHERRIFFS,

Mr Viner

3. The Reformation in England

1. UNDER HENRY VIII

To understand the Reformation in England one must know something of what the Church was like before it took place. First of all its power and influence had been enormous and were still very great. It was the Church which had kept learning and religion alive during the dark days after the fall of the Roman Empire. Churchmen had turned art, writing, music, and architecture to the glory of God, and we can see their work in our cathedrals and parish churches, in paintings and in beautifully decorated Latin service books. They had given alms to the poor, had done what they could to heal the sick, and had taught the word of God to men with its message of hope and love. The Church was universal or Catholic, and wherever you travelled throughout most

HEADPIECE. The massive head of Martin Luther; composite from three contemporary drawings of Europe you would find the same services going on, in the same language, Latin, which had been used for 1,200 years. The head of the Church was the Pope, and its headquarters the city of Rome.

Life was hard and death never seemed very far away, religion was real and important to everyone, and the parish church played a large part in people's lives. They came there to pray and hear the word of God, to attend christenings, weddings, and funerals, to see the solemn processions on the great festivals, and also for sheer entertainment from such activities as the church-ales, which were feasts to raise money for the upkeep of the church buildings. The central figure in all this was the priest. As very few people understood Latin, they depended on him to explain the Christian faith to them, and to tell them the stories of the Bible, and the lives of the saints. He taught them the Lord's Prayer, the Creed, and the Ten Commandments, all of course in Latin, and urged them to come to church regularly, and to lead good and honest lives. They turned to him for advice and help in their troubles, to him they confessed their sins, and in the name of the Church he gave them absolution (forgiveness).

But there were things about the Church which some people did not like. As time went on, it became exceedingly rich as well as powerful. Pious people left land and money to monasteries, so that often the monks spent more time than before in managing their estates, and collecting their rent, and less on prayer and study. Others founded chantries, or private chapels, and put them in charge of priests whose only duty was to say prayers for the soul of the founder. These priests, with not much to do and nobody to supervise them, often became careless and idle. Churchmen were almost the only educated people, and, as life became more civilized, and business ability more important than skill in fighting, their talents were used more and more for things that had little to do with religion. Bishops became the King's councillors and spent more time at Court than in their dioceses; they were better educated and more intelligent than laymen, and they were certainly cheaper, because they could be rewarded with promotion in the Church, which cost the King nothing. Many became more interested in politics than in their religious duties and more concerned with serving an earthly sovereign than the King of Heaven.

Other things besides politics and Court appointments occupied men, and women, in Holy Orders. Geoffrey Chaucer, a poet and Esquire of the Household in the reign of Edward III, wrote a famous series of stories, the *Canterbury Tales* (about 1387–1400). He described a party of pilgrims riding to visit the shrine of Thomas à Becket in the cathedral at Canterbury. There are some vivid descriptions of the churchmen in the party which show what many people thought about such men even as early as that. There we can see a monk, fond of hunting and good living, owning horses and swift greyhounds, and dressed not in the coarse habit of an order but with expensive fur on his sleeves and a gold pin in his hood. There is a friar who had long given up preaching to the poor but who knew the taverns well in every town. Such men troubled little about simple living, hard work, good learning, or the discipline of the true monastic life, and the prioress described by Chaucer, though kind and harmless, obviously thinks more about her dress, her gold bracelet, her manners, and her little dog than of a life of service to mankind. The only good and sincere clergyman among them was a priest from a poor parish. He never failed to visit the sick, however far away they lived, or however foul the weather, and he would go short himself rather than press a poor man for his tithes. Chaucer says that:

> Christs law and his apostles twelve
> He taught, but first he followed it himself:

but by no means all parish priests were like this. A special inquiry made in 1547 showed that, out of about 300 priests who were questioned, more than half did not know the Ten Commandments, ten could not even repeat the Lord's Prayer, and twenty-seven did not know who was its author, or where it was to be found in the Bible.

The Church courts were also very unpopular. They affected people's lives in many ways, for they did not only deal with offences by clergymen but with everything concerning marriages and wills, as well as matters like Sabbath-breaking, evil living, and heresy, or refusing to accept the Church's teaching, which was a serious crime. There were often complaints that they misused their power, and charged too much in fees. An official from one of these courts was among Chaucer's pilgrims, a Summoner, or prosecutor, who used his powers to extort bribes and blackmail. He was accompanied by another disreputable hanger-on of the Church, a Pardoner, whose job was to sell printed pardons for any sin you might have committed, and who carried a profitable side-line in bogus relics—a piece of wood, which he would sell as a fragment of the True Cross, or a 'glas of pigges bones' which were supposed to be those of some saint

> and with these relikes, when that he found
> A povre person dwelling upon lande
> Upon one day he gat him more monaye
> Than that the person gat in monthes tweye.

Of course John Wycliffe had protested against the faults of the Church and had translated the Bible into English so that people would not have to depend so much on the clergy. He had been declared a heretic, and his followers had been persecuted, but his ideas never died out, and prepared people's minds to accept the Reformation later on. Remembering these things, it is clear that when Henry VIII became king the idea of improving the Church had been in men's minds for a long time, though probably nobody went so far as to think of breaking away from the universal Church and the Pope's authority and setting up a separate Church in England. In fact, when Wolsey was in power, the Church seemed stronger than ever, and Henry VIII its most loyal supporter. In 1521 he wrote a book defending the Catholic faith against Luther, and was rewarded by the Pope with the title of Defender of the Faith—*Fidei Defensor*—which can still be seen in a shortened form on some of our coins. But the Church was not really so strong as it seemed. In spite of Henry's book, Luther's ideas were spreading in England, especially among the merchants of London, and at Cambridge. In London the clergy were so unpopular that Bishop Fitzjames begged Wolsey to intervene in a case in which a clergyman was accused of murder because 'if he be tried by any twelve men in London they be so maliciously set in favour of heresy that they will condemn any clerk [clergyman] though he were as innocent as Abel'. If it should ever come to a struggle between the King and the Church there was no doubt which side the country would be on. The struggle began in 1527.

Henry VIII had married Catherine of Aragon, his brother's widow, in 1509. This was forbidden by the law of the Church, but Pope Julius II had been persuaded to give special permission to allow the marriage to take place, though there had been some doubts at the time whether he was really able to do this. Henry and Catherine had been happy together at first, but their life was saddened by the fact that only one of their seven children had lived, a daughter named Mary, who would inherit the kingdom. Now the last queen who had inherited the throne had been Matilda, nearly 400 years before, and her accession had led to twenty years of civil war, and many people feared that this might happen again. Even if Mary became queen without trouble she would need a husband. If she married a foreign prince England would become part of a foreign kingdom; if she married an English noble the old quarrels which had caused the Wars of the Roses might begin again, and all the work of Henry VII might be undone. With so much at stake, Henry VIII came to believe that the lack of a son was a judgement on him for an unlawful marriage, and that the Pope was wrong to allow it in the first place. At the same time he was attracted by Anne Boleyn, one of the Queen's ladies-in-waiting, and from 1527 onwards he was thinking of persuading the Pope, Clement VII, to annul his marriage to Catherine. That would mean that Henry was still a bachelor, and could marry whom he liked, but it would insult Catherine and disinherit Mary.

As usual, Henry VIII expected Wolsey to arrange things for him, but the task was impossible. The Pope did not want to offend Henry, but he was not his own master: he was in the power of Charles V, the Emperor and King of Spain, whose troops had invaded Italy and sacked Rome— and Charles V was the nephew of Catherine of Aragon. The Pope simply dared not offend Charles V, and so for once Henry VIII did not get his own way. This failure ruined Wolsey, who was by now very unpopular. The nobles were jealous of his power; Parliament blamed him for heavy taxes, and the alliance he had made with France, which they feared might upset English trade with Flanders; the clergy resented his high-handed way of dealing with them; and Anne Boleyn and all her family hated him. It was only the King's favour that had kept him in power for so long and now the King had no more use for him. He was dismissed from all his offices in 1529. Very unwisely, he wrote to

HENRY VIII AND THOMAS CROMWELL, EARL OF ESSEX

the King of France, asking him to speak in his favour to Henry; for this he was accused of high treason, but died on his way to London for his trial, in 1530.

Henry did not give up hope of persuading the Pope to change his mind, but he was quite ready to defy him if necessary. He knew how laymen disliked 'proud prelates', hated interference by foreigners, and coveted the Church's lands. There would be no opposition there; it only remained to bring the clergy under his control. To do this, Henry used a law called the Statute of Praemunire, which had been passed in Edward III's reign, to prevent the Pope from interfering in English affairs, and which made it a serious crime to take orders from the Pope without the King's permission. Henry suddenly accused all the clergy of having broken the law by accepting Wolsey as the Pope's legate, which was a particularly mean trick as he had done the same thing himself. The penalty was imprisonment and the loss of all their property, but the clergy were allowed to buy a general pardon for £100,000. In return they had to admit that the King, not the Pope, was the Supreme Head of the Church of England, though he agreed to add the words 'as far as the law of Christ allows'.

As the Pope would still not give way, Henry got Parliament to pass an Act stopping the payment of Annates. This was the first year's salary of any newly appointed bishop or other clergyman, which, by old custom was paid to the Pope. The Act was not enforced at once, but, when Archbishop Warham died, Henry used the threat of it to persuade the Pope to appoint Thomas Cranmer as the new Archbishop of Canterbury. Cranmer was a Cambridge scholar, who had studied Luther's writings, though he was not one of his followers, and who was quite willing to accept the King as head of the Church. As soon as he was appointed, he declared the marriage of Henry and Catherine cancelled and married the King to Anne Boleyn. At once the Pope replied by excommunicating Henry, which meant that he was cut off from the Christian Church, and his subjects no longer had a duty to obey him. Excommunication had been a deadly weapon against John in 1206, but Henry, secure in the support of practically the whole country, simply ignored it. In 1533 Anne Boleyn was crowned as Queen, and, by a series of Acts of Parliament, appeals to Rome were forbidden and all payment of money to the Pope was stopped. In 1534 by the Act of Supremacy Henry was declared Head of the English Church, and by the Act of Succession the children of Henry and Anne were declared the rightful heirs to the throne. The Bishop of Rome, as the Pope was now called, had no more power in England.

In all this, Henry's closest adviser had been Thomas Cromwell. He was born in 1485; his father had been a blacksmith and brewer at Putney, who was often in trouble for selling bad beer. Thomas, as he admitted to Cranmer, 'had been a ruffian in his youth'. He had been a soldier in the French army, clerk to a Venetian merchant, a money-lender, and later Wolsey's secretary. After Wolsey's fall, he became Secretary to the King. He was a clever unscrupulous man, who allowed nothing and nobody to stand between him and what he wanted. He had two objects—to make the King all-powerful in England, and to make his own fortune at the same time. From the first, he urged Henry to marry Anne Boleyn and defy the Pope to do his worst; if there were resistance it should be crushed without mercy. The King must be able to do exactly what he liked, and claim absolute obedience from his subjects. The test of obedience was to be an oath which anyone might be compelled to swear, pledging them to be loyal to Henry, and to his children by Anne and to admit that he, and not the Pope, was the head of the English Church. To refuse this oath was treason and the penalty was death.

Almost the first man to suffer under this law was Sir Thomas More. He had opposed Wolsey, and Henry VIII, who liked and respected him, made him Chancellor in Wolsey's place. He was loyal to the Church, and when Henry's attack on it began he resigned, but he did nothing to oppose the King, though he would not deny the authority of the Pope. Another man who thought as he did was Bishop Fisher of Rochester, who had taken Catherine's part in the divorce. Both men were well known and respected abroad as well as in England. More, in particular, whom the Emperor Charles V had called a miracle of learning, was one of the outstanding men of his time—and Cromwell thought these two were his most dangerous opponents. He was sure that they would not go against their conscience by taking the oath, and knew that when they refused they would be at his mercy. He was right.

Both refused the oath, were imprisoned and, in 1535, executed for treason against the King.

Henry and Cromwell then turned on the monasteries. No doubt the chief reason was that Henry was short of money for by now he had spent what his father had left him, and by seizing the wealth of the monasteries he might become, as Cromwell said, 'the richest prince in Christendom' without having to ask Parliament for more taxes. Another reason, of course, was that the monasteries were too independent. They nearly all belonged to ancient orders, such as the Benedictines or Cistercians, with headquarters in France or Italy and branches in all Christian countries. Each order had its own Head, who was responsible only to the Pope, and the monks were not likely to agree to the Act of Supremacy, so Henry had really very little control over them. They would clearly be a dangerous centre of opposition to his plans.

All he needed was a good excuse to end this state of affairs, and one could easily be found. Henry had taken over the Pope's power to inspect the monasteries, and he appointed Cromwell to do so. The men Cromwell sent round, the Commissioners, made no attempt to be fair to the monasteries or their inhabitants, for they knew that they were expected to produce reasons for abolishing them, and it is no wonder that they gave a very bad account of what they found. But we do know from other people's accounts that many of the monasteries were no longer doing much good, even if they did no great harm. Fewer people were becoming monks, and many of those who did had no real vocation for religious life. Often they hired servants to do the work that monks used to do for themselves, neglected their Latin, and broke the strict rules of conduct whenever they could. One of their chief occupations, the copying of books by hand, was coming to an end with the invention of the printing-press. They did something to help the poor, but only a very little of their income was used for this, and when, later, distress in England became serious it was not caused by the closing of the monasteries, but by high prices and unemployment. In fact, although there were still many good monasteries, especially in the north, which were doing very useful work, the picture one gets is of a system which was beginning to break down, and the idea of using monastery property for more useful purposes was not a new one. Bishop Fisher had used the property of two small monasteries to found St. John's College at Cambridge, and Wolsey, with the Pope's permission, had closed no less than twenty-two of them to endow his new school at Ipswich, and Cardinal College (later Christ Church) at Oxford.

Many of the monastic houses were very small—some only held five or six monks or nuns—and these were the first to go (1536). Their inmates who wanted to stay in orders were allowed to enter the bigger monasteries, but they could not count on a welcome there, and a great many seem to have been glad to give up monastic life altogether. Most of the men were given permission to become parish priests. Abbots and priors were given a pension out of the monastery's property, and all who ceased to be monks had a small grant of money to start them in their new life. The nuns were much worse off, for there were no jobs for them to go to, and they were less well treated over grants and pensions.

The larger monasteries did not last much longer, and their end was hastened by the only serious rebellion of Henry VIII's reign, which was called the Pilgrimage of Grace. It broke out in 1536 in northern England where people were loyal to the old Church, and profoundly distrusted the work of the King and his officials, like Cranmer and Cromwell. They felt the loss of the monasteries more than people elsewhere, for the north was a hard and warlike part of the country, and the monks still did a great deal to help the poor and the sick, besides being good farmers and husbandmen. Rumours began to get about (and some of the displaced monks encouraged them) that the churches would be robbed, that taxes would be raised on christenings, weddings, and funerals. It was even said that soon one would not be allowed to eat wheaten bread or poultry without buying a licence, and that all unmarked cattle would be confiscated. Many of the nobles too were discontented. They despised and hated low-born counsellors like Cromwell, and they resented any attempt to prevent them from disposing of their estates as they wished by leaving them to the monasteries.

So rebellions broke out in Lincolnshire and Yorkshire. The leaders declared they were loyal to the King, but asked him to restore the monasteries, to protect the Church, to punish heretics, and to dismiss all 'evil counsellors and those of villein blood'—as well as to grant the optimistic request from Lincolnshire 'that we be no more taxed'. At

**A TYPICAL CHURCH AND GATEHOUSE OF A RICH ABBEY
BEFORE THE SUPPRESSION**

one time there were 40,000 men in arms, and the King, with no army, had to parley with them until he could raise one. The leaders could not prevent some looting and murders by their followers, and, as soon as he had collected some troops, Henry used this as an excuse to cancel his earlier offer of a pardon, and punished them with ferocious cruelty. The leader Robert Aske and many more were hanged, and a committee of the King's Council, known as the Council of the North, was set up to keep that part of the country in order.

The rising gave Cromwell an excellent reason for closing the rest of the monasteries (1539). His Commissioners did all they could by promises or threats, to persuade the monks to disband of their own accord, and most of them did, for it was no use resisting, and their only hope of receiving a pension was to submit at once. If they did not they were accused of all kinds of misdemeanours and an unfriendly monk or neighbour could generally be found to give evidence against them. Here and there a brave abbot tried to defend his monastery; what happened then can be seen from a note jotted down in Cromwell's handwriting: 'item: the Abbot of Glaston to be tried at Glaston and hanged there.'

A special office, 'the Court of Augmentations', was set up to deal with the monasteries' property, and committees of local gentlemen were appointed to carry out its orders. The furniture, books, vestments, and church ornaments were put up for sale, but the really valuable things, like jewelled crosses, and gold and silver communion vessels were sent to the Treasury in London. Even the lead from the roof and the church bells were taken and melted down. The fate of the monastery churches varied. Six of them, Westminster, Oxford, Chester, Gloucester, Bristol, and Peterborough, became cathedrals for the new bishoprics that Henry set up. Others were bought by the people who lived near them, and used as parish churches, though as a rule they could only afford to keep up part of them. But most were left empty and roofless, until they gradually crumbled away, or were pulled down by people who wanted the stone to build themselves barns or houses.

All the land was taken by the King, and the Court of Augmentations was busy for several years disposing of it. Most of it was sold, often very cheaply, to courtiers, country gentlemen, lawyers, or merchants. Some of the money it brought in was used for defence on the south coast, and some to found the new bishoprics, but most of it was quickly swallowed up in the day-to-day expenses of governing the country. The men who had bought the land became a very important class of people. Many were justices of the peace or members of Parliament and of course they were among the King's most loyal supporters, for they knew that any attempt to upset Henry's Church settlement and restore the old Church might mean that they would lose their lands.

Although Henry VIII had quarrelled with the Pope and destroyed the monasteries, he was not a Protestant, and still believed all the articles of the Catholic faith; but naturally his attack on the Church was bound to encourage the Protestants. Another thing which did this was the use of the Bible in English. Although both Wycliffe and, in Henry's reign, Tyndale had been declared heretics for translating the Bible, Cranmer persuaded the King to allow it, and in 1539 the Great Bible was printed, and orders were given that a copy should be put in all churches—where everyone might read it or hear it read—carefully chained so that it could not be stolen. People no longer depended on the priest; they could read for themselves what the Bible said, and they often found that a good deal of what they had been taught was not really in the Bible at all. They began to discuss the Scriptures among themselves and even to 'oppose the best priest in the parish and tell him he lies'. Henry had not foreseen this. In 1536 he complained that 'the commons rail on Bishops, speak slanderously of priests and rebuke preachers. I am very sorry to know how irreverently that most precious jewel, the word of God, is rhymed, sung and jangled in every ale-house'. But just when Henry was deciding that the reformers were going too far, Cromwell wanted to encourage them still more by making an alliance with the Lutherans in Germany; he thought their help might be needed if France and the Empire, should join forces against England. The alliance might be strengthened by a royal marriage. Henry had soon tired of Anne Boleyn; she had been accused of betraying him and had been executed in 1536, leaving a daughter Elizabeth. His third wife, Jane Seymour, had given him a son, but died immediately afterwards; so he was again a widower, and Cromwell suggested that he should marry Anne, daughter of the Lutheran Duke of Cleves. When she arrived in England she proved to be very unlike her portraits—in fact, Henry was rude enough to speak of her as a 'fat Flanders mare'. He refused to go through with the marriage, and was furious with Cromwell for advising it. It was not simply that he disliked Anne of Cleves; he had never been really keen on the Lutheran alliance, and had only agreed to it because Cromwell had insisted on the danger from the Empire and France. But soon these two were at war with each other, and there was no need for help from the Lutherans after all. Henry decided that Cromwell had tried to trick him into supporting heretics, whom he had always disliked. He was now no more use to Henry and like Wolsey before him was isolated from all men and hated for his power. So without the least warning, he was suddenly accused of treason, given no chance to defend himself, and executed in 1540 just ten years after the death of his master the Cardinal.

Shortly before this, Parliament, at the King's request, passed the Act of Six Articles, which laid down what the English Church was to believe. It included all the most important beliefs of the Church of Rome; the only differences were that the King, not the Pope, was the Head of the Church, and that the Bible and the Litany were to be in

English. This was the law for the rest of Henry's reign, and it was strictly enforced: Protestants who would not hear Mass were burned as heretics, while Roman Catholics, who were still loyal to the Pope, were executed as traitors. It must have been most bewildering for ordinary people. For the time the Protestants were checked, but their numbers still increased, and their chance came in 1547, when Henry VIII died, and was succeeded by his ten-year-old son Edward VI.

4. The Reformation in England

2. UNDER EDWARD, MARY, AND ELIZABETH

In the reign of Edward VI, the English Reformation was carried much farther, services were changed, and the Church became more Protestant. Henry VIII had laid down in his will that his son should succeed him, and that until he grew up the country should be governed by a council, the members of which he named himself. Just before his death, the old King had become rather less hostile to Protestants. After Cromwell his chief adviser had been the Roman Catholic Duke of Norfolk; but he was replaced by Edward Seymour, the Earl of Hertford and Henry's brother-in-law, a man much interested in Protestant ideas. Seymour at once took the lead in the Council, and within three months of Henry's death the young King made him Duke of Somerset, and the Council allowed him to become Lord Protector of the realm.

Somerset was a successful soldier, and as a statesman he had many sensible ideas. He wanted to stop the enclosing of land, and to impose a tax on sheep which would give the King a steady income, and at the

HEADPIECE. Philip II of Spain and Mary I of England, with arms impaled

49

same time check the increase of sheep farms, which was causing unemployment, but he failed in this because of the opposition of powerful landlords. He wanted to make a union with Scotland by a marriage between Edward VI and the five-year-old Scottish Queen Mary, whose father was dead and whose French mother, Mary of Guise, was planning to marry her to a French prince, and so strengthen the old alliance of Scotland and France, so hostile to England. He failed in this too, because, by trying to bully the Scots into an English alliance which they naturally resented, he only made them closer friends of France, and Mary married not Edward but the Dauphin Francis (later Francis II of France). Again by trying to check the greed of the landowners and protect the ordinary man's common land, he turned the rest of the Council, all of them landlords, against him. It was only in his reform of the Church that he had any success, and even here he did not go far enough to satisfy the most ardent Protestants.

Somerset did not believe in persecution, and he cancelled the Act of Six Articles, and the old law De Heretico Comburendo by which heretics were to be burnt alive. In 1549 he approved a new Prayer Book in which the old services were translated into English and made more simple but most carefully worded, so that both Catholic and Protestant could use them, and each interpret them in his own way. The new book was mostly the work of Cranmer, and it shows the Archbishop at his best, a scholar who could write fine and dignified prose. An Act of Uniformity made its use compulsory in all churches, and abolished the Latin Mass.

The new Prayer Book was popular in and around London, where there were many Protestants, but in the more distant parts of England, where people were very slow to change their ways, it was hated, and in Devon and Cornwall a rebellion broke out. The rebels complained that the new service seemed to them 'like a Christmas game' and demanded that the Mass should be restored. Although many of the local gentry were Protestants, now owning lands which had once belonged to the Church, they could not stop the trouble and either fled or were imprisoned in their houses. The rebels besieged Exeter, which was in great danger of capture, until an army was sent by Somerset to attack the besiegers and drive them off. Most of the leaders were caught and put to death. One priest who had helped the rebels was hanged from his own church tower 'in his robes, having a holy water bucket, a sprinkler, a sacring bell, a pair of beads, and the like Popish trash hanged about him' as one grim triumphant Protestant put it.

Somerset had other troubles to cope with. French pirates seized English ships in the Channel, and Somerset's brother, the Lord Admiral, instead of trying to stop them, appeared to be in league with them. He was a restless ambitious man, who had married Henry VIII's widow, Catherine Parr, and had been made guardian to Elizabeth, the daughter of Henry VIII and Anne Boleyn. If Edward VI and Mary died without children, Elizabeth would be queen, and so when Catherine died, the Admiral secretly planned to marry the Princess and perhaps one day become King of England. Somerset had him arrested and executed on a charge of treason, which was probably justified, but which seemed a harsh and cruel way for Somerset to treat his own brother.

In 1549 another rebellion, this time in Norfolk, caused Somerset's fall. It had nothing to do with religion—in fact the rebels held regular services every day using the new Prayer Book—but was caused by poverty and unemployment. Rising prices, low wages, and greedy landlords, who turned out their tenants to use the land for sheep farms, and helped themselves to the common land which had for centuries been free for everyone—all these things drove the poor country people to the verge of despair and led to violent riots. In many places the new fences put up round the old common lands were torn down. The leader, Robert Kett, himself a country gentleman, argued that the enclosures were illegal, and that his followers were only enforcing the law because the justices would not do so. This was quite true, and Somerset had a good deal of sympathy with the rebels, but with 16,000 of them in arms and controlling most of Norfolk, something had to be done to restore order, and while Somerset hesitated, his great rival in the Council John Dudley, Earl of Warwick, a bold and ambitious man, led an army into Norfolk. Within a few weeks the rising was crushed, Kett himself and many of his followers were caught and hanged, the fences were put back round enclosed fields, and the attempt to hold out against the changes in farming ended in disaster. And not only for the rebels; disaster too for Somerset. The rest of the Council blamed him for the rising: they feared his sympathy for the distressed country folk, and his rival,

SOMERSET'S IMPORTED GERMAN AND ITALIAN TROOPS

Warwick, who now became Duke of Northumberland, took his place as the head of the Council.

Northumberland had none of Somerset's honesty, or of his genuine desire to help the poor. He was concerned only with his own wealth and power. The son of Henry VII's hated tax collector Dudley, and despised by the old nobility as an upstart, his best hope lay in the support of the merchants, and the newer landowners who had bought monastery lands—and these were the men most interested in Protestant ideas. So, although he had no strong religious views of his own, he encouraged the extreme Protestants, who thought that the Reformation had not gone far enough, and that the English Church was still too like that of Rome. Bishops like Gardiner of Winchester and Bonner of London who were strong for the old faith were imprisoned, and replaced by Protestants. In 1552 another new Prayer Book was drawn up, which was much more Protestant than the 1549 one. Clergymen were ordered to use the new book, and those who did not were dismissed from their posts and fined or imprisoned. Their places were taken by earnest reformers, many of whom had been abroad to Germany or Switzerland

and brought back with them the ideas of Luther and Calvin. At the same time the churches were robbed of much beauty, because silver and gold vessels, crosses, and ornaments were taken away, on the grounds that they were not needed for the simpler services. Zealous reformers pulled down altars and statues of the saints, and blotted out the wall-paintings, which had done so much to teach Englishmen their religion. The reformers thought such things were 'idols' which led people away from real worship, but the churches lost much cheerful beauty and colour, which could never be replaced. Protector Somerset had ordered the dissolution of chantries in 1547. Now the last of them were closed and their property taken by Northumberland and his friends.

All these things were done in the name of Edward VI, the solemn, clever little boy who was very much in earnest about his own royal dignity and his religion. Northumberland deliberately set out to flatter him and win his confidence. In this way he became the real ruler of the country, but his whole position depended on the life of Edward VI, and Edward was very delicate. If he should die his sister Mary, who all through her unhappy childhood had clung obstinately and passionately to her mother's memory and her mother's Church, the Church of Rome, would be queen; then Northumberland would be faced not with an inexperienced boy, but with a grown woman, who had all her father's strength of purpose, and a bitter hatred of Protestants.

By 1552 Edward's health was failing, and Northumberland, who saw that the loss of all his power was now very near, became desperate. He worked on Edward's deep devotion to the Protestant religion, and convinced the boy that it was his duty to save it in England at all costs. His father, said Northumberland, had settled the succession in his will, and Edward should do the same, and disinherit Mary, for only so could he prevent the restoration of the Mass and the Papal power. But it would not be enough to dispose of Mary. Northumberland had no desire for the Princess Elizabeth to be queen. She also had far too much of her father's spirit to suit him. There was, however, the Lady Jane Grey, second cousin to the King, descended from Henry VIII's younger sister Mary, a gentle quiet girl, learned and devout, and, as Northumberland had carefully arranged, the wife of his son, Guildford Dudley. If she became queen, Northumberland would be safe, and more powerful than ever. Edward VI readily agreed to make a will leaving Jane his heir, and although both the Council and the judges had grave doubts whether this was legal, they were persuaded in the end. Cranmer may well have had his doubts too, but he saw that the Reformation was in danger, and he did not inquire further when he was told that the judges had approved. Soon after signing the will Edward VI died (1553).

At the time of her brother's death, Mary was on her way to London to see him. If she had arrived she would have been arrested, and Northumberland's plot might have succeeded, but she was warned in time, and turned back to Norfolk. The danger was acute, but Mary at once proclaimed that she was the rightful queen, and demanded the loyalty of her subjects. She was popular; most Englishmen were sorry for her and admired her courage. Besides, she was old King Henry's daughter, and without doubt his rightful heir, so although the Council, at first obedient, and Northumberland proclaimed Jane queen in London, thousands of supporters, both Catholic and Protestant flocked to join Mary, and when Northumberland led his troops against her his men deserted in such numbers that the Council saw the game was up. Hastily they deposed Jane, and proclaimed Mary queen. Northumberland could only give himself up: he was brought back to London, and beheaded as the traitor he was.

Mary was thirty-seven years old when she became queen, which in the sixteenth century, when so many people died quite young, was thought much older than it is now. She was not strong physically but had a will of iron. In her portraits she looks strained and wary, for her childhood had been shadowed by the divorce of her mother and her own ill treatment by her father and the spiteful Anne Boleyn. Her mother died when she was twenty, and after that Mary was very much alone. Her religion and her loyalty to her mother's Church became the most important things in her life. She believed it a sacred duty to bring England back to the old faith and this belief made her persecute and torment people who refused to acknowledge that faith. Yet Mary was not a cruel woman. She was surprisingly merciful to Northumberland's supporters and the unfortunate Lady Jane Grey was at first only imprisoned and not executed, as she would certainly have been under Henry VIII.

Mary's first act was to release Gardiner and Bonner. Gardiner became again Bishop of Winchester and Lord Chancellor and Bonner Bishop of London. Next, Archbishop Cranmer and the leading Protestant bishops, Latimer, Hooper, and Ridley, were arrested, and all over England Protestant clergymen, many of whom were married, were replaced, often by their own predecessors who, because they would not use the new Prayer Book, had been turned out in Edward VI's reign. Without much difficulty the Queen persuaded Parliament to cancel the religious laws of Edward VI and to restore the Latin Mass. Parliament agreed to all this with surprising readiness, as if most of the members cared very little what sort of parsons and services they had. One thing, however, they utterly refused to do—give back to the Church its former lands, and Mary saw that she could do nothing there.

Almost at once the question of the Queen's marriage came up. Her counsellors, her Parliament, and her people were all anxious for her to take a husband, but equally anxious for him to be an Englishman. Mary thought otherwise. Her cousin, the Emperor Charles V, urged her to marry his son, Don Philip, heir to the throne of Spain, and to Mary the suggestion seemed perfect. By such a marriage England would be firmly united with Catholic Spain and with her mother's family, the Hapsburgs of Spain and Austria, and she herself would have a constant and enthusiastic helper always at her side in the task of restoring England to the Catholic faith. The prospect was delightful to her. Disregarding all protests and advice Mary pressed on with the arrangements for the marriage. It was to be the greatest mistake of her life, but nothing would turn her from it—not even when early in 1554 a serious attempt was made to get rid of her and to put her sister Elizabeth on the throne. English dislike of foreigners in general, and particularly the thought of a foreign king, led to a rebellion under Thomas Wyatt. It began in Kent, a county which was wealthy, Protestant, and near enough to London for a rebellion there to be dangerous. But the scheme to crown Elizabeth was betrayed, and the rebellion suppressed, largely because of Mary's cool courage in remaining in London when Wyatt's men were at the very gates of the city. Wyatt himself and many others were executed. Other results followed. The innocent Lady Jane Grey and her husband, who had been imprisoned in the Tower since

SHERRIFFS

THE END OF WYATT'S INSURRECTION, 1554

Northumberland's attempt to crown Jane, were executed, and Mary's suspicions of her young sister became acute. Elizabeth was sent to the Tower and for a time was in grave danger, but there was no proof that she had known anything about the plot to put her on the throne— indeed Wyatt at his trial swore that she knew nothing—and Mary was not unjust. In spite of her dislike of her cool and wary sister, and of the urgings of the Spanish Ambassador, she would not consent to Elizabeth's death. Instead she released her from the Tower and sent her to Wood- stock, near Oxford, to be kept in semi-captivity. But perhaps the most important effect of Wyatt's rebellion was on Mary herself—she was more than ever determined to marry Philip, for it seemed imperative that she should have a child, an heir to whom her throne and her mis- sion should pass, and whom she could trust, for otherwise Elizabeth would succeed her. And she felt she must press forward with her mis- sion—the restoration of the Catholic Church in England—with greater severity than before.

In the summer of 1554 Don Philip of Spain arrived and the marriage took place with great solemnity in Winchester Cathedral. Soon after another visitor arrived in England, Cardinal Pole, Papal Legate and special envoy sent from the Pope to heal the breach between England and Rome. Pole solemnly pronounced the re-admission of the nation to the Catholic Church, and Parliament repealed the Act of Supremacy and all the other anti-papal laws of Henry VIII. They still utterly refused to consider the return of any land or money or treasures. At the marriage ceremony Mary wept for joy, but there was little happiness in store for her. Philip, who was years younger than his wife, did not love her and disliked England. He soon departed to his own realms, return- ing only once for a short visit. Moreover, there were no children. In fact the only clear result of the marriage was that England was dragged with Spain into a disastrous war against France, which she could not afford and from which she gained nothing.

After her wedding and her husband's departure Mary went on with her great task. On the advice of Cardinal Pole she revived the law by which heretics were burnt. Probably she expected that a few sharp examples would be enough, as they had been in her father's time, and did not realize how much things had changed since then. For during the reign of Edward VI the English Prayer Book had become part of the people's lives, and the Protestant faith had come to be something that hundreds of English people were prepared to die for. The Protestant bishops were among the first to do so. Latimer and Ridley were burnt at Oxford and faced this horrible death very bravely. Cranmer, old and frail, was forced to watch the burning of his two friends, and at the sight his nerve failed: he signed a confession of his sin of heresy, and begged for a pardon. But Mary could not forgive his conduct to her mother twenty years before, and he was told that he was to die in spite of his confession. At this the Archbishop's courage returned, he withdrew his confession, declared himself a Protestant, and went to his death as bravely as his friends. The burning of this old and respected man, who had been the friend and counsellor of Henry VIII, sent a wave of horror through the country. 'The burning of the Archbishop', men said, 'hath harried the Pope out of the land.'

Urged on by Pole, Mary went ahead with the persecution of Protestants, hating the suffering she inflicted, perhaps even uncertain of its success, but blindly believing it a duty from which she must not shrink. About 300 Protestants were burnt. They were all kinds of people—well-known figures like Cranmer, and humble tradesmen and farmers, women as well as men. Many were Londoners, who were burnt at Smithfield just outside the city walls. In spite of the burnings, the Protestant religion was not crushed. Some of the bravest suffered martyrdom, but the majority submitted outwardly, and longed and prayed for Mary's death and the accession of Elizabeth. Good-will towards Mary turned to hatred, and most Englishmen were filled with a horror of the Roman Catholic faith and everything to do with it—a horror which was to last for more than 200 years. For when the actual memories of the fires and torture began to fade, the sufferings of the Protestants were recalled by *The Book of Martyrs*, written by John Foxe in 1563, which formed an important part of the upbringing of English children for many years afterwards, and kept alive the idea that the Pope and the Catholics were the cruel and unsleeping enemies of 'God's Englishmen'. Severe and cruel these persecutions certainly were, but even so they cannot be compared with the sufferings endured by Protestants in other European countries, for instance in Philip's own dominions.

By 1557 Mary's health was failing; her husband neglected her, her subjects hated her, and her life was made bitter by the knowledge that Elizabeth, now her only possible heir, would undo all her work. The war with France went badly, and Calais, England's last outpost in France, was lost. Like all the Tudors, Mary was proud and patriotic, and this last blow overwhelmed her. She died in 1558, one of the most courageous, honest, and sincere of all our rulers—and one of the unhappiest and least successful.

Her sister Elizabeth had seen the English Reformation pass through three stages. First Henry's breach with Rome and its result, a Catholic England without the Pope. Secondly, under Edward, a more Protestant Church with the new Prayer Book in English and the pillage of the Church buildings. Thirdly the Catholic revival under Mary and the persecution which so greatly strengthened the Protestant faith.

Her first task was to settle the religious question in a way which could be accepted by most people, Catholic and Protestant alike. In 1559 a new Act of Supremacy declared that she was 'Supreme Governor of the Realm as well in all Spiritual things as Temporal', which, though it did not say in so many words 'Head of the Church' meant much the same thing. Another Act of Uniformity laid down that the English Prayer Book should be used, that all must attend church, and that anyone who did not could be fined, unless he could produce a good excuse. The fines, 12d. per Sunday, were not always enforced, but the Act provided a useful test of who was reliable and who was not, and in times of danger, such as the war with Spain, the 'recusants' as those who refused to go to church were called, were firmly dealt with by the magistrates. The teaching of the Church was explained more fully in the Thirty-nine Articles, and the effect was to leave it much as it had been in the time of Protector Somerset. Both the Prayer Book and the Articles were worded very carefully, so that there was little for anyone to object to, and on the whole Elizabeth's Church settlement was acceptable.

Of course it did not please everyone. There were Roman Catholics who did not accept Elizabeth's authority over the Church. They did not attend church, paid the fines when they had to, and held their own services privately. Later on, some of them supported Mary Queen of Scots, and took part in plots against Elizabeth, but it would be a mistake to think that all Roman Catholics were like this; most of them were loyal subjects. At the other end of the scale, there were Protestants who did not think the Church was Protestant enough, and who came to be known as Puritans. Some of these only wanted to make the services more simple, as they thought they had been in the early days of the Christian faith, and to cut out some of the remaining ceremony, which reminded them of the Mass. Others went farther and objected to the whole idea of a Church governed by bishops: they thought it ought to govern itself by means of an elected Church Assembly. Such people got their ideas from John Calvin, who had set up a Church like this at Geneva in Switzerland, and they were known as Calvinists or Presbyterians. Elizabeth thought such ideas were a danger to her authority and, later in her reign, when the Presbyterians were becoming stronger, she suppressed them. A special Court of High Commission was set up to deal with them, and many were punished by this and by the Star Chamber for writing or preaching against the bishops; but once again it would be wrong to think of them as rebels, for they were loyal to the Queen, though they wanted some changes in the Church. The Presbyterians were held in check by Elizabeth, but they were not crushed, and their number steadily increased under the Stuart kings.

In spite of those Roman Catholics who preferred to pay fines rather than attend church to hear the Prayer Book read, and of Presbyterians who disliked the bishops, Elizabeth's settlement did one great thing. By satisfying the majority of her subjects it gave England peace from religious strife. It was most fortunate that it did, for the Queen had plenty of dangers and difficulties to face without a civil war about religion.

5. Dangers to England

To this day, we still 'remember the 5th of November', but for more than 200 years our ancestors kept another November anniversary—the 17th; for 17 November 1558 was the beginning of the reign of Queen Elizabeth I, who brought to its greatest success the Protestant monarchy which Guy Fawkes tried to destroy with his 'gunpowder treason and plot' in 1605.

It was a joyful day for England. The crippling war with France, the loss of Calais, the marriage with Philip, the hated Spaniards who had often thronged the Court in Mary's time, the 'fires of Smithfield'—all these were forgotten in an outburst of loyalty to the new queen. Elizabeth I entered London, dressed in purple velvet, and riding at the

HEADPIECE. Mary Stuart 'en deuil blanc', from the portrait in Dumbarton Castle, with a sample of her elegant handwriting

head of a brilliant procession of nobles and gentlemen, and the whole
city greeted her with 'such a roaring of guns as was never heard afore,
and with trumpets playing, and melody, and joy and comfort to all true
English men and women'. From then until her coronation she stayed
in London, and showed that she well knew how to win the hearts of her
people. She rode about the city, being gracious to all, high and low—
never at a loss for a kindly word, so that crowds turned out to cheer her,
and old men who had known her father in his prime chuckled to each
other, 'Remember old King Harry the Eighth', though her easy manner
made the dignified Mantuan Ambassador think that 'she exceeded all
the bounds of gravity and decorum'. The coronation was a gorgeous
affair, with pageants and processions and banquets; but when it was all
over, and Elizabeth settled down to the business of government, she had
to deal with many difficulties.

Everyone expected that the new queen would marry—but whom?
She had plenty of suitors, for many foreign rulers were anxious for a
marriage alliance with England; but Mary's reign had shown the
dangers of marrying a foreigner, and the dangers of marrying an English
nobleman were almost as great. In the end, Elizabeth never married,
though she made very clever use of the possibility that she might do so
one day. Then again, government was thought to be entirely men's
business, and her sister had not been a successful queen, so that even if
she did not marry, Elizabeth unless she was very careful would find
herself completely controlled by her Council. She was clever enough to
avoid this and to keep matters of state very much in her own hands.
Her knowledge of languages helped, for she could speak Latin,
French, and Italian fluently, and could deal with foreigners herself.
She was careful, too, to consult her advisers one at a time, so that she
could pick their brains and decide the question herself. This often
meant that she hesitated a long time before making up her mind but,
when she did so, she was usually right. Like her father, she was quick
to recognize an able man and one of her best choices was William Cecil.
He was at the time a man of thirty-eight, who had been secretary to
Protector Somerset, and then to Northumberland. He was a Protestant,
but he had managed to avoid trouble during Mary's reign, and was
always more interested in politics than in religion. Elizabeth at once

made him a member of her Council. 'This judgement I have of you,'
she said to him, 'that you will not be corrupted by any manner of gifts,
and that you will be faithfull to the state, and that, without respect of
my private will, you will give me that counsel you think best.' She was
quite right, and for forty years Cecil's loyalty, caution, and common
sense made him her most trusted adviser, even though they had many
disagreements. But there was never any doubt who ruled the country.
'She seems to me', wrote the Spanish Ambassador, 'incomparably more
feared than her sister, and gives her orders as absolutely as her father
did.'

For all that, Elizabeth's position at first was exceedingly difficult, and
in fact it was never easy during her long reign of forty-five years. According to Roman Catholics, she was not the rightful queen; the real
heiress was her cousin Mary Queen of Scots, who was married to King
Francis II of France. Mary was therefore Queen of Scotland by birth,
of France for a time by marriage, and of England by right in the eyes
of many people, and the French hoped to put her in Elizabeth's place.
While she was at the French Court, her mother, Mary of Guise, ruled
Scotland for her, with a French army, and so England might be attacked
from two places at once. Elizabeth's best defence against this was Spain,
for, although France and Spain were both Roman Catholic powers,
they were also enemies, and she could continue her father's game of
playing one off against the other. Indeed Philip II of Spain was so
anxious for English support that he actually proposed to marry Elizabeth, and though she refused him he helped her to make peace with
France in 1559; but not to get Calais back.

Elizabeth's other great advantage was the outbreak of civil war in
Scotland. The Scottish nobles were still very like the English barons of
Richard III's time—powerful, turbulent, and jealous of each other.
They disliked the French regent as a foreigner and a Roman Catholic,
and were greedy for Church lands, so they supported the Protestant
leader John Knox, and in 1557 a number of them, calling themselves
the Lords of the Congregation of Jesus Christ, attacked the French, and
asked Elizabeth to help them. Elizabeth could not afford a war, and
she did not like helping rebels against their lawful queen, but this was
a wonderful chance to get the French out of Scotland, so she began to

help the Lords secretly by sending them money. In spite of this they got the worst of the fighting. An English fleet was sent to the Firth of Forth, which prevented the French from landing reinforcements; but even this was not enough, and it was clear that the only way to save the Lords from defeat was to send an army as well, and risk open war with France. Cecil insisted that the risk was worth taking, and in the end Elizabeth was persuaded. Cecil was right. France had troubles of her own at home where civil war soon broke out between the Catholics and Protestants (or Huguenots). The Regent of Scotland died, and her supporters, the Scottish Catholics, could hold out no longer. Cecil was sent north to discuss terms of peace, and in 1560 both sides agreed to the Treaty of Edinburgh. The French left Scotland: Mary gave up her claim to the English throne (though she later revived it) and agreed that Scotland should be governed in her absence by a council consisting of the chief Protestant nobles, who were naturally friendly to England. It was suggested that Elizabeth should marry one of them, but this she gracefully refused to do.

The Treaty of Edinburgh was a great success for Elizabeth, but when Cecil tried to weaken France still further by sending an army to help the Huguenots in the hope of recovering Calais, the expedition was an expensive failure. Calais was lost for good. The Scottish and French wars left Elizabeth nearly bankrupt, but, for the time, the French were no longer a serious danger. After the death of Mary's young husband Francis II in 1560, France was really governed by the crafty Italian queen mother, Catherine de Medici, who tried to keep the power in the hands of her feeble sons by playing off the Catholics and Huguenots against each other. In this way France became so weak and divided that it was more than 100 years before she was again a real danger to England, though this was not realized at once, and many people still thought of France as our worst enemy. Yet because of the stormy and tragic career of Mary Queen of Scots, Scotland and its affairs kept Elizabeth and her Council fully occupied, even after the French had been driven out.

Mary was nineteen when, on the death of her husband, she returned to Scotland—'a vain, artful, bewitching creature', tall and graceful, with brown eyes and dark chestnut hair. She had been brought up at

SHERRIFFS

YOUNG QUEEN ELIZABETH AND WILLIAM CECIL IN A GARDEN
AT HAMPTON COURT, ABOUT 1560

C

the French Court to a life of what John Knox angrily called 'joyousity'. She was generous and impulsive, and, unlike the cautious and politic Elizabeth, apt to be carried away by love or hate, and to act recklessly without counting the cost. She was sometimes weak, but in a crisis she had a gay light-hearted courage which was most attractive and made even her enemies respect her.

Elizabeth and Mary rather naturally distrusted each other from the first. A struggle between the Catholic and Protestant powers of Europe was bound to come sooner or later, and it might easily begin by Mary marrying someone who would claim the English throne in her name. Elizabeth wanted her to marry an Englishman and suggested her own favourite Robert Dudley, Northumberland's son, whom she made Earl of Leicester, so as to make him more Mary's equal in rank. Mary did not do so: she married her own cousin the Earl of Darnley. He was a Catholic like herself and he had many enemies among the Scottish lords. Even worse, from Mary's point of view, he was like a spoilt child, jealous, ill tempered, and fickle. Mary soon came to despise and hate him, and turned more and more for advice and help to an Italian, David Rizzio, who had been one of the Court musicians and became her private secretary. Not only Darnley, but all the Scottish nobles were jealous of this low-born foreigner, and they planned his murder. One evening in March 1566, when Rizzio was at supper with Mary, Darnley and others burst in and seized him. He clung to Mary's dress, crying to her to save him, but they dragged him out, and stabbed him to death outside the door. Mary was overwhelmed by horror and grief, but this soon gave way to hatred for Darnley. 'No more tears', she said, 'I will think on revenge.'

Soon afterwards, Mary fell in love with the Earl of Bothwell, 'a glorious rash and hazardous young man' and one of the greatest scoundrels in Scotland. He was a Protestant, and was married already, but that did not stand in his way when he saw a chance to be king. The only problem was to get rid of Darnley, and Bothwell planned his murder as Darnley had planned Rizzio's. People still argue fiercely as to whether Mary was an accomplice or not, but at the time her actions looked suspicious. She pretended to be reconciled to Darnley, which was made easier by the birth of their son, the future James I, in 1566; she nursed her husband devotedly through an attack of smallpox, and early in 1567 she brought him with her to Edinburgh, still weak from his illness. On 9 February she suddenly remembered that she had promised to attend a masque, and went out, leaving Darnley practically alone in the house. At about 2 a.m. the whole city was shaken by an explosion, and the house was blown up: Darnley's body was found in the garden: he had apparently escaped the explosion, and seemed to have been strangled. Nobody really knows just what happened that night, for the murder was never properly investigated. There was an inquiry, but thongh everyone suspected Bothwell nobody dared to give evidence. Mary would hear nothing against him, and to complete the scandal, they were married three months later, after Bothwell had got a divorce from his wife. The marriage ruined Mary. The Protestant ministers, who had always hated her as a Catholic, now accused her of murder and adultery, and the nobles, who had been glad enough to get rid of Darnley, but disliked even more the idea of Bothwell as king, rose in rebellion. Mary's supporters were defeated, and she herself was brought as a prisoner to Edinburgh, while a howling mob, urged on by their preachers, cried out for her death. Bothwell fled with a band of pirates to Norway, where he was recognized and denounced by the first of his deserted wives, and eventually went mad in prison.

The Lords imprisoned Mary in the island castle of Loch Leven, while they decided what to do with her. If they had succeeded in killing Bothwell, or if Mary had been willing to divorce him, they might have restored her to the throne, but she was still devoted to him, and her first act would have been to bring him back if she could. Meanwhile they had found some letters which Mary had written to Bothwell before Darnley's murder, which seemed to prove that she was as guilty as he. By threatening to publish them, and charge her with murder, they forced Mary to give up the throne in favour of her infant son, with one of themselves, the Earl of Moray, as regent. Many of them wanted to go further, and put Mary to death, but at this Elizabeth protested so strongly that they spared her. In the midst of it all Mary escaped, and again raised troops, but within ten days her small force was scattered, and Mary only saved her life by a desperate flight across the dangerous sands of the Solway to take refuge in England.

Her arrival set Elizabeth and Cecil a new problem. What was to be done with her? Elizabeth's first instinct was to restore her to her throne in Scotland, but she knew the Scottish lords would fight rather than have her back, and Elizabeth could not afford to make enemies of them. Next, Mary asked that if Elizabeth would not herself help her to regain her throne, she would at least allow her to go to France and ask her friends there for help. It was not easy to refuse—after all, Mary was a queen in her own right and not one of Elizabeth's subjects—but if she did go, and managed to reconquer Scotland with French troops, England would face the same danger as she had before 1560 with 'the French king bestriding the realm with one foot in Calais and one foot in Scotland'. The only thing left was to keep Mary in England. The excuse for doing so was that she was suspected of a part in Darnley's murder, and that Elizabeth could do nothing to help her until she had been cleared of this charge by a full inquiry. The inquiry was held, and was very carefully managed. The Scots lords produced the letters Mary had written to Bothwell and claimed that they proved her guilt, but at this stage Elizabeth quickly stopped the inquiry: she now had a good reason for not pressing the Scots to have Mary back, and that was enough: she did not want matters to go any further.

So Mary was kept in England in a kind of semi-captivity: she had failed in Scotland, but she had never given up hope of becoming Queen of England, and, as she was not very strictly guarded, she began to build up a party of English supporters. There were many Roman Catholics among the nobles and squires of the north, and Mary used all her wiles to win them over to her. She kept in close touch, too, with France and Spain. France was too distracted by civil war to be able to do much for her, but Spain was the most strongly Catholic of all the European powers, and Spanish friendship with England was beginning to wear very thin. Philip was not particularly anxious to have the half-French Mary Queen of England, but he was beginning to think that even that might be better than the insolent heretic Elizabeth. He was too busy on the Continent to risk open war, but it was worth his while to encourage anything that would weaken England. In this way Mary became the centre of various plots to depose Elizabeth with Spanish help.

The first of these was the northern rebellion of 1569—the only open rebellion that Elizabeth had to deal with during her reign. The north was the home of lost causes, and had not changed very much since the Wars of the Roses. There great nobles like the Nevilles of Westmorland or the Percies of Northumberland, were in some ways as powerful as the Queen herself, and they could still call out armed retainers, veterans of border raids against the Scots. They were jealous of men like Cecil who were not of the old nobility, and wanted in fact to be the power behind the throne. Most north-countrymen were still Catholic; they had already made one attempt to restore the old faith by the Pilgrimage of Grace, and they were ready to try again, but this could only be done by deposing Elizabeth and making Mary queen. A plan was made to arrange a marriage between Mary and the Duke of Norfolk, and to settle the succession by making Elizabeth accept them as her heirs. Norfolk was Elizabeth's cousin, and the only duke in England, but he was neither a Catholic nor a very brave man and, although he was quite willing to marry Mary, he did not really intend to be a traitor to Elizabeth. He found, however, that he had gone too far to draw back and had committed himself to leading a rising of the northern Catholics. Elizabeth's spies discovered the plot, and the Queen summoned Norfolk to Court to explain his suspicious conduct. At this his nerve failed; although Mary and her friends urged him to act boldly, he meekly returned to London, and was imprisoned in the Tower, after writing to the northern earls warning them to call off the rebellion. His submission upset the whole plan, for while the Earls of Westmorland and Northumberland were still wondering what to do, they too received a summons to Court. The only hope now was to fight. By November they had collected 1,500 cavalry and 1,000 infantry—a small force, but enough to make them masters of northern England, at least for the time being. They got as far as York, intending to march south and rescue Mary, who had been moved to Tutbury in Staffordshire; but by December loyal troops had been collected in the Midlands, no help had come from Spain, and the rebels were hopelessly outnumbered. Their army melted away without a battle. The leaders fled to Scotland, but Northumberland was captured by the Scottish regent, handed over to Elizabeth, and executed. A last effort by Sir Leonard Dacre was defeated early in 1570, and about 600 of the rebels were hanged.

THE ST. BARTHOLOMEW'S DAY INCIDENT, 1572

In spite of this failure, Elizabeth's enemies, at home and abroad, continued their efforts. Philip still kept up a show of friendship, but the Pope had never been anything but an open enemy—though, so far, what Cecil called his 'evil-will, cursing, and practising' had not done England much harm. In 1570, however, the Pope solemnly excommunicated Elizabeth; this meant that to Roman Catholics she was no longer lawful queen but a usurper, and it was their duty to overthrow her. Although it came too late to help the northern rebellion, the excommunication encouraged new plots, and in 1571 Cecil, whom Elizabeth had made Lord Burghley, discovered a dangerous one. Once again Norfolk, who had been released in 1570, was involved: he was to marry Mary, depose Elizabeth, and restore the old faith with the help of 6,000 Spanish troops, to be sent over by Philip's general, the Duke of Alva, from the Netherlands. Ridolfi, an Italian banker living in London organized it, but he was not a good conspirator, and Burghley managed to intercept his letters, which betrayed the whole plan. Norfolk was condemned as a traitor, but in spite of all her Council could say, Elizabeth could not bring herself to put him to death. When Parliament met in 1572, the members spoke even more strongly and demanded Mary's death as well. 'Cut off her head and make no more ado about her', said one member, 'a general impunity to commit treason was never permitted to anyone.' It was impossible to save Norfolk: sadly, after much hesitation, the Queen signed his death warrant, and he was beheaded on Tower Hill. But for Elizabeth's firmness, Mary would have died too. As it was, her execution was postponed for another thirteen years, but it was perhaps bound to come in the end. Even Charles IX of France, her brother-in-law, realized this. 'Ah the poor fool', he said, 'she will never cease her plotting till she lose her head. In faith they will put her to death: I see it is her own fault and folly. I see no remedy for it.'

News of the terrible massacre of the Huguenots on St. Bartholomew's Eve (23 August) 1572, when something like 4,000 people were killed, appalled all Protestants, and led to new demands for the death of Mary. It was her relations who had let loose the Catholic mob in France, and the massacre was believed to be only one part of a vast Catholic plot which threatened England as well. All this was bound to affect the position of Roman Catholics in England.

For the first ten years of Elizabeth's reign the great majority of English Catholics had in fact been perfectly loyal, and had not been seriously interfered with. Elizabeth had declared that as long as they kept the law there should be 'no examination or inquisition of their opinions in matters of faith': but she probably hoped that, by excluding them from schools and universities and forbidding their services, she might so weaken the Catholic religion that in time it would die out. To prevent this, a group of English exiles set up a college at Douai in Flanders specially to train Catholic missionaries for England, and in 1579 the Pope himself started another college at Rome for the same purpose. Between 1575 and 1580 these colleges sent over to England a steady flow of brave and gifted men, who went about in disguise, encouraging the English Catholics, and making new converts. They lived dangerous, hunted lives, moving at night from one country house to another, and hiding during the day in secret passages and 'priests' holes', some of which can still be seen in old houses. In 1580 the Jesuits took over the work, and sent over a secret mission led by Edmund Campion. 'My charge', he said, 'is of free cost to preach the Gospel, to instruct the simple, to reform the sinners, to confute errors.' He said he had no idea of interfering in politics, but with a heretic queen on the throne this was practically impossible, and indeed his companion, Parsons, took an active part in plots against Elizabeth. Everywhere there was much activity among those who stuck to the old Church. Parliament replied with much stricter laws against Roman Catholics. The penalty for holding a Catholic service was increased to £135 and a year's imprisonment, while the fine for recusancy went up from 12d. a week to £20 a month.

In 1581 Campion was arrested. First promises of pardon, then torture were used to make him give up his faith, but, when both failed, he was accused of treason. 'If you call my religion treason', he said, 'I am guilty; as for other treason, I never committed any as God is my judge.' But, since the excommunication, all Catholic missionaries could be regarded as traitors, for they were after all sent by the Pope to harm Elizabeth, and Campion was sentenced to death. Other executions followed, and since to be an open Catholic meant ruin and imprisonment, many turned to secret plots in favour of Mary. Strangely enough, in spite of the Ridolfi plot, Mary was not very closely guarded, and could still write to her friends. In 1573, however, Burghley became Treasurer, and the Queen appointed a new Secretary, Francis Walsingham. He was a stern Protestant, a solemn dark-featured man (Elizabeth nicknamed him the 'Moor') who had been an exile in Mary Tudor's reign, and who had seen with his own eyes the horrors of St. Bartholomew's Eve in Paris when he was the English Ambassador there. He knew there could be no peace for England as long as Mary was alive, and he set himself to destroy her. In 1583 his spies discovered another plot, and, although there was no direct proof against Mary, a wave of fury ran through the country. A 'Bond of Association' was drawn up, which pledged all who signed it to kill Mary at once if any plot should lead to the murder of Elizabeth, and thousands of signatures came in from all over the country. Mary was much more strictly guarded, and could no longer write or receive letters, but she still had a pathetic faith in secret hiding places, ciphers, and the like, and Walsingham used this to trap her. In 1585 he arranged what Mary believed to be a secret way of smuggling letters in and out of the house in the weekly deliveries of beer to the household. She used it at once to write to the Spanish Ambassador, to France, to the Pope, and to her English friends; but all the letters were brought straight to Walsingham, who deciphered them, made copies, and sent them on. They told him all he wanted to know.

By August 1585 he had full evidence of another plot organized by a Catholic gentleman called Babington. The leaders were quietly and swiftly rounded up. One day Mary, who suspected nothing, was invited out to hunt, and while she was away her secretaries were arrested and all her papers seized. There was plenty of evidence against her now. In October she was taken to Fotheringay Castle and tried for treason. She defended herself vigorously but there was never any doubt about the verdict: the only question was whether Elizabeth would consent to her death. When Parliament met, both Houses again insisted that Mary must die, but not till February in 1587 did Elizabeth bring herself to sign the death warrant. On 8 February Mary was beheaded. She met her death with great courage and dignity, declaring that she died a martyr to her faith, and leaving her claim to the English throne to Philip of Spain.

By this time the war with Spain, which had been threatening so long, could not be put off much longer. Ever since Elizabeth's accession, the old friendship between England and Spain, started by Henry VII, had been changing to hostility. Philip II was a strong Roman Catholic, and apparently the most powerful ruler in Europe. In his own dominions he stamped out heresy by means of the Inquisition, but as long as the heretic Elizabeth ruled, England would always be a rallying-point for Protestants—Dutch, French, Scottish, or German—and heresy would never be really crushed. At the same time Spain's real enemy in Europe was France, and while France was powerful it would be dangerous for Philip to make an open enemy of England as well. Even if he conquered England it would do him no good, for as long as Mary was alive he could not overthrow Elizabeth without making Mary queen—and that would mean an alliance between France, England, and Scotland which would make France stronger than ever. The outbreak of the religious wars made France rather less dangerous, but Philip still had not his hands free to deal with England. He had to fight the Turks in the

Mediterranean; French pirates from the Huguenot base of La Rochelle attacked his shipping (with some English help); and there was discontent in the Netherlands which in 1567 broke out into open rebellion. A strong army, under Philip's most able general, the merciless Duke of Alva, partly crushed the revolt, and reoccupied most of the rebellious provinces; but the Protestants of Holland took to their ships and carried on the struggle at sea. Elizabeth saw the advantage of keeping Spain busy on the Continent, and allowed the 'Sea Beggars', as the Dutch seamen were called, to refit their ships and sell their plunder in English ports.

In 1568 Elizabeth took a bigger risk still. In order to pay Alva's army, Philip borrowed from the merchant bankers of Genoa a large sum of money, which was sent by sea up the Channel. The ships carrying the money met rough weather which forced them to put into Plymouth for shelter. The money did not become Spanish property until it was actually handed over at its destination, and Elizabeth, after making a private agreement with the Genoese agent, calmly announced that she was borrowing the money herself, and had it unloaded and brought to London. Philip was furious; he gave orders that all English property in his dominions was to be seized, and forbade English trade with the Netherlands. Fifty years before, the interruption of our trade with Flanders would have been a disaster, but by this time English merchants were beginning to find other markets in the Baltic and the Mediterranean, and even across the Atlantic. More serious was the danger that Philip would at once declare war, for he had the largest army and fleet in Europe, and England with her small population seemed to stand little chance against the might of the whole Spanish Empire. But, as Elizabeth had guessed, Philip was not yet ready for a war with England as well as the revolt in the Netherlands, so the danger passed, and the inevitable war was put off for a little longer.

6. Sea, Ships, and Spaniards

In the first half of the sixteenth century, Spain was the greatest world power. The discoveries of Columbus and Magellan had given her a long start in the race for overseas possessions and for some time she had no serious rival in the Atlantic. The Portuguese were busy on the African coast and in the Far East, and the English were more interested in France and Scotland. Spain conquered, without much difficulty, the islands of Cuba and Hispaniola (now San Domingo), Mexico, the Isthmus of Panama, the north coast of the South American Continent ('the Spanish Main'—or mainland), and Peru, stretching along nearly the whole Pacific coast of South America. These colonies were thinly settled by Spaniards, and produced sugar, tobacco, grain, and indigo, but much more important was the fact that Mexico and Peru also produced gold and silver. The Spanish government tried to protect the

HEADPIECE. Sir Francis Drake, from an unsigned portrait dated 1591, with a facsimile autograph natives (who were still called 'Indians'), but could not prevent the Spaniards in America from treating them so cruelly that in many places they died out, and a steady supply of slaves was imported from Africa to keep the colonies going.

The treasure of the New World enriched Spain, but it also encouraged other people to attack her, and Spain was not always able to defend her wealth—partly because her ships and her colonies presented such a big target, and partly because she was slow to develop a suitable fleet. For hundreds of years, the Mediterranean had been the centre of the world, and all the Mediterranean powers (of which Spain was one of the biggest) had used galleys—a type of warship which had changed very little since Roman times. They were long narrow craft, driven by oars, and they were fast and handy, but they could only carry heavy guns in the bows and stern, and they could not make long voyages or stay at sea in rough weather. A fight between galleys was like a land battle between two forces of calvalry. They charged, and tried to sink each other by ramming. Failing that, they grappled together, and the crews fought it out hand to hand. The greatest of all such battles was Lepanto, in 1571, when a Spanish fleet under Don Juan of Austria defeated the Turks.

Because of conditions in the North Sea and the Atlantic the English had never made much use of galleys. They, like their northern neighbours, used sailing ships which, with no slaves or oars to take up space, could mount heavy guns well down in the hull, which were able to fire broadside. Henry VIII took a great interest in ships. He experimented with different types, and really laid the foundations of the modern navy, setting up a royal dockyard at Deptford, and giving a charter to Trinity House—a guild of master mariners, with the Controller of the Navy at its head. His first warships, such as the famous *Great Harry*, were rather clumsy, but later designs improved, and the English captains worked out ways of manœuvring so as to cripple enemy ships by gunfire instead of trying to ram them. The Spaniards also developed these 'galleons' or 'great ships', but they were slow to change their ideas. They still thought in terms of stopping the enemy and then getting alongside and boarding him. Their ships had high 'castles' fore and aft, and they carried many light guns for clearing the enemies' decks, and a great many soldiers who were useless for working the ship and despised the sailors. This ill feeling between soldiers and sailors was apt to crop up on board English ships too, but Drake would have none of it in his crews. 'I will have the gentlemen', he said, 'to haul and draw with the mariners.'

The first people to challenge Spain in the New World were the French. The peace between France and Spain in 1559 made no difference to what happened outside Europe, and although the civil wars weakened France, the Huguenots, from their base at La Rochelle, kept up their attacks on Spanish shipping. It was not until 1562 that the English appeared on the scene. In that year John Hawkins 'having made divers voyages to the Canaries, and being assured that negroes were very good merchandize in Hispaniola, and that store of negroes might easily be had on the Guinea coast' made his first voyage to the Spanish Main. Sailing to the West African coast, he bought slaves from native dealers, and took them to the Spanish colonies. Those who survived the horrors of thirst, heat, and disease, on the 'Middle Passage' were sold to the Spanish settlers at a good profit. It was a grim trade, but for many years after most people saw nothing wrong in it.

Hawkins at first hoped that the Spanish government would allow him to go on supplying slaves, but Spain meant to keep the trade of the New World to herself and wanted no trespassers—especially heretics. On his third voyage in 1567 he ran into trouble. This time Hawkins had six ships, one of which, the German-built *Jesus of Lubeck* belonged to the Queen, and he was accompanied by his young cousin, Francis Drake. After selling the slaves, they put into the small Mexican port of San Juan d'Ulloa (now Vera Cruz) to refit before the voyage home. While they were there a fleet of thirteen Spanish ships arrived outside the harbour. After a parley, a truce was arranged, and the Spanish ships entered the harbour and berthed alongside the English while the crews mixed with each other on shore. Suddenly the Spaniards made a carefully planned and treacherous attack. Taken by surprise, the English resisted fiercely, but only two of Hawkins's ships got away—his own ship, the *Minion*, and the *Judith*, commanded by Drake.

This was a turning-point in English dealings with Spain. In their earlier voyages they had hoped for peaceful trading, and some English merchants had carried on their business in Spain itself; but now every English seaman was out for revenge on the Spaniards, and war was bound to come sooner or later. The man who did most of the avenging was Francis Drake. He was born in 1545 in Devon, but his Protestant parents were driven out by the western rebellion of 1549, and he grew up near Chatham. He learnt his seamanship in the coasting trade, until he joined his cousin John Hawkins in his slaving ventures. After San Juan, both Hawkins and Drake resolved to make the Spaniards pay for their treachery, and each in his own way succeeded. Hawkins became the Controller of the Queen's Ships and used his experience to make them the most efficient fighting machines of their day, while Drake spent the rest of his life in daring attacks on Spain.

His first voyage to the Caribbean in 1571, was to gain information and to find a base from which he could attack the Spanish treasure ships. Much of the gold came from Peru, being brought by sea to the Pacific coast of the Panama Isthmus, and then taken by strings of pack-mules across to Nombre de Dios to be shipped to Spain. Drake decided that this was the point to attack. In 1572 he set off with only two ships and seventy-three men—a small force, but very well equipped, with 'three dainty pinnaces made in Plymouth, taken asunder all in pieces and stored aboard, to be set up as occasion served'. The English set up a base on the Panama coast, fitted up the pinnaces, and used them to play havoc with Spanish shipping. With the help of friendly Indians whom they called the 'Maroons', mostly escaped slaves able to tell them all about the habits of the Spaniards, they surprised Nombre de Dios and held it for some hours. But they found no treasure there and Drake himself was wounded. Undaunted by this, they tried to ambush the next treasure convoy in the hills of the Isthmus. They were only partly successful, but even so the plunder they took, as Drake put it, 'made the voyage'. It was during this expedition that Drake saw, from a great tree high up in the hills, the farther shore of the isthmus with the Pacific Ocean stretching away to the west. He resolved to sail that ocean before he died.

His chance to do so came in 1577. By that time relations with Spain were very strained, and there were two parties at the Court: the younger counsellors like Leicester and Walsingham thought that the time had come for open war, but the more cautious Burghley was anxious to keep the peace as long as possible. The Queen kept everyone guessing, now inclining to one side, now to the other. Drake was careful to conceal his plans from Burghley, but it was obvious that he was fitting out ships, and it was not difficult to guess what for. So he took the extra precaution of sailing a day or two before he was expected to, and in this way he just escaped an order not to go. He had five ships of which the biggest was the *Pelican* of 100 tons, and 158 men. He planned to reach the Pacific by Magellan's Strait, which had—and still has—an evil reputation among seamen. The Spaniards had given it up as too dangerous and built their ships on the Pacific coast. Drake was taking a big risk, but if he did get through he would take the Spaniards completely by surprise.

It was a difficult voyage. The two smallest ships, the *Swan* and the *Marigold*, had to be scrapped, and, there was even something very like a mutiny. It was led by Thomas Doughty, who had been a close friend of Drake's, but who had given away the plans of the expedition to Burghley, and had made a lot of trouble among the crews. He may well have been briefed by Burghley to prevent Drake from reaching the Pacific for fear of provoking Spain to declare war. Drake dealt firmly with the situation. He called a court martial which tried Doughty for 'mutiny and contention', and sentenced him to death. After this a fresh start was made. At the approach to the Straits, the ships were separated by rough weather and the *Elizabeth*, after a vain search for the *Pelican*, turned back. Drake got through the straits with great difficulty, but met a terrible gale, which drove him back to the south-east. In this way he discovered that the land to the south of the straits was not, as everyone thought, a great southern continent, but only a small island with Cape Horn at its southern tip.

When the gale abated, Drake headed northward into the Pacific. Here he changed the name of the ship to bring better luck, naming her the *Golden Hind*. Sailing north along the coast of Peru, he found the Spanish settlements utterly unprepared for an enemy. He raided Valparaiso, and seized the port of Lima, plundering eleven ships in the harbour. Here he heard that 'the Cacafuego galleon' a great treasure ship, had just sailed for Panama, and at once set out in pursuit. The

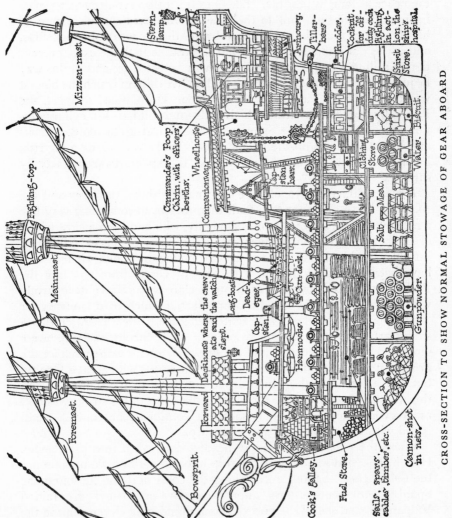

Mizzen-mast.

Stern-lamp.

Armoury.

Tiller-bars.

Rudder.

Cockpit for dirty cock fighting in action.

Spirit Store.

tion the ships hospital.

Commander's Poop Cabin with officers' berths.

Wheelhouse.

Companionway.

Fighting-top.

Capstan bars.

Molding Store.

Biscuit.

Water.

Salt Meat.

Mainmast.

Gun deck.

Log-boat.

Dead-eyes.

Deckhouse where the crew ate and the watch slept.

Forward

Foremast.

Capstan.

Hammocks.

Gunpowder.

Bowsprit.

Cook's Galley.

Fuel Store.

Cannon-shot in nets.

Sails, spars, cables, timber, etc.

CROSS-SECTION TO SHOW NORMAL STOWAGE OF GEAR ABOARD
A 20-GUN ELIZABETHAN FIGHTING SHIP

galleon was found and captured after a short fight, and the *Golden Hind* was ballasted with silver and gold. Drake treated his prisoners well, sending them home in the ships he captured, and some of their accounts give a good picture of life on the *Golden Hind*, where Drake and his officers dined in state in the great cabin, using gold and silver dishes, and with music playing. They were very much impressed with his dignity and good manners, and with the efficiency and discipline of his crew.

Drake's next problem was to get safely home with his plunder. The whole Pacific coast was now on the alert, and even if he escaped the Spaniards, he would still have to face the perils of Cape Horn. He first tried to get back by means of the North West Passage, and sailed along what is now the coast of California 'towards the Pole Arcticke' to about latitude 48 degrees. Here he abandoned the attempt and decided to head westward across the Pacific to the Spice Islands, and so home via the Cape of Good Hope. Before setting out on this immense voyage he put into a bay on the Californian coast to refit and take on supplies of water. He claimed the land for England, 'setting up a faire great poste, a plate whereon was engraven with her Majesteye's name'.

Setting out from 'Drake's Bay' in July 1578, he sailed for more than three months to the south-west, without sight of land, until, in November, he reached Ternate, one of the Molucca Islands, where the ruler who hated the Portuguese, made a treaty of friendship with Drake and sold him a consignment of spices. Drake called at several islands in the East Indies, and once the *Golden Hind* ran aground on a reef, and was lucky to escape wreck. But he crossed the Indian Ocean safely and reached the Cape in June 1580. He returned by way of the West African coast, and got back to England in November, after a voyage of nearly three years, with 67 of the 157 men who had set out, and a cargo worth a fortune.

Much had happened while Drake had been away, and he must have been uncertain what kind of a reception he would get from the Queen. Bitter complaints about his activities had been coming in from Spain, for Philip was now King of Portugal too, and all Drake's plundering had been at his expense. This voyage had certainly made war more likely, but the Spaniards were still occupied with the Dutch, and were not ready to attack England. Elizabeth had her own grievances, for Spain was helping rebels in Ireland as well as backing Roman Catholic plots. Besides, she could not afford to hand back the booty which Drake had taken. So she ignored Philip's protests, dined with Drake on board the *Golden Hind*, and afterwards knighted him as a reward for what he had done.

But war was sure to break out in the end. The Spanish expedition to Ireland, and the English help to the Dutch, as well as the Jesuit mission to England, and the intrigues of Mary Queen of Scots with Spain, all increased the tension between the two countries. In 1585 the Dutch resistance began to weaken, and Elizabeth saw that she must openly send help or see her friends defeated, and be left to fight alone. She sent an army under the Earl of Leicester, but it did not achieve very much. There was not enough money to equip or pay the troops properly, and most of what there was found its way into the pockets of the courtiers whom Leicester made his officers. But the troops fought well, and the gallant death of Sir Philip Sidney at Zutphen showed that some at least of their commanders knew their duty.

After this events moved quickly. In 1586 Drake made another voyage to the Gulf of Mexico, and did great damage. Philip decided that the English must be beaten, and began to prepare an Armada, or expeditionary force, for an invasion. Next year the execution of Mary Queen of Scots gave him a good opportunity to claim the English throne for himself. But the Armada did not sail in 1587, because the English got their blow in first. While the Spanish fleet was slowly assembling and fitting out, Drake sailed from Plymouth with six ships to 'singe the king of Spain's beard'. He made a completely unexpected attack on Cadiz, which had no proper defences, sailing into the harbour and burning eighteen ships. For three weeks he cruised off the Spanish coast, and captured or sank twenty-four more ships. This raid completely upset Philip's plans, and the sailing of the Armada had to be put off till the following spring. Drake finished off his cruise by capturing a Portuguese galleon from the East Indies with a cargo worth £100,000, so the expedition showed a handsome profit.

Philip patiently set to work to repair the damage. But in February 1588 he suffered another blow, for Santa Cruz, the greatest of Spain's admirals, died. Philip appointed the Duke of Medina Sidonia to succeed him but it was not a good choice, for Medina Sidonia had no experience of the sea, and was most reluctant to take command. He found many excuses for delay, and it was not until the end of May that the Armada put to sea. It did not get far, for it was dispersed and badly damaged by a gale, and had to put into Corunna for repairs. Medina Sidonia wanted to abandon the whole enterprise. He wrote that, 'neither officers nor men were as efficient as they ought to be, and he could find few, and indeed hardly one, who understood his duties'. Of course this was an exaggeration, but it shows his state of mind.

His orders were to sail up the Channel to the North Foreland, and there cover the invasion fleet of the Duke of Parma which was to sail from the Belgian coast bringing his troops from Flanders. Neither Parma nor Philip seems to have realized that an invasion would be impossible unless the English fleet had been either destroyed or else blockaded in harbour. In England too there was some confusion about the best kind of defence. Drake and Hawkins, as soon as they heard that the Armada had been delayed by a storm, wanted to make a raid on the Spanish coast and destroy it before it could put to sea again, but this very sound plan was thought to be too risky, and the ships were kept at home. There were two dangers to guard against—Parma in the Netherlands and the Armada itself, and Parma seemed the more serious. Troops were raised, and the main force concentrated at Tilbury, where they could protect London against a landing in the Thames estuary. Levies were called out in all the southern counties, and a system of beacons was arranged to give warning of the enemy's approach. The fleet was divided, part of it, under Lord Thomas Seymour, watching the eastern end of the Channel, and the main body at Plymouth with Lord Howard of Effingham, Drake, Hawkins, and Frobisher. The English commanders, unlike Medina Sidonia, were eager for a fight. Sir William Winter, aboard the *Vanguard* in the Downs wrote: 'Our ships do show themselves like gallants here. I assure you it would do a man's heart good to behold them: and would God that the Prince of Parma were upon the seas with all his forces and we in view of them: then I doubt not that we should make his enterprise very unpleasant for him.'

In July the Armada again set sail. It was sighted off the Lizard on

19 July. The English ships had to be towed out of the harbour against the wind, and if Medina Sidonia had taken the advice of his best captains and made straight for Plymouth, he would have taken them at a great disadvantage, and might have destroyed them; but his orders were to sail up the Channel, and he would not disobey them. During the night the English ships crossed the course of the Spaniards, and, making a circuit to the south-east, got behind and to windward of them, in a good position to attack. There was much less difference between the two fleets than people often think. The total tonnage of the Spanish fleet was probably greater than that of the English, but tonnage is not the same thing as fighting power. Many of the Spanish ships were primarily transports full of soldiers. Their high 'castles' and many small guns made them suitable for fighting in the old-fashioned way with the ships, as Raleigh put it, 'clapped together'. But Howard and Drake had no intention of fighting like that. Their ships were handier and faster, and they carried much heavier guns, so they were able to engage from outside the range of the Spanish ships, and avoid their attempts to get to close quarters. In a fight of this kind, the advantage lay with the English.

The first action was fought off Plymouth. Neither side did the other much damage, though two big Spanish ships collided and a third was damaged by an explosion. The Armada sailed on up the Channel, in variable winds, with the English attacking whenever they could, and the Spaniards from time to time turning on their pursuers. There were battles off Portland and the Isle of Wight, but they were not decisive, and on 27 July the Armada anchored off Calais, almost within reach of their objective.

In a running fight lasting a week, they had only lost two ships, and Medina Sidonia must have felt that things were going well. In fact, he was in serious danger, for the English fleet was waiting for him outside and the anchorage at Calais was too exposed for his ships to stay there long, while Parma's forces were still not ready. During 28 July he could see activity in the English fleet, and guessed that an attack was coming. It was made by fire-ships. These were old vessels, filled with pitch and tar to make them burn; volunteer crews sailed them as near the enemy as they dared, then lashed the helm, and sent them drifting down

ENGLISH FIRE-SHIPS MOVE IN TO CALAIS HARBOUR, 1588

among his fleet. Drake had prepared six of these, and during the night he sent them into action. If the Spaniards had kept their heads, they could easily have towed them aside, but they fell into a sudden panic. Some of them perhaps remembered that at Antwerp the Dutch had done appalling damage with fire-ships like floating mines packed with explosives, and thought that these were the same kind: in any case they did not wait to find out. In a wild scramble to get out of harm's way, they cut their cables (leaving their anchors behind) and struggled out to sea in complete confusion.

The English at once attacked. Medina Sidonia, with about one-third of his fleet turned to meet them and fought bravely, but most of his ships were being driven by a north-west wind towards the dangerous sand-banks of the Belgian coast and could give him no support. His squadron was very badly battered, but the English had used up most of their ammunition, and did not continue to attack closely because it looked as if the whole Spanish fleet was drifting to certain destruction on the shoals. The Spanish pilots, had given up hope of saving a single ship, but they were saved at the last moment, for 'God was pleased to change the wind to southwest' and the Armada was driven out into the North Sea, with the English still in pursuit. They may have had hopes of turning back and joining Parma, but the gale continued and they could only run before it. The English followed them as far as the Forth, until they had little food and water left.

Just a fortnight after the Armada had first been sighted, Howard turned back, leaving the Spaniards, with their crippled ships full of sick and wounded, alone in the grey North Sea. The worst part of their ordeal was still to come, for their only way home was round the north of Scotland and out into the Atlantic. After rounding the Orkneys, they met the full force of the Atlantic waves, and were dispersed into groups of two or three or single ships as the worse-damaged vessels fell behind. Some were driven on to the west coast of Scotland. One was wrecked in Tobermory Bay, and many attempts have been made to raise it, and recover the treasure it was supposed to have had aboard. Many more were caught by a westerly gale off Ireland, and either foundered at sea or were wrecked on the rocks of that grim coast. Most of those who escaped the sea were massacred either by the Irish or by the English army of occupation.

Medina Sidonia and part of his fleet got back to Spain in September. He had lost sixty-four ships. At first it was not realized in England how complete the victory had been, and there was still anxiety about invasion, but when it became clear that England was saved there were great rejoicings. Medals were made to commemorate the victory bearing the words, in Latin, 'God blew with his winds and they were scattered'. It is true that more Spanish ships were destroyed by the sea than by the English fleet, but it was the fleet that had saved England. The defeat of the Armada was 'the first naval campaign of the new era, when sail and gun replaced oar and sword'. It was the real beginning of that English sea-power which was to shape our whole history.

The defeat of the Armada was not the end of the war. It was only the beginning of many years of fighting against Spain which occupied all England's wealth and energy. The war was fought in the Netherlands, in France, and in Ireland, as well as on the sea. From 1585 onwards there was an English force of about 6,000 men in the Netherlands, and, under leaders like Lord Willoughby and Sir John Norris, they did good service in helping to liberate Holland. In 1589 the war spread to France, for Henry III was murdered, and the heir to the throne was Henry of Navarre, the leader of the Huguenots. The Catholic party would not have a heretic as king, and made an alliance with Spain. This was so dangerous to England that, although Elizabeth was very short of money, and had already failed once in an attempt to interfere in France, she promptly made an alliance with Henry. Between 1589 and 1595 she sent five separate expeditions to help him, and even when he changed his religion and became a Catholic, in order to get the support of Paris, Elizabeth still supported him as long as he was fighting against Spain.

The most important front of all was the sea, for, in spite of the defeat of the Armada, the Spaniards were tough and determined enemies. Very few of the English naval expeditions were completely successful, while some were costly failures. In 1589, for example, Elizabeth sent out an Armada of her own to invade Portugal and liberate it from Spain. Troops were landed at the mouth of the Tagus, but there were quarrels between Drake who commanded the fleet, and Norris who commanded the army, the Portuguese did nothing to help, sickness broke out, and the forces had to be withdrawn. After this failure, which cost £60,000 and 8,000 men, 'combined operations' were given up, and a small force of warships was based on the Azores to patrol the approaches to Spain and intercept the treasure ships. A lot of damage was done to Spanish shipping, but not enough to win the war, and the Spaniards were still able to keep their fleet at sea. In 1591 the blockading squadron was very nearly caught by a force of fifty-three Spanish ships. The admiral, Lord Thomas Howard, managed to get away in time, with five of his ships, but the sixth, the *Revenge* commanded by Sir Richard Grenville, was cut off and surrounded. For twenty-four hours the *Revenge* fought on alone until at last, with the ship sinking under him, and almost his whole ship's company dead or wounded, Sir Richard surrendered. He died of his wounds on board the Spanish flag-ship.

In 1595 another big naval expedition was sent out with Hawkins and Drake in command to the Isthmus of Panama, to cut off the treasure at its source. By this time the Spanish Main was much better defended. The only hope lay in a surprise attack, and the Spaniards had ample warning of the expedition. Hawkins died before they reached the Isthmus; and though Drake again captured Nombre de Dios and advanced towards Panama, many of his men died of fever, and the rest were driven back to the coast. Drake himself fell ill: they managed to get him back to his ship, but they could not save his life. He died on board, and was buried at sea in Nombre de Dios Bay, on 28 January 1596.

The long war gradually wore down Spanish sea-power, and, by the end of Elizabeth's reign, England was fast becoming the greatest naval power in Europe.

Some of the fiercest fighting of the whole war took place in Ireland. From 1595 onwards, there was trouble in Ireland—a rebellion by the powerful Ulster chief, Tyrone. Elizabeth had very few troops to spare, and Philip saw his chance to play the same game in Ireland as she had played in the Netherlands. In 1596 he sent a fleet and an army of 10,000 men to help the rebels. If this force had landed it would probably have driven the English out altogether, but twice the ships were scattered by storms. In 1598 Philip died, worn out with toil and struggle, and the Spanish war effort began to slacken. But the Irish rebellion went on without foreign help, and was the worst problem of Elizabeth's last years.

With so many troops already fighting elsewhere and with very little money available, the English did not have much success in dealing with Tyrone, and in 1598 Elizabeth sent out the Earl of Essex to take command, giving him great powers and many troops. Robert Devereux, Earl of Essex, was in some ways the most brilliant of all Elizabeth's courtiers. He was handsome, daring, and spirited, much admired by the army, and popular with the citizens of London. Elizabeth herself liked him and behaved towards him like an elderly and affectionate aunt with a spoilt young nephew. In fact there was a good deal of the spoilt child about Essex, who was rash, conceited, jealous, and selfish, and apt to become sullen and treacherous if he did not get his own way. He was bitterly jealous of Sir Walter Raleigh and of Robert Cecil, Burghley's son, who was taking his father's place as the Queen's chief adviser. He hoped that he would win such a success in Ireland that he would oust his rivals and win Elizabeth's favour for good.

Like other Englishmen, before and since, Essex quickly found out that Ireland was a much tougher proposition than he expected. Tyrone had built up a strong army, and Essex put off attacking him to make a raid into the south, which did no good. Elizabeth sent angry messages to him, urging him to get on with the war, but Essex seemed more interested in building up a party of supporters among his officers. He made some of them knights, although he had no power to do so, and he answered Elizabeth's protests by appeals for more troops. At last he could find no more excuses for delay, and set off into Ulster; but he had little hope of success. He knew that his enemies at Court were making the most of his failure. He dared not risk a defeat, and wanted only to get back to England, and try to win back Elizabeth's favour. Instead of fighting, he arranged a truce which left Tyrone practically supreme in Ireland. Soon afterwards he crossed to England, and rode post-haste to London. Elizabeth was very angry, and put Essex under house-arrest in the charge of another member of the Council. In August 1600 he was released, but still banished from Court. He could still count on a gang of supporters, 'swordsmen, bold confident fellows and discontented persons', so he resolved on a desperate plan to seize the Court, the Tower, and the city, and force Elizabeth to dismiss his rivals, and take her orders from him. The Council discovered the plot and summoned Essex to appear before them. He knew that the game was up unless he could strike first, and, with about 200 men he rode into the city where he had always been popular and called on the Londoners to defend him. But he got no help; his house was soon surrounded, and he gave himself up. Within three weeks he was beheaded. His successor in Ireland, Mountjoy, was one of the most skilful soldiers of his time. In 1601 the long-awaited Spanish troops reached Ireland but they were too late. Tyrone's rebellion was already waning, and Mountjoy routed the Irish and Spanish forces in a great battle at Kinsale in 1602.

This was the last triumph that Elizabeth was to see. In March 1603 her health at last began to fail, and she as well as her subjects knew that the end was coming. Everyone assumed that James VI of Scotland would become king, and already many courtiers were taking care to get in touch with him. On 11 March a proclamation was drafted to make James king; then, with that matter settled, Elizabeth waited for death. It came early in the morning on 24 March, and the greatest reign England had ever known came to an end. The war still went on —but not for long. England had fought Spain to a stand-still, had saved herself and the Protestant cause in Europe, and had laid the foundations of her future strength on the sea.

7. Land and People

1. GETTING AND SPENDING

RICHARD III was the last of the Plantagenet kings of England, and after his violent death at Bosworth five members of the Tudor family between them occupied the throne for 128 years (1485–1603). All the five were remarkable, and in some cases, spectacular men and women, and during their reigns many changes took place in England, many very important events occurred, and many Englishmen of towering greatness lived and died. So it is quite natural that their family name should have been attached to that period of 118 years, and that it should often be called after them—the Tudor period—and quite natural too, that the reign of Elizabeth I, who 'though only a woman made herself feared by Spain, by France, by the Emperor, by all!', should be specially marked out and called after her—the Elizabethan period. Such labels as these attached to certain periods of history are very useful but they can be dangerous. They may give a false idea that history can be chopped up into neat time-compartments, each with a label and a clear beginning and end—

HEADPIECE. 'The Tudor beastes', heraldic supporters and badges. The white cock was peculiar to Henry VIII and the falcon to Elizabeth the Middle Ages up to 1485 and then the Tudor period till 1603—and so on. It is perilously easy to talk as if the moment Henry VII was crowned everything in England stopped being medieval or Plantagenet and suddenly became Tudor, almost as if people quickly changed into a completely new kind of clothes, looked round for a ruff, and moved into a Tudor house which had conveniently sprung up in the night. That is, of course, an absurd exaggeration, but sometimes books and people give the impression that it is true, and so it is exceedingly important to remind ourselves that, though by the end of the Tudor reigns immense changes had taken place in the daily life of English people— their homes, habits, food, work, and amusements and in their ideas— they had done so very gradually. Such changes had begun almost invisibly, years before the wary Henry VII settled his family so securely in 'the king's palace of Westminster' and they went on long after Elizabeth, the last and most magnificent of that family, was dead. And it was also true, as we shall see, that there were ways in which England and Englishmen had hardly changed at all since the Norman Conquest.

Nowadays a large number of books are written every year about England, describing the countryside, the farmer's year, the ancient buildings, and the bygone customs of our forefathers, and although books are not by any means the only way of finding out such things—the best being to poke about for oneself among churches, houses, pictures, museums, and so on—they are extremely helpful. From them we can find out a great deal about life in these islands at the present time, and also a certain amount about life in the past. The fashion of journeying about, of discovering and describing this land that we possess and live in is a popular one today, but it was really first begun in the reign of Henry VIII, by a man named John Leland, Keeper of the King's Libraries who, as he said of himself, 'was totally inflamed with a love to see all . . . this ample realm', and who for nearly ten years (1534–43) travelled and rummaged about and in so doing noted 'a whole realm of things very memorable' and presently wrote them down. Since then there have always been men passionately interested in their country, 'the most famous Iland of all the world', who have found out and recorded for us much that would otherwise have been forgotten; those who immediately followed John Leland's example tell us a great deal

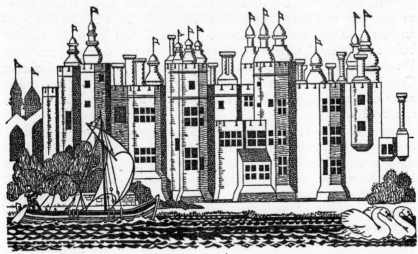

'RICHMONT'S FAIRY PALACE AT SHEEN IN SURREY'

about 'the Iland' under the Tudor and Stuart sovereigns, and make it easier for us to imagine what it was really like.

Now Leland noticed, among many other things, 'three kinds of ruins', and these alone give us some very useful information. First he noticed many 'lofty towers downrazed', and these were the remains of feudal strongholds, keeps, and castles which had been 'downrazed' because they were no longer necessary for safety, as they had been in former days of violence. The work of Henry VII had been successful. He had crushed in one way or another the insolent lawless owners of such strongholds and made violent ways unprofitable. No one in their senses would want to go on living in these keeps and castles unless it was absolutely necessary, for they were dark, dank, and intolerably draughty, and people were beginning to realize that there were other more comfortable possibilities. Their owners, if they could afford it, usually preferred to build themselves new houses where they could look out of quite large glass windows instead of arrow slits, and where the first thought was not 'Are we safe?' but 'Are we living comfortably and pleasantly?' Thus many warlike houses crumbled, and others, more graceful and peaceful-looking, were built, beautiful houses, large and small, which all of us can visit in almost any part of England. At Chartley, in Staffordshire, Leland found the castle 'in ruine' and 'a goodly manor' built a 'flite shot' away. Some castles were not deserted however. Warwick and Kenilworth, Raglan and Dunster, and Little Stokesay Castle on the Welsh Marches, were altered and made more convenient and went on being used as family houses. Warwick and Dunster are still lived in.

Secondly Leland noticed that the walls of many towns were crumbling. Here again the more peaceful times made these stone curtains, which in the Middle Ages had been so vital for the safety of little communities inside them, less necessary, and in many cases houses had spread and were spreading far beyond them. The walls of London with its seven gates, and of a good many other towns, remained, but their day was over in England. Except in a danger-spot like Berwick-on-Tweed, on the Scottish border, no one would ever again attempt to build a new wall around the spreading towns. In any case they were not much use for defence, for the days of bows and arrows, hurled spears, and stones cast from giant catapults were past, and cannon-balls propelled by gunpowder were another matter altogether. By 1592 the private secretary to the Duke of Wurtemburg, when on a visit to England, could write in his diary that 'Reading *like all English towns* is without walls', and at Oxford he noted down, 'walls razed and falling into decay'.

The third kind of ruins which Leland saw were, to him, very recent ones—the monasteries—standing, since 1540, roofless and silent, except where, here and there, the smaller ones had already been altered and occupied by the men who had bought them along with the land from the King.

From information like this collected by Leland, and by Camden, Harrison, Fynes Moryson, Stow, and many others who wrote after him, we can build up a reasonably clear picture of what England was like during the 200 years between 1485 and 1688, and in some ways the picture might surprise us. Of course we should not expect to see great towns, railways, factories, dockyards, and airfields, but it might, for instance, be quite a shock to find that there were far fewer people. There were, in fact, only four million instead of fifty million people living in this island, so that they would be noticeably thinner upon the ground, and the country would have seemed to us distinctly empty. Indeed there were more sheep than people—three sheep to every human being. We should miss the crowds and, again, we should miss entirely the impression of neatness, of the orderly parcelling out of the countryside into compact farms, and rather small fenced or walled fields. Instead the land would strike us as shaggy and untidy. There were villages of clustering houses, usually grouped round a church, and surrounded by unfenced fields, running off and away as far as the eye could see, disappearing into woods, or merging with irregular patches of rough common land where the geese and cattle grazed. These fields made a patchwork of different-coloured strips among dark masses of woods, so that the villages and their cultivated land seemed to be almost shouldered out by the remains of vast forests. Arden, Sherwood, Epping, and Dean still stood, dark and of almost impenetrable thickness, even though by Elizabeth's reign the government were getting alarmed at the rate that trees were being felled for house- and ship-building, and for industry too. Of course, round the towns the forests were thinning rapidly, but in places they were still as thick as the Forest of Westward between Carlisle and Cockermouth, into which, since the north remained wild and lawless far longer than the south, men still drove their cattle for safety and knew that they could not easily be found. In the forests were wild pigs, wild cats, and, of course, deer in plenty. Narrow twisting roads, running naked over moors and hills in the north and Wales, or deep between banks or hedges in the warmer parts of the country, linked the villages, usually atrocious roads impassable in winter with mud, and choked with dust in summer. Only a few of the main highways, like the London to Bristol, or the Stratford–Oxford–London road, along which Shakespeare travelled, were cobbled where they passed through a town or a large village.

In the villages the houses were built without any ordered plan, facing this way and that, straggling along the tracks, and grouped irregularly round the church. Many of them were miserable places still with the wooden frame and wattle-and-daub of earlier times, and an earthen floor—poor enough to deserve the contempt of a Spaniard travelling in England who said that 'the English have their houses of sticks and

dirt'. Even quite prosperous farmers like Robert Smalley, who died at
Galby in Leicestershire in 1559, had only a living room, 'the hall', and
a private bower or bedroom, often called 'the parlour', both on the
ground floor, though another Galby farmer, John Power, had an upstairs bedroom into which he probably climbed by a ladder poked
through the parlour roof. There were, however, three changes coming
everywhere which gradually made even the poorer homes more comfortable. First, the fire had usually been moved from the middle of the
floor, under a hole in the roof, to a hearth against a wall, with brick- or
stone-work behind it, and a stone hood jutted out to catch the worst of
the smoke and conduct it out through a hole higher up in the wall. As
time went on, this was improved upon by a stone or brick chimney,
carrying off the smoke above the roof, and it made a vast difference to
the inside atmosphere. Secondly, the windows, once closed by wooden
shutters or by fine lattices of wood, or at the best by small panes of horn
fitted into a wooden framework, were now coming to be filled with
glass, since, by the middle of the sixteenth century, this was quite cheap.
Thirdly, rather fewer domestic animals shared the living-rooms with the
family, for usually their sheds and sties were built a little away from
the house itself. Apart from these improvements there was not much
that we should call comfort in the smallest houses, whether in village or
town. The furniture was of the roughest—clumsy wooden tables and
three-legged stools, home-made of course, like the plain chest in which
clothes were kept, and the wooden bowls and platters and spoons. There
were still few bedsteads, but other things were improving and people
slept if possible on mattresses filled with flock, that is, rough wool,
instead of straw and, one is thankful to realize, they had flock or feather
pillows instead of 'good round logs'. If possible, too, a family would
collect a few treasures such as pewter mugs and pewter spoons and
candlesticks, and these were handed down from father to son.

If these had been the only houses in the Tudor village, there would
have been little to distinguish it from a medieval one. But in practically every place in the land there were new and more solid houses
going up. It was a great time for building. Some were magnificent
mansions for noble and wealthy families, but others were quite modest
places yet solid and comfortable. They were carefully planned, often

built round quadrangles or in the shape of an H or an E, and were usually built of whatever material was most easily obtained in the neighbourhood—stone where there were quarries, bricks where good bricks were made, and so on. All of them had chimneys, glass in the lattice windows, and inside staircases, and no doubt their owners were very proud of these new things. At any rate they liked people to notice chimneys and often made them ornamental and even fantastic, while the staircases were elaborately and beautifully carved so that visitors could not help noticing them as soon as they entered the house. Chimneys and glass windows meant, of course, less smoke, more warmth, and more light, things which people were beginning to enjoy as a matter of course. Rooms were made snug with tapestries or painted cloths, or panelled with wood, 'whereby', said William Harrison, writing in Elizabeth's reign, 'the rooms are made warm and much more close'. They were not, however, made dark, for though when you go into one of these houses now you are apt to exclaim 'How dark it is!' it would not have been so when the panelling or tapestry was new. Then the wood would be a beautiful pale colour and the bright tapestries or cloths would glow on the walls, so that the houses must have seemed full of rich colours, and especially when filled with people in bright elaborate dress.

Even if the new house was for a farmer or a parson or a small land-owning squire, the furniture would not be at all magnificent. It was made locally in the village or nearest town. The tables, stools, and high-backed settles of wood were heavy and clumsy. The master and mistress of the house had solid-looking armchairs, made more comfortable by loose home-made cushions. There were chests for clothes in nearly every room, and in the houses of better-to-do people one or two carved cupboards, and buffets or, as we should say, sideboards, on which specially treasured glasses and pieces of pewter or silver were displayed. For everywhere private possessions were increasing. We can tell this from the lists of things which were left by people in their wills. These included long tables, armchairs, carved bedsteads with down mattresses, hangings and quilts, cups of silver and porcelain, and of course salt-cellars, which were often magnificent: Queen Elizabeth was given one at her christening by Lady Burghley: 'a salte of golde, in the form of a globe enameled grene with a cover enameled white with a lion in the toppe of the cover.'

There were curtains for the windows, and sometimes mats of plaited rush for the floors, though many people still had stone floors strewn with rushes or hay. When Erasmus first came on a visit to England in 1519, he noticed this custom and said the hay often smelt horrible, which is not surprising considering that people freely threw bones and unwanted scraps of food upon the floor, and left them either to go mouldy or be cleaned up by the dogs. Erasmus may have been unlucky, however, for in 1581 a Dutch doctor visiting England said 'the neate cleanliness of the chambers rejoysed me and the strawing of them over with sweete herbes refreshed me'. It cost as much as 16s., probably about £6 in our money, to renew the rushes for a large house.

In some ways people were keeping their houses and themselves cleaner than before. There were public baths in towns, and Windsor Castle had a bathing room. Most people used a wooden tub, and home-made scented soap, though in 1524 there was a soap factory in London and household soap could be bought for 4d. a pound. Toothbrushes were not used: people preferred to pick their teeth clean, and the very fashionable carried a case of gold picks around with them. All of this, the warmer, pleasanter houses, the increase in furniture and possessions and in comfort and cleanliness, showed that at least some Englishmen and their families had more money to spend and more leisure to enjoy themselves and that for a good many the standard of living was going up.

Just as there was a growing interest in the building of houses and in furnishing, and a desire for more comfort generally, so there was a new taste for the setting in which the houses stood. All but the most miserable hovels had always had small patches of ground around them, roughly fenced in and used for growing necessary but not particularly attractive plants—cabbage and onions, parsley, garlic, and thyme and other herbs, but little else. Now, however, orchards and gardens were more highly thought of. William Harrison says: 'If you look in to our gardens how wonderfully is their beauty increased!' And they certainly were becoming more than merely plots where vegetables and fruit were grown, and where the mistress of the house had her herb beds from which she could concoct the necessary drinks and preserves, both pleasant and un-

pleasant, with which she delighted or dosed her family and servants.
Harrison gives a good long list of fruit grown in England: apples, pears,
plums, apricots, peaches, figs, strawberries, mulberries, with walnuts,
almonds, and filberts. He also says he has seen oranges and lemons
growing, but these were usually imported and could be bought at 7 for
4d. All the herbs we know, like mint and sage, lavender and rosemary,
and many more besides, were grown and were very important. As in
the Middle Ages, they were used for seasoning meat, which in winter
was not fresh, as well as for medicines and ointments. Every woman,
even if she lived in the town, was expected to understand their uses,
from the amount of rhubarb to put in a dose, to the making of complexion water and 'violet confects' (which were little sweets made by
dropping violets into thick syrup and letting the sugar crystallize on
them) or hair cream from stewed apples and lard! The herbs and
vegetables were often planted out of sight, at least of the main windows
of the house, but the flower gardens were planted in full view and greatly
enjoyed. Often they were elaborately laid out with smooth lawns and
trees trained to make shady walks, with neat beds called knots and stiff
little hedges of box and lavender. There were

> Sweet smelling beds of lilies and of roses
> Which rosemary banks and lavender encloses.
> There grows the gillyflower, the mint, the daisy
> Both red and white, the blue veined violet,
> The purple hyacinth, the spike to please thee,
> The scarlet-dyed carnation bleeding yet.

Englishmen had begun to grow flowers as they do today, not simply
because they were useful for food or for medicine but for their colour
and shape and scent. In Elizabeth's reign a certain Humphrey Gifford
wrote a collection of prose and verse and showed his interest in flowers
by giving it the title 'a Posie of gilloflowers (wallflowers), eche differing
from other in colour and odour, yet all sweete'. Shakespeare's plays are
full of passages which show how interested he, for one, was in flowers,
and the Dutch doctor Lennius wrote in 1581, 'theyr nosegays of fragrant
flowers in theyr chambers cheered me up and entirely delyghted my
sences'.

Houses, chimneys, windows, furniture, gardens, all these showed great changes during the years 1500–1700 which were obvious to everyone, and were clearly improvements. No wonder that towards the end of Elizabeth's reign the old men of Radwinter village in Essex told their rector, the Rev. William Harrison, that they thought everywhere there had been a 'great amendment of lodging' since they were boys. There were also other changes taking place in village and in town, which often broke with customs and traditions so old that no man knew when first they began, and which often caused distress and deep discontent. These did not come suddenly. They had, as we shall see, begun quietly and almost unnoticed even before Bosworth was fought, but as they quickened they were felt and discussed, and either approved or hated.

First of all, life in the villages was undoubtedly changing all through the reigns of the Tudors and Stuarts, although when Henry VII became king it was going on very much as it had done for many years. The humblest of the houses in the country, the least likely to be improved, belonged to the *cottager*, who paid a small rent of a few pence a year to the lord of the manor and earned his living as a farm worker. He usually managed as well to keep a pig, a few geese and hens, and possibly a couple of sheep, and these animals he could turn out to feed upon the common grazing land round the village. His living conditions had not altered much since the Peasants' Revolt in 1381. In fact, even as late as 1700 a poem was written which says that the cottager's pigs lived under his bed, while his hens roosted over his head.

Rather more prosperous than the cottager, certainly more important, and probably living in a better house, with pigsties and henhouses apart, was the *copyholder*, and this rather curious name must be explained. It had long been the custom for the lord of the manor to keep a written record about his land, how much was let out, to whom, and on what terms. The lord's steward kept the record and it was called the manor roll. Each tenant received a written copy of the particular entry which concerned him and his portion of land, and this copy could be produced as proof that he held such land and of the terms on which he held it. The name 'copyholder' gradually stuck to the man who held by copy, and both the name and position were far more popular than that of villein. For to be a villein, as you may remember, had originally meant that you were personally unfree, that you could not leave the village, or marry, or allow your children to marry, or send your son to train as a priest, without first getting your lord's permission, which was often refused. Moreover, a villein had held his land in return for irksome and often much-resented services, week work for perhaps three days a week, and boon work, always at the busiest times of the year. Changes in these matters had already occurred all over England, and by 1500 most villeins had won the right to pay money rent instead of service for their house, garden, pasture rights on commons, and the thirty or fifty acres of land from which they got their living. In fact, only one out of every hundred people in England was personally unfree and tied to the land and to the lord when Elizabeth I came to the throne, but all the same it is easy to understand why the name 'copyholder' was much more pleasant than 'villein', with its old taint.

To be a *freeman* or a *freeholder* was still better than to be a copyholder, especially in one way. For when a freeholder died his son inherited the family land by right or 'at will' if he still paid his small fixed rent to the lord of the manor—whereas the son of a copyholder had to apply for it to the lord, and to pay a sum of money, or 'heriot', before he could take it over; and besides this, if it were the lord's pleasure, the right to take over the land could be refused or the terms could be altered, so that the copyholder was always less secure than the freeholder. These changes in name (copyholder for villein) and in payment (money rents for services) had come long before the Tudors, first here and there throughout the land and finally almost everywhere in England, and they were important.

But one thing had changed remarkably little, and that was the system of farming itself. Still around the church and houses of most villages in the south and midlands there lay three or four vast un-hedged stretches of land—the open fields; and here each farmer had his land scattered in strips and plots, some good land and some bad. Thirty acres was a traditional amount, made up of some strips in each of the ploughed fields, and the farmer would have his share of smaller strips in the hay meadow. And still in most places the rotation of crops, the times for ploughing, sowing, and harvesting, were agreed upon for the village as a whole and were binding upon everyone. No one could plan for himself except in the little croft round his house, or try any new crops or methods unless, which was most unlikely, he could persuade the whole community to try them too. Farming then was very different from that of today. The system had worked well enough in many villages for hundreds of years and by it men had got their living. But at times it was a bare one; and in a bad year, when the harvest was poor or one sickly beast in the common pasture had infected all the cattle or sheep in the village, starvation was very near by the end of the winter.

The system certainly had great disadvantages, and if you can imagine for a moment a farmer with his land scattered in strips over three or four fields and his beasts mixed up with those of other men, working on a farming plan which he could not alter, it is not very difficult to make a list of these disadvantages, and to guess what changes an energetic farmer would want to make, if he came to realize that what one writer called this 'mingle-mangle' of open fields was getting out of date. Of course, one of the first things to do was to try to get his strips lying all together and dig a ditch around his fields, drain them, and plant a hedge or build a wall. Such a man could soon be more than a 'subsistence' farmer—that is, he could produce more than he and his family needed to eat or wear upon their backs, and could sell the surplus for cash. Gradually more and more people began to see the advantage of enclosing and of better farming. Two things drove them on. First, there was a growing demand for food and farm produce. The population was increasing and so was trade and industry, and in the towns there were far more people entirely engrossed by their work, weaving or building or shoe-making and the like, and quite unable to spare the time to grow their own food. They became dependent on the food grown by someone else. This obviously made the farmers try as never before to produce a surplus of corn and cattle, and to send their wives into the nearest town two or three times a week with eggs, butter and cheese, frumenty and apples to sell. They found they could sell all they could grow, and so became hungry for more land and ready to try new methods. Some of them urged on the need for enclosure—it was one of these who scornfully called the open fields a 'mingle-mangle'. Others, like Anthony Fitzherbert of Derbyshire, wrote books describing how to look after the land well, how to plant 'Quycksette hedges', how to plough and sow, reap and mow, and how wise it was to keep one's oxen in a good enclosed pasture and 'the byggeste cattell from the weykeste'. His *Boke of Husbandrie* came out in 1523, and a little later another enthusiastic farmer, Thomas Tusser, wrote a long poem about farming in which he said, among other things,

> The country enclosed I praise
> T'other delighteth me not.

So, as Leland travelled about England, he must have seen that farmers were busy in many places getting strip beside strip and enclosing fields and, because they were land-hungry, fencing in and using parts of the old thickety wastes, bits of downland, and edges of forests and swamps which had never been cultivated before. As long as this went on amicably and slowly there were few complaints and a good deal of approval. But even in Henry VII's reign there were difficulties appearing. The demand for food, all the food they could grow, was the first thing that drove farmers to produce more; to do this they usually had to improve their farming, and often this meant that they tried to enclose their fields. The second thing that drove them on was strong enough to affect everyone else as well—the plain fact that prices were going up during the reigns of all five Tudors. Every family in the land began to find it needed more money to buy even the necessities of life like sugar and nails and mugs and needles and knives, not to mention luxuries like new clothes, silver tankards, ornamental daggers, or 'a boke for my lybrary'. Of course some people found it impossible to get the money to pay for all they wanted, and many were forced into great poverty, but naturally anyone who could tried to increase his income. So the farmer tried to produce a bigger surplus and sell it, the craftsman worked longer and harder so as to have more goods for sale, and the merchant did his best to increase his trade. It was the only way to make both ends meet, and those who could not increase their spending money found themselves in a most uncomfortable position. Such people were often landowners, for their land was all let out to their tenants, great and small, at fixed rents, and many of them began to find that, though they were obliged to spend much more, they were getting just the same income from their rents as

A PEASANT BEING DISPLACED UNDER THE ENCLOSURE SYSTEM

before prices began to climb. Obviously they were compelled to find some way of getting more for their land—not because they were all thoroughly unpleasant and greedy, but because they had no other alternative. Some landlords fenced in their waste lands which had never been used except for hunting, and either cultivated these new fields themselves or let them to farmers who, as we know, were hungry for more land. This enclosing of waste land harmed nobody, but other landlords enclosed for their own use those common lands on which the whole village could turn their animals to graze, and had done for centuries, and this was another matter altogether, and far more serious. Geese, pigs, and sheep cannot graze in a cottage garden, and loss of commons meant that many village people could no longer keep their few beasts, and so lost the bacon and lard from the pig and the wool from the sheep. It was more serious still when a landlord chose to ask higher rents from his tenants, or a heavier heriot when a man took over his father's land. A tenant who could not find the extra was turned out in bitterness of soul and saw his strips let to one who could. Sometimes this was a prosperous farmer who had no need of the cottage that went with the land. Then an unscrupulous lord would pull the little ancient house down, and its former owner found himself homeless as well as landless, and in a desperate plight. For instance, at the village of West Sandford in Berkshire John Baybrooke had a house and sixty acres of land, and he had the house pulled down so that 'by the said cause six persons went out from their habitations wandering elsewhere'. And, indeed, sometimes whole villages were emptied of cottagers and copyholders.

But the change which at this time did most to drive families from their homes in search of work was the increase in sheep farming—and this again, for the landlord or farmer, was a thoroughly sensible way of making both ends meet. The 'golden fleece' of English sheep had, for centuries, been in great demand, chiefly in the markets of Flanders and Italy. It was still in great demand in the sixteenth century, and not only as the raw wool straight from the sheep's back, but also in the form of English cloth woven by English weavers, which had become well known and very popular. Merchants found they could sell abroad almost any amount of good cloth such as Stroudwater scarlet, Coventry blue, and Worcester whites, and so the wool grower, like the food grower, was sure of an easy sale for all he could produce. Wool was cheap to grow, too, compared with corn, for one shepherd and his two dogs could manage a large flock of sheep while a dozen or more men were needed to

> Plough and sow
> Reap and mow,

and many a shrewd landlord and farmer put his land down to grass, dismissed his labourers, and happily calculated the golden fleeces growing on his sheep; while the unhappy workless labourer muttered the jingle

> Horn and thorn
> Hath made England
> All forlorn.

Cottagers and small copyholders suffered badly, losing their common rights, driven by higher rents to give up their little holdings of land, and more than ever to depend on daily wages at the very time when employers were doing their best to cut down the number of workers they kept. Their hardships caused men like Sir Thomas More to blame everything on cruel landowners and greedy sheep farmers. 'Sheep', he wrote, 'eat up and swallow down the very men themselves.' Yet in spite of such protests, in spite of many Acts of Parliament passed in the reigns of Henry VII, his son and his grandson, to try and stop enclosures, and in spite of riots and rebellions—the worst being in 1549—the movement away from open fields went on, not in a wholesale way but steadily. Only when, in Elizabeth's reign, corn growing became more profitable than sheep farming, did it almost cease for the time being to attract attention and cause distress. For as the price of corn went up, even the most wool-minded of farmers thought twice before putting land down to pasture, and began to take on more labourers to grow wheat, barley, oats, and rye, not only to feed the English nation, but to export. So that by the time James VI of Scotland followed his cousin Elizabeth, nearly all country people were better off than their grandparents had been.

But before this came about, enclosure and sheep-farming between them brought trouble to many English people. In fact they were the chief causes—an increase in population and a decrease in private warfare being others—of a problem which seriously worried the government of the sixteenth century, the problem of unemployment. For the first time it had to contend with a permanent body of workless people unable to support themselves and their families. Hungry and homeless, some of them dangerous ruffians, most of them simply helpless, they roamed the country, no one responsible for them, nowhere—after the destruction of the monasteries—to turn for succour. In the reigns of Henry VIII and Edward VI they were treated as wrongdoers, as people who preferred to steal or beg rather than do an honest day's work. They were beaten, they were branded, but the problem did not disappear—it was too big to be cured by severity only, and at the end of Elizabeth's reign, a new system of dealing with unemployment and poverty was established—the Poor Law of 1601. Under it the helpless poor, old, young, sick, and unfortunate, were to be fed and cared for, the children being taught a trade as soon as they were old enough. The able-bodied unemployed were to be found work of a suitable kind, the idle scamps who would not stick to the work were to be punished and forced to labour. All this cost money, which was raised by a poor-rate levied on the householders in every parish, and the Justices of the Peace were held responsible by the government for seeing that the money was collected and that overseers were appointed to carry out the law and cope with the poor and the workless. This system worked well for about 200 years until, again partly because of enclosures, the amount of poverty and unemployment became too big for it, and a new one had to be evolved.

The person who came best out of all these changes, and who went on steadily becoming more prosperous and powerful, was the freeholder. The price of all the things he had to sell went up, and the rents of his neighbouring copyholders went up, but his was fixed, and not to be raised. Soon these fortunate men were holding land worth many times more than the tiny sums they had paid for it, and growing crops for which they got the new high prices. No wonder William Harrison said 'that many freeholders come to great wealth and sette their sonnes to the Universities', no wonder that they were able to build comfortable new farm houses, complete with chimneys and glass in every window, and when they died to leave their families feather beds, hangings, carpets, 'a silver salt and a dozzen of spoons'.

8. Land and People

2. LONDON AND THE COURT

THE greatest of all the towns in the land was London, which had a population of over 150,000 in the year Queen Elizabeth I died. It is not easy to be quite sure of population numbers, for in those times governments were not so much concerned about counting heads as they now are. But it is clear that other towns came far behind London. Norwich had about 15,000 in 1601, Bristol averaged 6,000 during the sixteenth century and there were probably the same number, 6,000 people, living in Edinburgh. The numbers are very small, of course, compared with the populations of these places now, and this as a rule would be true of all towns—they were far smaller, or indeed not towns at all in our sense of the word, but simply villages.

HEADPIECE. The Aldgate about 1600

Almost all of them which bore the name of city or town had certain things in common—walls, for example. Although Leland had noticed that many city walls were crumbling, there were still plenty of them to be seen. They were certainly in good condition at Bristol, Chester, Carlisle, Edinburgh, and many other places, and London was still circled by its medieval wall, pierced by the seven great gates of Aldgate, Ludgate, Newgate, Moorgate, Cripplegate, Aldersgate, and Bishopsgate, even though it was in bad repair in some places. Besides their walls, towns might be further strengthened by a deep ditch dug right up to the walls and filled with water. The London ditch, first dug in 1213, had originally been 200 feet wide and in Henry VIII's reign was so deep that it held a great store of 'verie good fish of divers sorts'. But the defence of the city was no longer constantly urgent and few people wanted to spend money on clearing out the ditch, so that in Elizabeth's day it was described as 'a verie narrow filthy channel and in places quite stopped up and houses and gardens builded on it'. It was last cleaned out properly in 1569.

Everywhere the town authorities had become carefree of the defence of their cities, and as it was quite as safe for people to live outside the walls as inside—for the greatest dangers of fire and disease and thieves were at least as bad within the walls as outside them—most towns had burst their seams, so to speak, and had houses sprawling beyond their medieval boundaries. All around London was a dirty unpleasant rash of dwellings, and when John Stow, a master tailor in the city, wrote his famous book *The Survey of London*, he continually mentioned how fast the capital was growing and how rapidly the pleasant country lanes around were becoming 'filthy passages, both sides built up with small base houses'. Stow greatly feared the spoiling of the country near London, and he bemoaned the spread of buildings almost half a mile into the common fields which ought, said he, 'to lie open and free, a faire and pleasant way for people to walk on foot'. Stow lived in London from 1525–1605, so he spanned the reigns of four Tudors and the first Stuart. Even when he died the south bank of the curving Thames was still green, its waters were clear and gleaming, and flocks of swans swam among the shipping and smaller craft. He remembered and loved the country customs and pastimes which, when he died, were fast dying too—the dancing round the Maypole set up at the top of Cornhill when streets would be hung with garlands of fresh flowers, and pleasant Midsummer Eve, when everyone decked their door and windows with white lilies and the green boughs of birch, so that even the smelly streets were filled with country scents, and men like Stow could easily 'walk in the sweet meadows and greene woods there to rejoice their spirits with beauty'.

Inside the walls houses were closely packed along narrow streets. Many were tall and gabled, with their upper floors jutting out over the lower ones, making the downstairs rooms extremely dark. The streets were cobbled, or were simply earthen tracks; in either case they were usually dirty, and rubbish and, in summer, flies were everywhere. The shops were quite small, a single room with its door opening straight on to the street and a front window fitted with a wooden shutter. When this was let down, as it was if the shop was open, it could be propped up to form a rough counter outside. On this and round the doorway the shop goods could be displayed. The shopkeeper and his workmen made their goods in the shop as well as selling from it, and the younger apprentices loudly called the attention of passers-by to the fine things they had for sale.

There were a good many difficulties to be tackled or to be endured in the towns of the sixteenth and seventeenth centuries. For one thing, as we know from Stow, there were slums of small base houses, dirty and ramshackle. The streets, too, were dirty—and their narrowness made them so dark that it was most unsafe to be abroad in them at night. A few feeble lanterns hung outside the inns and the houses of the rich, but otherwise the narrow ways must have been as black as pitch, and you risked not only your money but your life if you went out at night. The watchmen and parish constables did what they could to protect people and to catch thieves and rogues, but many wrongdoers escaped, even when the watch was alert and conscientious, and not as nervous as Dogberry and his men were in Shakespeare's play *Much Ado about Nothing*. It was, of course, quite common to see the stocks which stood in the streets occupied with rogues, or to meet thieves being whipped through the town for their crimes. But it was not only criminals who made the ways unsafe. Apprentices were always apt to

make trouble either by their ferocious games of football, by their baiting
of unfortunate foreigners, or simply by the tremendous fights they had
among themselves. The cry of 'Clubs! Clubs!', would bring a score of
them into the street spoiling for a row.

Water was another problem. This was either pumped from the river
when there was a river handy, or drawn from springs and wells. It must
often have been most impure, and positively dangerous to drink, but
people knew less about such matters then and did not turn a hair, even
when they drew drinking water from the river a few yards below the
place where housewives washed the dirty clothes. Elizabethan London
had two mechanical force pumps in the Thames, and during the Tudor
reigns eight new water points were set up in the city, so that the supply
there was good compared with other towns, where drinking water was
often short, and there was very little available for any emergency. Fire
was always likely to occur, and was of course a most terrible menace.
With houses so close together, built largely of wood, and with thatched
roofs, you can imagine the peril and the terrible speed with which it
could spread, the sparks leaping from house to house. There were no
hoses or engines then, only leathern buckets and clumsy instruments to
claw down the thatch and even the house walls, when they were burning, or in danger of catching fire. It is not surprising that half London
was destroyed in 1666, when the Great Fire, which started in a baker's
chimney in Pudding Lane and was driven by a strong south-east wind,
raged for five appalling days. Samuel Pepys, the Londoner who wrote
a famous diary, and of whom you will hear more later on in this book,
went out to watch the city in the grip of what he called 'the most horrid
malicious bloody fire, not like the fine flame of an ordinary fire'.

But there were many other things besides the excitement of great
fires, which drew the people of London, or of any other town, out of
their houses and into the streets. There were markets, of course, and
there were processions of all kinds from the magnificent spectacle of
'the marching watch' of London on Midsummer Eve, in which 2,000
men took part guided by the light of 1,000 torches, with the mayor and
sheriffs in shining armour and crimson surcoats, to the simple dances
which men performed everywhere on May morning in greeting to the
coming of summer. The craft gilds acted their plays at Whitsun or on

OLD LONDON BRIDGE SHOWING THE DRAWBRIDGE SECTION

the feast of Corpus Christi, the actors standing and strutting well above the heads of the crowd on movable stages or pageant carts.

Many games were played in the streets, such as football, and hockey, and dancing, while on all the open spaces within and without the walls men practised at archery, wrestling, jumping, and throwing the hammer. Rich people built themselves tennis courts in which to play the old royal game from which lawn tennis has been developed. Henry VIII was very fond of this game and made a court at Whitehall and another at Hampton which still exists; James V of Scotland had an excellent one at his palace of Falkland in Fife, and this, too, you can see today.

In the country, of course, hunting, hawking, shooting, were the most popular sports, and you could hunt with all the magnificence of Elizabeth, who went to the chase from Hatfield in 1557 with 120 mounted men and 50 archers—she loved hunting—or else in a humble but equally satisfying way with mongrel dogs chasing a rabbit or hare, and everyone running after them hot foot and yelling. But it is worth remembering that, because towns were small, because they still—even London—

contained orchards and small paddocks within their walls, because the fields themselves came close up to their very gates, there was no such sharp distinction between town and country amusements as there is now, so that a man might fish almost as pleasantly in the great town ditch as in the Warwickshire Avon, and skate there just as well.

London, of course, had many special attractions. There was the mighty bridge spanning the Thames on twenty arches, with houses and shops upon it and a troop of special warders to look after it and keep the structure safe. This was one of the wonders of the world. Then there were the numerous performances given by companies of actors, either strolling players or employed by some great nobleman like the Queen's favourite, the Earl of Leicester. Their plays were first given in inn-yards, with spectators crowding all the windows and the wooden galleries which ran round the yard, or standing in the cobbled ground itself, called the pit. These performances, and the players too, were detested by the city authorities, being often rowdy and riotous, and they were so strongly discouraged that, as time went on and men began to build theatres on the pattern of the inn yards, they were all outside the city boundaries, where the authorities could not interfere. When Shakespeare was in London, acting and writing his plays, they were produced chiefly at two playhouses, the Theatre belonging to an actor called James Burbage, and the Globe built by his sons, Richard and Cuthbert.

Of course, other towns besides London had fair bridges and companies of players even if they were not quite so numerous and amusing, but there was one thing that only the capital enjoyed, and that was the frequent presence of the Sovereign and the Court; and the stir of the coming and going, and the glimpses of stately ceremony which surrounded the throne, must have made life very exciting for Londoners.

Whitehall Palace, which Henry VIII took from the fallen Cardinal Wolsey, was the chief Royal residence until its destruction by fire in 1697; Henry built on a sumptuous gallery, a tennis court and a bowling alley. It lay, a rambling confusion of buildings, on the north bank of the Thames, not far from Westminster Abbey; the present street of Whitehall runs about through the middle of its site. The Court always spent Christmas there and usually part of the spring as well. But there were other royal palaces not far away and, as in the Middle Ages, the

King of England was a traveller. Then he travelled from one royal house to another in order to live on the produce of his estates, now he had discovered the value of moving about so as to show himself and become known to his subjects, and perhaps to find out something of what they thought and felt. And not only did the King and Queen travel. Their children, even when quite young, were constantly on the move, either with their parents or, when they were a little older, with their own households. In 1520, when Mary Tudor was four years old, she and her attendants stayed in seven different palaces between October and Christmas, and each time all the household stuff, even down to brass pots, frying pans, and trumpets, had to be packed up and loaded on the wagons. So, although Whitehall probably saw most of the sovereign, other royal houses were not left empty for long. There was St. James—separated from Whitehall only by a park and garden—a pleasant place where Henrietta Maria, wife of Charles I, went for the birth of her first child (Charles II), because it was so quiet and peaceful. Then there was Greenwich across on the south bank of the Thames, and the Tower, and Hampton Court, Richmond, Oatlands, Nonsuch, and Windsor—not to number the smaller royal manors round London, Eltham and Enfield, and Hatfield, where the hunting specially pleased Elizabeth.

Some of these royal houses, those that were least used, remained simple enough, only being decked and furnished for the actual period of residence. But others became increasingly magnificent within and without, especially during the reigns of the Tudors, for every one of that family loved splendour in their houses, as well as in their clothes and in the ceremonies with which they were attended. Henry VII, who in general was distinctly careful about money, built Richmond Palace, with eight tall towers each one bearing a weather-vane with the royal arms painted on it in brilliant gold and blue, and a fine marble fountain in its courtyard. Inside, the Great Hall, chief living-room of the palace, was splendid with coloured glass in the windows and a timber roof most craftily carved. At Hampton Court, too, the Great Hall blazed with colour from its windows and its roof painted as blue as a summer sky, and spangled with gold stars. In the Long Gallery the ceiling bore no fewer than 1,250 balls of burnished gold.

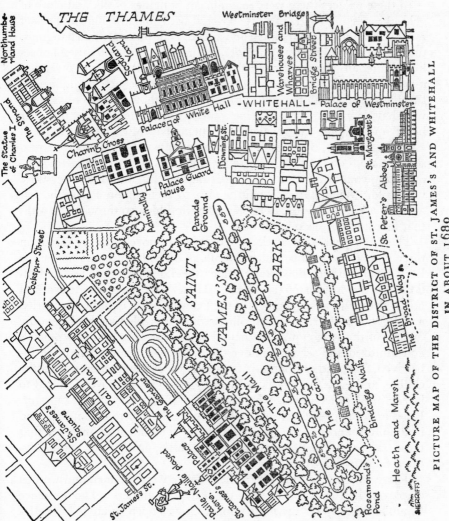

PICTURE MAP OF THE DISTRICT OF ST. JAMES'S AND WHITEHALL
IN ABOUT 1680

In these palaces there were magnificent hangings of silk and cloth of gold, thrones and chairs of estate covered with gold and blue and russet red, and elaborate beds painted and gilded. The furniture and hangings, though some remained permanently in the most frequently used houses like Whitehall, were still carried from place to place as the sovereign moved. Strange, too, seems the fact that, in spite of such magnificence, the floors, at least till the end of Elizabeth's reign, were still only strewn with hay or rushes, carpets being kept to adorn the walls or put over beds; and though the royal family themselves always had chairs of estate to sit upon, their visitors and attendants only had stools or possibly cushions on the floor. These royal palaces were magnificent without being comfortable, or even particularly clean, and often they were very cold. When James I paid a visit to Kensington Palace he left again in a hurry because, as he said, the wind blew so through the walls that he could not sleep in his bed.

The Court, whether stationary or on the move, was organized in three chief departments under three high officials—upstairs under the Lord Chamberlain, downstairs under the Lord Steward, and out-of-doors by the Master of the Horse. These three men were always of noble birth, and were members of the Privy Council. They each carried a white staff as the sign of their office, which was solemnly broken at the funeral of the sovereign. The actual work was done by lesser officials and multitudes of servants under them, some of whom were often ill-behaved, lazy, and dishonest. Apparently the scullions often wore filthy clothes, and even those responsible for waiting on the sovereign had to be reproved for having dirty hands and for wiping them on the tapestry. Rules and advice for servants and courtiers of every rank can be found in the Ordinances of the royal household, even down to an order that those 'nearest to the Presence should not tattle, or mumble' about anything done by his Grace.

Those who saw most of his (or her) Grace were the men and women employed in the Presence and the Privy Chambers. The Presence Chamber was by far the most public. It was open to anyone who by birth or office had the right to attend the Court, to the ambassadors of friendly powers, and to other visitors from home or abroad with special permission. For instance, one Sunday in 1598, a German called Paul

Henztner stood among those who waited in Greenwich Palace to see the Queen's Majesty. He had been given a permit by the Lord Chamberlain, and he carefully observed all that went on and afterwards wrote down what he remembered in his journal. He said that there were rich tapestries on the walls and hay on the floor, that no one spoke to the Queen unless they were kneeling, and that 'where ever she turned her face as she was going along everybody fell down on their knees'. Paul was much impressed by Elizabeth's majesty and grace in spite of the fact that, as he noticed, she wore a red wig and had blackened teeth from eating too much sugar. Paul did not himself expect to be presented to the Queen, but he was quite close to her when the gentleman dressed in velvet with a gold chain, whose business it was to introduce any person of distinction, brought forward a Bohemian baron, named Slawata. The baron fell upon his knees and the Queen gave him her right hand to kiss, the jewels sparkling in her rings as she did so.

Although Elizabeth was easily to be seen in the Presence Chamber, she disliked the custom of dining in public and very seldom did so. James I revived this habit, and dined in public in great pomp, eating off gold plate 'exceeding massy, fair and sumptious'. It was said, rather unkindly, that he did so 'to show himself in glory to the Scots'. At any rate such crowds attended that barriers were erected to keep them from pushing too near the royal tables. But whether the sovereign dined in public or private, the food was served with elaborate care and ceremonial by the Yeomen of the Guard, 'tall strong large men like half-giants' dressed in scarlet with a golden rose embroidered on chest and back. Their hands had to be covered before they might lay the table-cloth or take up the knives, spoons, and salt-cellars, and under the watchful eye of a high official they had to perform the solemn ritual of the assay, the tasting and trying of morsels of each dish before it was eaten in case of poison.

In the Privy Chamber the sovereign was served only by the closest personal attendants, who carefully watched the doors and kept the rooms as private as possible. Here sat Elizabeth with her ladies, and the famous maids-of-honour dressed all in white—as indeed maids-of-honour still are when they occasionally attend the Queen. Their business was to wait upon the Queen, to play and sing and read with her, to catch her cloak if she walked out in the garden and carry her books when she went to prayers—in other words, to be in close personal attendance all day and often late into the night. It must have been a most exhausting job.

All these courtiers, guards, maids-of-honour and so on down to the scullion pages, attended the sovereign, or were supposed to do so, wherever he went, whether settled for the winter in Whitehall or trailing through the country-side on the summer progresses so much enjoyed by Elizabeth. Sometimes towards the end of her reign, when her courtiers, like herself, were growing old and found these summer journeyings very exhausting, they tried to escape and have a brief rest themselves, which annoyed the Queen greatly.

Not only were royal progresses sometimes exhausting to those who attended, but even when the Court was stationary the perpetual round of entertainment must have palled at times—banquets, masques, and plays which were performed by the children of the Chapel Royal or the courtiers themselves, or by amateurs who desired to entertain the sovereign at their own expense. Henry VIII not only sang, danced, and diced with his courtiers, but would get up at 4 o'clock in the morning to hunt from daylight to 10 o'clock at night, and James I, after sitting up two whole nights watching entertainments, was 'so wearied and sleepy that he had no edge to it' on the third, which annoyed the players who performed before their nodding king. James was never a very dignified person, being noisy, garrulous, and amused by horseplay. His Court was garish and disorderly, and drunkenness was common among courtiers of every rank. The King himself often drank till he could not stand, and once on getting up to dance formally at a reception for a foreign visitor, he fell to the ground and had to be carried off to bed. At the wedding of his daughter Elizabeth to the Elector Palatine he was oddly dressed. One onlooker wrote 'the king, methought, was somewhat strangely attired in a cap with a feather, a Spanish cape and a long stocking'!

Charles I was very different from his father, and his household was different too. Serious and dignified, he had held aloof from rowdy courtiers even when Prince of Wales, and he would not tolerate disorder or rough behaviour. He was always exceedingly courteous himself and expected others to be the same. He at once refused a place at Court to the Earl of Anglesey, saying he would have no drunkards about his person, and in 1637 he dismissed Archibald Armstrong, the old king's jester, because his jokes were too vulgar. Charles liked elegance and gaiety, but of a different kind. He would never have appeared strangely attired, for his tastes ran rather to delicate lace for his collar and cuffs and an occasional diamond ornament. Instead of being amused by noisy talk and rough loud laughter, he preferred to discuss painting with the Court painter, Van Dyck, and to watch the crates of pictures, bought for him by his agents in Italy and France, being opened, and to decide which of them to buy. For Charles was 'a most excellent judge and great lover of painting, carvings, gravings and other ingenuities', and it was he who first started the royal collection of pictures, which is now one of the best in the world.

9. Land and People

3

*'The very persons of our noble story
As they were living.'*
SHAKESPEARE, *Henry VIII*

WHEN we remember the centuries which have passed since the first Tudor reigned and since the last Stuart, Queen Anne, died, it is remarkable how much is left to help us when we try to reconstruct the life of the people of those times, and the England they then knew. We have still many lovely churches, though these are plain and severe inside compared with their former glory before they were stripped of their ornaments, hangings, and rood-screens, and before the glowing colour of their walls was scraped off or whitewashed by reformers of one kind

HEADPIECE. What William Shakespeare may have looked like. Based on the engraving by Martin Droeshout in the First Folio edition or another. Besides churches we can also visit some of the houses lived in by English people from king to cottager, and the schools and colleges in which they studied. We can see and even at times handle the things that our ancestors used, their weapons and tools, their pewter mugs, their furniture and spurs and spits; we can see too some of their very clothes, their hats and gloves, shoes and shirts, and from these faded, fragile garments get some idea at least of their outward appearance.

But even so these relics are not really enough to tell us what people were like in character and behaviour, and the best way to find that out is to read either what they wrote about themselves, or what foreign visitors thought when visiting England, and to look at their portraits and other pictures painted at the time. Fortunately there are plenty of all these sources from which we can dig out information. Already we have used the writings of the Rev. William Harrison and of John Stow the London tailor, and we have noted the remarks of a Dutch doctor and a German traveller. Later on we shall certainly hear something from the diaries of a clerk in the Navy office, and a lady of leisure with a passion for travelling. As for portraits, there are plenty, for from the reign of Henry VIII onwards it became the fashionable thing to be painted by some well-known artist. Two men who excelled at portraits were Hans Holbein the Younger and Sir Anthony Van Dyck.

Holbein was a German but he lived mostly in England from 1526 till his death in 1543, and was Court painter to Henry VIII. He had many duties. He designed decorations for state occasions, and costumes for plays and pageants; he made goblets and weapons. But his main work was to paint portraits of the royal household, and he had an unfailing eye for the look and expression of each individual who sat for him. His pictures are not dramatic, they are rather quiet, but the longer you look at them the more you begin to think that besides seeing the build, and the colouring and the best clothes of the sitter, you can also discover something about the personality. It may be the King himself with his masterful legs and cold little eyes, or his eldest daughter with her wary watchful look, or Master Robert Cheseman quietly holding his favourite hawk, hooded and motionless, on his gloved hand. The portraits are all faithful records and you can find out a great deal from them.

Van Dyck was a Fleming. He became Court painter in 1632, and his portraits are as different from Holbein's as chalk from cheese, not only because the two artists were very different, but because the people they painted were different too. Like Holbein, Van Dyck was inundated with orders from wealthy people who longed to see themselves painted in his cool elegant style, and many of them had to content themselves with a picture in which much of the work was done by his pupils and only perhaps the head and hands were painted by the master himself.

Now of course only the rich could afford the fees of Holbein or Van Dyck, or of Hilliard or Oliver, who were fashionable in Elizabeth's reign. The humble people are not found in their pictures, except occasionally when the family servants appear in some big group, like the one Holbein made of Thomas More and his household. Nevertheless there are plenty of portraits to be found, not done in oils but in words. And if you take the trouble to look for them, say in the plays of Shakespeare or of Beaumont and Fletcher, you may discover even more than from painted portraits. For people do not always look completely natural posing in their best clothes, and with what they hope is their best expression, but Nick Bottom, and Ralph the prentice and his master and mistress, had no idea when Shakespeare or Beaumont and Fletcher were watching them or that they would appear before future generations of English people upon the stage, and we can be sure that they are drawn to the very life.

Gradually from these sources we can discover that in Elizabethan England people were divided into distinct classes and few thought this at all peculiar and unjust. It was generally taken for granted that classes or estates (for there are two meanings of the word estate) had been arranged by God, and therefore it was right and normal—not bitterly unfair—to see a rich man in his castle and a poor man at his gate. Later on, of course, people began to challenge this, and by the time of Oliver Cromwell there was a group calling themselves Levellers, who wanted to reduce all men to one level and do away with every rank and title.

The sovereign was above all ranks of men, and in a very different position from the violent days of the Wars of the Roses, when the great nobles thought themselves as good as, or possibly slightly better than, the King. That idea had quite disappeared. Below the King came the gentlemen, and these included the nobles of the realm as well as the ordinary country squires with quite small estates (that is the other meaning of the word) and snug manor houses. A noble gentleman would be addressed as 'My Lord' and his wife as 'My Lady', but the rest wrote 'Esquire' after their names and were addressed as 'Master So-and-So' and their wives as 'Mistress'. Today the courtesy titles of 'Mr. and Mrs.', the shortened forms, are used by everyone. There was a great variety of gentlemen, some immensely rich, well-educated, and famous, others quite poor, and crude and hardly able to read. The one thing they had in common, however, was that either they or their fathers all owned land. In fact ownership of land automatically put you in this class, and many families were able to enter it for the first time under the Tudors, not only because a grant of land and a title was a usual way of rewarding faithful royal servants, but also because the lucky purchase of monastic lands made many a solid merchant into a gentleman. For it was quite possible for a man to move up a class, as Malvolio the steward in *Twelfth Night* hoped to do by marrying the Lady Olivia, or to move down as, in the same play, Sir Toby Belch seemed to be doing.

It was from this class chiefly that the Justices of the Peace were appointed, the unpaid magistrates to whom the central government in Tudor times gave more and more work, so that they came to be responsible in their own localities for fixing wages, collecting the poor rate and appointing the overseers of the poor, arranging for highways and bridges to be repaired, inns licensed, recusants fined, and other law breakers brought to justice. Without them the machinery of government in England could not have worked.

In the next class came citizens of importance, such as merchants and lawyers, and often they were as rich or richer than any noble. These were the men who frequently sat as members of Parliament for the towns, and who were usually very keen to buy land and so enter the class of gentleman.

Next to them came the yeomen farmers from the country, both freeholders and prosperous copyholders, and the highly skilled craftsmen from the towns, solid, hardworking and prosperous. These men were addressed as 'Goodman' and their wives as 'Goodwife'. William Harrison

ELIZABETHAN 'BARE-KNUCKLE' STOOL-BALL

admired them greatly and believed they were the backbone of the English nation. He liked to think they were well-known and feared by foreigners. 'These were the men', he wrote, 'who in times past made all France afraid.'

Lastly came the day-labourers in town and country, together with farmers whose holding of land was too small to support them unless they worked for wages as well.

Of course foreigners coming to England formed very mixed opinions of all these people, and some of them wrote in their diaries descriptions which they probably hoped would remain private, but which, luckily for us, have not. Frankly, most of them found the English people puzzling and distinctly formidable, being tumultuous, proud, and boastful, quick to quarrel and having little fear of death—'When their rage is up', wrote one traveller, 'they will not easily be pacified for they have high and haughty stomachs.' They were suspicious of foreigners and frequently scoffed and laughed at them in public. And if a stranger objected to this, then street boys and apprentices would collect and 'strike unmercifully'. Evidently this attitude was one of the things in

England which had not changed, for right back in 1421 the citizens of Coventry were well-known for throwing things at unknown people who came to their city. On the other hand, Doctor Lennius from Holland found English people 'very civil to those well-stricken in years', and he also mentioned that they were joyous and fond of music and dancing. Some things evidently amused foreigners a good deal. Apparently Englishmen loved 'great noises that fill the ear such as firing of cannon and ringing of bells', and the German, Paul Henztner, said 'In London it is common for a number of Englishmen to go up into a church steeple and there ring the bells for hours together.' Another strange characteristic which struck Henztner was that they had such a passion for new-fangled clothes. They seemed to be always following fresh fashions. Shakespeare, too, realized this and joked about it in his play *The Merchant of Venice*, and in one book written in Elizabeth I's reign there is a funny drawing of a naked man with a balloon coming out of his mouth in which is written:

> I am an Englishman and naked I stand here,
> Musing in my mind what raiment I shall wear,
> For now I will wear this, and now I will wear that,
> And now I will wear I cannot tell what.

Practically everyone found the English very hospitable to guests in their own homes, however unpleasant their manners might be in the street. They ate enormously themselves and liked to see others do the same. In 1577, when the Queen was staying for three days with Lord North, his household ate, among many other things, 1,200 chickens, a cartload of oysters, 2,500 eggs, and 430 pounds of butter. There were only two meals a day, dinner at 11 or 12, and supper at 6 or 7, but they were usually vast ones, at any rate for the rich and the comfortably off. There were quantities of meat, fine white bread, tarts and jellies of many colours, and very sweet and highly spiced puddings. The food was eaten off pewter and silver, and washed down, not of course by tea or coffee or lemonade, but by wine and ale. William Harrison knew of eighty-six different kinds of wine being drunk in England besides ale, cider, perry (made from pears), and mead, which he obviously hated for he calls it 'a kind of swish-swash'. Even the poorer people ate more and better food than ever before, with bacon, fowls, fruit, cheese, and eggs. They liked barley or rye bread because they found 'it lies longer in the stomach', and ate it as new as possible 'so as it be not hot'. They used wooden plates and dishes and coarse glass or horn cups of English make.

We should have found table manners thoroughly bad even though people in England behaved on the whole much more quietly at meals than in France and Holland. Each man sliced off his own meat—and his neighbour's too if she was a woman—and cut it up with his own knife, but for eating everyone used his fingers. As late as 1608 a certain Tom Coryate saw forks for the first time in his life when he was in Italy and said, evidently in great surprise, 'The Italian cannot endure to have his food touched with fingers seeing all men's fingers are not alike clean.' To carry your own fork and toothpick about with you was considered grand but very fussy.

There were, however, some things about which there was no disagreement. One of these was the love of games and sport to be found everywhere in the land. Among some of the most popular, both in town and country, were quoits, ninepins, bowls, and shooting at butts, all reasonably quiet entertainments, at least if the silent concentration of present-day bowlers and archers is anything to judge by. But there were the rougher and more energetic sports too, leaping, running to base, stool-ball (the ancestor of cricket), and wrestling, all of which went on in the long summer evenings after work, on holidays, and at the organized festivals of games, sports, and dancing, which were held on special days like 1 May. One of these festivals only died out in the middle of the last century. For 400 years it was held on 8 May on Dovers Hill at Chipping Campden, Gloucestershire, high up above the wide Avon Valley, with its peaceful fields and farms spread out below.

Men in village and town alike played football, then a most violent and dangerous game, so violent that often schoolboys were forbidden to play it and it was entirely prohibited among undergraduates at Oxford. It was certainly not much like the football we play now, for a game might last all day, with an unlimited number of players taking part, goals three miles apart, and no rules at all. Naturally there was plenty of scope for foul play and even, at times 'beastly fury, murder and extreame violence'. But it is of course important to remember that the sight of violence and cruelty, in sport or in anything else, did not affect people as much in England in the sixteenth and seventeenth centuries as they do now, and men, women and children thoroughly enjoyed amusements which most of us would find revolting. For instance they flocked to see cock-fighting or cock-stoning and bull- or bear-baiting, either in a specially built ring like the one at Southwark in London, or on the village green; and they were enthralled by the ugly sight of a wretched animal chained to a stake and set upon by every cur in the neighbourhood, or of a cock buried to the neck in sand and then stoned to death. Enormous crowds also turned out to watch all executions and burnings, and it was taken as a matter of course by most people, at least until the reign of Charles I, that offenders like Prynne should have both ears cut off simply for writing a pamphlet which seemed to criticize the Queen, and that persons might be tortured to extract their confessions or force them to betray their accomplices.

Among country sports hunting, chiefly of deer and hares, but not the fox, was continually popular—though of course it tended to be an amusement of the well-to-do. But as time went on it changed greatly. This was because the ancient elaborate skill of training and flying hawks for hunting gradually went out of fashion, and gave place to the shot-gun and the chasing of prey with dogs only. In fact by the eighteenth century the word mews had quite changed its meaning and instead of the hawk house—so-called from the incessant mewing noise which the birds made as they sat on their perches—it came to mean simply stables and coach-houses.

England was also famous for its music, and this was another matter upon which all foreign visitors agreed. It was a fame which had grown with astonishing speed, for the unquiet time before 1485 had driven many musicians out of the country. During the Wars of the Roses there was little or no employment for them at the Court or in noble households, and many went abroad to Italy or the Netherlands. But the coming of Henry VII changed this. He himself recalled a skilful musician, John Hothby, from Italy to his Court; and in Elizabeth's reign some German visitors wrote 'it is the custom that even in small villages the musicians wait upon you for a fee'. In 1587 London was said to be so full of pipers and fiddlers that when a man entered a

tavern there were two or three at once hanging about waiting to give
him a dance tune before he left—also for a small fee of course. There
were four favourite instruments in use, the lute, the viol (forerunner of
the violin), the virginals (forerunner of the piano), and the recorder,
and every well-bred person was expected to be able to perform on at
least one of them. But it was not only the accomplished people who
made music. A very large number of the quite humble and ordinary
could play the viol, or squeak out a passable tune on a home-made pipe,
and it was a perfectly normal thing for families and friends to collect
together of an evening to sing part songs and madrigals by the hour.
Indeed all well-known English composers like Thomas Tallis, William
Byrd, and Orlando Gibbons, who were known all over Europe for their
music, composed much of it for songs as well as for instruments, and
Shakespeare, and Ben Jonson, and Robert Herrick, the Devonshire
parson, wrote some of the most lovely lyrics (songs) in the world. So it
is not surprising that many of these such as *Where the bee sucks there suck
I* and *Drink to me only with thine eyes* and *Cherry Ripe*, are still well known
and often heard today. Not only these great poets, but many others less
well known wrote beautiful song-lyrics, and indeed what is now perhaps the most famous of all Elizabethan songs *There is a lady sweet and
kind*, was written by someone whose name we do not even know.

In 1605 a careful inventory was made of the contents of Wardour
Castle, the home of Thomas, Lord Arundel, and among the items listed
in it are many books of music. All of them were clearly made to stand
wear, being covered with strong parchment. Six contained 'songes of
3, 4, 5, 6, 7 or 8 partes', 5 were called 'bookes for the consert', 5 contained 'fa-laes' or songs with choruses, and 5 contained 'musicke for
pavannes, galliardes, measures and cuntry daunces'. For dancing was
an amusement enjoyed by everyone. Men and women, kings and commoners, danced indoors and outdoors, after the state banquet as well as
the harvest supper. Henry VII and Henry VIII employed composers
of dance music, Elizabeth excelled at dancing and loved it, Prince
Henry, the eldest son of James I, who died without coming to the throne,
danced with 'as great perfection as could be devised'. Beyond the Court
with its stately formal measures, Tom, Dick, and Harry danced round
their maypoles, in and out of their houses in jig, morris, furry and every

AN EARLY PRODUCTION OF 'HAMLET'

kind of 'cuntry daunce' like *Gathering Peascods, Haste to the Wedding*, and many others which only comparatively few people can dance today.

But there was another amusement which was then growing in popularity and importance, and which has not lost its fascination for the general public, as to a great extent madrigals and morris dancing have, and that was the drama. Acting is an instinct with most human beings, and from very early times it was a necessary part of all religious ceremonies and rituals. The Greeks held drama festivals in honour of the gods, and built vast open-air theatres, and you can still visit some of these and walk up the stone steps, quite worn down in places by the feet of people, who, more than a thousand years ago, clambered up to the stone seats and watched the plays written by Aeschylus or Sophocles or Euripides. In England in the Middle Ages the Church was the chief producer of plays, using them to teach stories from the Bible, the lives of saints, and other holy mysteries, for there were few better ways of impressing such matters on the minds and hearts of men. As time went on these miracle or mystery plays were acted in all the chief towns of England, usually by the craft gilds. Because they took place in the open, in the churchyard or the streets, they were held in the summer when the days were long and fine; and as they grew from the plays produced by the Church they were about sacred subjects, though that is not to say that they were all serious. Some were often very funny, especially the tale of Noah and his family and their adventures in the Ark, or Jonah and his encounter with the whale. It is easy to imagine that here and there a few particularly gifted journeymen or apprentices, with the fascination of acting strong upon them, might leave their masters, form themselves into a little group of players and try to earn a living by their art. At first, perhaps, they would simply visit the near-by manor and the outlying farms in the Christmas mumming play about St. George and the Dragon, but later they might take to the road and become a company of strolling actors. In his play *Hamlet* Shakespeare writes about some of these travelling players arriving to present their plays, and Hamlet, who is the son of the house, receives them with enthusiasm. 'You are welcome masters, welcome all. I am glad to see thee well', he says, and tells his chamberlain to see that they have all they want, and are well used. They have evidently visited this great house frequently, for Hamlet knows the chief actor well enough to call him 'old friend'. That kind of welcome must have been what every strolling company dreamed of, for usually their life was hard enough. As well as visiting the houses of noblemen they tramped from town to town, and when they arrived they would at once seek out the biggest inn and get leave from the host to act there. Many inns were built round a square or oblong yard, and the doors and windows of its rooms opened on to the yard. There would be a wooden balcony running round at first floor level on to which you stepped when you came out of your room. It was a most convenient place. The actors played in the yard, on an improvised and, no doubt, often rickety stage hurriedly erected by laying boards on top of barrels and benches. Some people, guests at the inn and those who could pay for a good view, watched from the balcony or upstairs windows, while the ordinary townsfolk stood gaping and marvelling in the yard itself, and paid a penny or two for doing so.

By the reign of Elizabeth there were a number of companies of players in England, and their plays were no longer religious. They were stories from history and legend, about kings and heroes and lovers, with fools and comic characters to keep the laughter going. The most desirable thing for a company was to be adopted by a nobleman or the Queen, for this meant more or less permanent work if they gave satisfaction. Shakespeare himself belonged to a strolling company before he began to write plays. We do not know how he first became attracted to the stage, whether he acted as a boy at Stratford Grammar School, or was inspired by strolling players visiting the town and so resolved to become a professional actor. Whatever it was must have been strong indeed to draw him away from the small town and the woods and meadows of the Warwickshire and Cotswold country which he loved so much, and later so clearly saw in his mind's eye as he wrote his plays. First he acted, then he began to write parts for his fellow actors, then to alter old dramas, and finally to write his own famous and immortal plays.

As you will have read in the last chapter, the town authorities usually disliked the strolling players, for they thought they were idle and dishonest ne'er-do-wells—some of them certainly were—who drank and quarrelled and attracted the worst and roughest sections of the town wherever they happened to be acting—and that was probably true too. Certainly in London the first theatres were built in the suburbs of Southwark and Shoreditch because they were forbidden inside the walls.

They were very like the inn yards, open to the air with galleries running round, and the audience either sitting in these or standing round the stage itself. The players, who were all men or boys, wore costumes, but there was no scenery, and because there was no roof there were no performances in wet weather. People knew when a play was about to begin because a trumpet was blown and a flag was run up above the roofs of neighbouring houses. Then into the play flocked the audience, to pay their 2*s.* 6*d.* for a stool right on the stage itself, or 1*s.* for a seat in the gallery or a 1*d.* for standing or sitting on the ground itself, when they chewed and spat and laughed, and interrupted or watched in silence the plays written by Christopher Marlowe, or Thomas Dekker, or Ben Jonson, or Will Shakespeare, for their entertainment and delight.

10. Parliament and King

PARLIAMENT, and especially the House of Commons, played an important part in Tudor government. Henry VIII said 'We at no time stand so high in our estate royal as in time of Parliament, when we as head and you as members are knit together in one body politic'; and the Tudor kings and queens managed to get Parliament to approve all their important actions. This was a great help in such matters as Henry's

HEADPIECE. James I and Henry, Prince of Wales, hawking

133

quarrel with the Pope, for it showed that he had strong backing for what he did; but of course it meant that Parliament tended to think itself more important, and in Elizabeth's reign its power undoubtedly increased.

For one thing, the House of Commons became much bigger: in 1559 there were 398 members, but by the end of the reign there were 462. This increase was because many more towns sent members to Parliament, though only a few of them were actually townsmen. Indeed most towns preferred to elect country gentlemen, who owned their land and could afford to pay their own expenses. The importance of the Commons is indicated by the very fact that such people now wanted to become M.P.'s instead of trying to avoid it. Generally the heads of the leading county families were 'knights of the shire' or county members (unless they were nobles and then of course they sat in the House of Lords), while the less important represented the towns. They were usually elected unopposed, and it was only when there were two rival families in the same district that there was a real struggle, for then to get oneself elected became a test of popularity and influence. For example, the election of 1593 nearly led to a local war in Nottinghamshire, between supporters of Sir Charles Cavendish and Sir Thomas Stanhope. M.P.s were often related to each other, and they formed family groups which worked together in the House.

As Elizabeth's reign went on, she called Parliament more often. There were 15 sessions of Parliament during her reign—an average of one every 3 years—and their average length was about 9 weeks. The ruler was still expected, like any other landowner, to live chiefly on the rents and dues from his tenants: anything beyond this had to be granted by a special vote of the Commons. All through her reign, Elizabeth was desperately short of money. She had inherited a big debt when she came to the throne, and her wars in Scotland and France, and above all with Spain, were very expensive. To make matters worse, her income like everyone else's at the time was worth less than it had been, because the price of everything was going up. Elizabeth spent as little as she could; she saved money by staying for quite long periods with wealthy subjects, and she made the most of any windfalls that came her way, like the plunder Drake took from the Spaniards. But even so she had to ask the Commons for money, and this made them more powerful by the end of her reign.

Elizabeth handled her Parliaments very cleverly. She kept in close touch with them, because most of her Council were important members of either the Lords or the Commons, and she always knew what was going on. When things did not go as she wished, she took a hand herself. She would send down to the Commons a message forbidding them to discuss this or that, or she would summon the Speaker of the Commons, or a deputation from both Houses, and tell them what she expected of them. Occasionally she went down to the Parliament House herself and spoke, and when she did this she generally sent members away satisfied: for though she was sometimes in a towering rage, and scolded them like children, she also knew how to be gracious, and would often give way over some unimportant point, thus both winning their gratitude and getting her own way in things that really mattered to her.

But from quite early in her reign, Elizabeth had differences of opinion with her Parliaments. First the Commons, who were anxious about the succession, urged her to marry. Elizabeth realized the difficulties of this much more clearly than they did, and put them off with a vague answer, but they raised the matter again, and when she forbade them to discuss it, they actually dared to hold up a vote of money. In the end she reluctantly allowed them to discuss the succession, and at the same time reduced her demand for money, whereupon the Commons thanked her for her gracious speech and voted the money. But later more serious disputes arose, especially about religion, for a number of Puritans were elected to Parliament who wanted to reduce the power of the bishops, and make more changes in the Prayer Book. Elizabeth considered this an abominable interference with her powers as Governor of the Church, and forbade members to discuss such matters. A Puritan member, Peter Wentworth, protested at this and asked 'whether there be any council that can make laws but only this Court of Parliament; and whether free speech be not granted to everyone in Parliament house by law?' This was practically a claim that Parliament was the real ruler of the country. Elizabeth dealt with it firmly, and Wentworth, who had very few supporters, was promptly imprisoned in the Tower. But the incident shows that Parliament had changed since the days of Henry

VIII. It was beginning to learn its strength and to feel very strongly about certain matters; and though Elizabeth was able to hold her own, trouble began almost immediately after her death in 1603.

The middle-aged Scotsman who now became James I was not a very attractive person. He had weak rickety legs, a thin straggling beard, and a tongue too large for his mouth, 'which made him speak full in the mouth, and drink very uncomely'. He was timid by nature, and had his clothes made very wide and padded so as to be 'stiletto proof'—and he never changed them till they were quite worn out. He was well-read and intelligent, and liked nothing better than a learned argument, in which he could hold his own with anyone. He prided himself on his wisdom, but he knew very little about England, and he was a bad judge of men, depending too much on personal friends who had attractive manners and were willing to flatter him. His first adviser was Robert Cecil, Earl of Salisbury, son of Elizabeth's faithful friend, Burghley.

Salisbury made a much-needed peace with Spain in 1604, and arranged a very popular marriage between James's brilliant and beautiful daughter, Elizabeth, and Frederick, the Elector Palatine, one of the chief Protestant princes of Germany. Salisbury was Lord Treasurer till his death in 1612, but he had many rivals. One of these was Sir Walter Raleigh: he was one of the ablest men of his time, but James distrusted him from the first, and he soon lost all his influence at the Court. In 1603 he was accused of taking part in a plot to overthrow the King, and, although there was little real evidence against him, he was imprisoned in the Tower for fourteen years. Perhaps if James's eldest son, Prince Henry, had lived a little longer, Raleigh would have been set free, for the Prince was a great admirer of his. 'Why does my father keep such a bird in that cage?' he said to a friend.

As soon as James became king, he had to deal with questions of religion. Both the Roman Catholics and the Puritans expected favours from him, for his mother had been a Roman Catholic, and he had been brought up as a Presbyterian: but both were disappointed. A small body of Roman Catholics, resolute men with nothing to lose, determined to try force. Led by Robert Catesby, they planned the Gunpowder Plot in 1605, with the object of destroying the whole government, King, Lords, and Commons, by blowing up the Parliament House when they were all assembled for the state opening of Parliament. In the confusion which was bound to follow, they hoped to seize power and appeal for help to Spain.

Catesby got Guy Fawkes, who had served in the Spanish army, to prepare the gunpowder and fuses in a coal cellar under the House of Lords, which the plotters had managed to rent, and by the end of October everything was ready. But at the last moment, one of the plotters lost his nerve. He sent a letter to his brother-in-law, who sat in the House of Lords, warning him to stay away from Parliament, 'for they shall receive a terrible blow and shall not see who hurts them'. This mysterious letter was shown to the Council. Although they still did not know what danger to expect, the Council ordered a search of the House to be made and Guy Fawkes, waiting to light up, was caught. He was tortured to make him betray the others, but they betrayed themselves by a desperate attempt at an armed rising, and were quickly rounded up and put to death. The whole thing made people fear and hate the Roman Catholics more than ever and there was no chance of James granting them any concessions.

The Puritans had no idea of using force; they believed the King would listen to reason. As soon as he reached England, they presented him with a petition asking for certain changes in the Church. In 1604 James invited some of them, and some of the bishops, to a conference at Hampton Court to discuss matters, with himself as chairman; but though he listened attentively to both sides, he decided everything against the Puritans. He had no intention of giving up any of his power over the Church, and in the end he lost his temper. 'If you aim at a Scottish presbytery', he cried, 'it agreeth as well with monarchy as God with the Devil. I thus apply it—no bishop, no king', and he dismissed the conference with the final threat, 'I will make them conform or else I will harry them out of the land.' He was as good as his word, and in the next few years a number of Puritan clergyman were dismissed for refusing to carry out the services according to the Prayer Book. His treatment of the Puritans made him many enemies. He did not realize how strong they were in the country, or how much Parliament would resent his making rules about the Church without consulting them as well as the clergy; perhaps even if he had known, he would not have cared.

One of James's strongest beliefs was that a king was something quite apart from ordinary men: he was God's personal representative, and his power came directly from God, so he was above all laws, and need not observe them unless he chose. He might allow his subjects certain liberties, but if so it was only out of kindness, and he could withdraw them whenever he liked. He told his first Parliament, 'As to dispute what God may do is blasphemy, so it is sedition in a subject to dispute what a King may do. I will not be content that my power be disputed on.' It was quite clear that if Parliament should dispute about James's power there would be serious trouble. In fact disputes began almost at once both over religion and, even more, over money. The trouble was that the King's normal income was not big enough, even though the Commons had voted him the customs duties, or 'tunnage and poundage', for his lifetime. Elizabeth had just managed, by being as careful—even as mean—as possible, but even so she had had to sell some of the royal land, which meant that there was less for James. James was more extravagant, but even if he had not wasted money on his favourites he still would not have had enough to keep his family, pay his debts, and govern the country. He began by increasing the customs duties. The Commons objected that this could not be done without their consent, but the judges supported James. Since the King both appointed them and could dismiss them, the judges were less likely to act against his wishes than they later became. The merchants had to pay the extra duties, but the Commons stuck to their opinion, so James angrily dismissed his first Parliament in 1611, and his second, the 'Addled' Parliament in 1614, was dismissed almost as soon as it had met, without voting any money.

Parliament did not meet again till 1621, and in the meantime much had happened. Some time after Salisbury's death in 1612, James became much attached to George Villiers, whom he made Duke of Buckingham. Buckingham was a brave and gay young man, but he was also selfish, fickle and irresponsible, and he owed his position entirely to the King's affection for his handsome face and easy manners. James could deny him nothing, and he practically ruled England from 1617 till his death in 1628. Most people detested him for his conceit and truculence and utter lack of wisdom, but his greatest failure was in his dealings with foreign countries. Although peace had been made in 1604, many people still thought Spain our worst enemy and wanted to renew the war. Partly to please them and partly to fill the treasury, Buckingham persuaded the King to release Raleigh, so that he could lead an expedition to discover a gold mine in South America. James really wanted an alliance with Spain and was reluctant to trespass on the Spanish Main, and before the expedition sailed, Buckingham had changed his mind and come round to James's idea. Raleigh was therefore sent out with the impossible task of seizing Spanish gold without fighting the Spaniards. Of course he failed, and, on his return, he was most unjustly executed on the old charge of treason.

In 1618 war broke out between the Catholic powers, Austria and Spain, and the German Protestants. James's daughter and son-in-law were driven out of their territory by the Austrians and the Spanish, and asked James for help. Most English people wanted to help them, and thought the best way to do it was to make war on Spain. James was anxious to help them too, but he hoped to do it peacefully. His plan was to arrange a marriage between his son Charles and the King of Spain's daughter, and then to persuade the Spaniards to restore Frederick's territory to him. This was just at the time when James, still in urgent need of money, summoned his third Parliament. The Commons demanded war with Spain; but James, who was quite set on the Spanish marriage, forbade them to discuss foreign policy at all, and, when they passed a resolution claiming the right to discuss anything, he dismissed them, and himself tore the resolution out of the records.

As Spain did nothing more about the marriage, James grew impatient. He sent Prince Charles, accompanied by Buckingham, to Madrid to woo the Princess himself. The Spanish Court had slow, elaborate rules of behaviour about such things, and was scandalized. Charles was not allowed even to see the Princess, and Buckingham's haughty and ill-mannered behaviour made matters worse, so they soon came back thoroughly disgusted with their treatment. When Charles returned without a Roman Catholic bride, there were rejoicings all over the country. Bells were rung, bonfires were lit, crowds turned out to cheer and, for the first and only time in his life, Buckingham found himself a popular hero. This, and his indignation with the Spaniards, swung him right round, and he urged James to summon Parliament and declare war on Spain. Parliament was delighted; it voted money without argument, and an expedition was raised to help the German Protestants. But it was a wretched force, quite untrained, badly led, and badly supplied. It landed on the Dutch island of Walcheren, and there it remained. Half the soldiers died of starvation or fever, and the rest were brought home. Buckingham was blamed for this disaster, and lost all his new popularity. Meanwhile James I died in March 1625.

Charles I was in many ways a better man than his father. Though he was less learned, he was a man of good taste and was the patron of the painter, Van Dyck, and the architect, Inigo Jones. He was dignified, handsome, and sincerely religious. But, like James, he believed that the King should have supreme power in Church and State; he was just as devoted to Buckingham; and he was changeable and unreliable. His first act, on Buckingham's advice, was to marry Henrietta Maria, the sister of Louis XIII of France, a gay and beautiful girl of fifteen. Charles soon became devoted to her, and was very much guided by her advice. Parliament was not consulted about the marriage; in fact Buckingham put off calling it together until the marriage was safely over. He knew that the Commons would disapprove of a French queen almost as much as a Spanish one, for she too would be a Roman Catholic, and, to make matters worse, one of the conditions of the marriage was that the English Roman Catholics were to be given more liberty. When Parliament did meet, it was in an indignant mood. It only voted tunnage and poundage for one year, instead of for the King's lifetime, and tried to reform the Church on Puritan lines, so Charles promptly dissolved it.

For the next three years, the quarrel grew worse. Charles expected the Commons to vote money for the war with Spain, and he was soon at war with France as well, for he found he could not carry out his promise to help the Catholics, and, when Cardinal Richelieu, the head of the French government, complained, Charles banished all his wife's French followers from the country. The Commons, however, would not vote any money unless he would dismiss Buckingham, which he flatly refused to do. He tried to carry on the war without their help, but an expedition against Cadiz in 1626, and another in 1627 to help the French Protestants to defend their fortress of La Rochelle against Richelieu, were utter failures, for the troops were unpaid, badly equipped, and badly led. Charles tried to raise money by forcing wealthy men to lend it to him, and imprisoning those who refused, but this did not produce nearly as much as he needed. As he could not support the soldiers himself, he had to compel people to lodge and feed them in their own homes, which was a great grievance, for undisciplined troops robbed and insulted their unfortunate hosts. Things became so bad that whole districts were put under 'martial law' to restore order, and not only soldiers but civilians as well were tried by military courts, in which harassed officers dealt out very rough justice.

In spite of everything, Charles had to call another Parliament together in 1628. The members, ignoring all other business, drew up the Petition of Right, which declared it illegal to raise taxes without the consent of Parliament, to imprison people without trial, to compel anyone to take in soldiers (except inn-keepers, who were to be properly paid for it), or to put any civilian under martial law. Charles reluctantly agreed, hoping that now they would vote some money for the war, but they would still do nothing to help him as long as Buckingham was in power. Soon afterwards Buckingham, who was at Portsmouth trying to fit out a second expeditionary force to La Rochelle, was murdered by an unpaid officer called Felton. Charles was heart-broken, but his subjects were delighted, and there were open rejoicings, especially in London. Parliament met once more, but it did not last long. With Buckingham out of the way, they now turned to attacking the Church and the bishops, so Charles sent a message ordering them to adjourn. The Speaker rose, to bring the debate to an end, but some of the members held him down in his chair while the Commons voted that anyone who 'brought in any innovations' in religion, or who paid any tax not granted by Parliament, was an enemy of the kingdom. Immediately afterwards Parliament was dissolved, and Charles imprisoned some of the leaders. Most of them were soon released, but Sir John Eliot, who refused to apologise for anything he had done, was kept in the Tower till his death.

For the next eleven years (1629–40) Charles ruled without a Parliament at all. He made peace with France and Spain, and was as careful as possible over money. There was practically no opposition, because without a Parliament there was no way of organizing it. In any case most people cared very little whether the King consulted Parliament or not. One important change was that Sir Thomas Wentworth, who had been one of the leaders of the Commons against Buckingham, came over to the King's side. He was a determined and able man, who wanted efficient government. This had been impossible while Buckingham was in power, but, now that he was dead, Wentworth thought it was more likely to come from the King than from Parliament. The members had no experience of governing, and were too much concerned with details of religion which Wentworth, though he was a good Christian, thought 'things purely and simply indifferent'. Charles made him Lord Deputy of Ireland, where he raised an army, restored order, and encouraged trade, though he made many enemies by his high-handed methods.

Charles's other adviser was William Laud, whom he made first Bishop of London, then Archbishop of Canterbury. Laud was a devout, honest, but narrow-minded man, who had strong and not unreasonable ideas about how the Church should be run. He thought that it should have discipline and unity, and, as he said, 'that the external worship of God should be kept up in uniformity and decency and in some beauty of holiness, for I found that with the contempt of the outward service of God, the inward fell away apace'. For this reason he thought that the forms and ceremonies of the Church were important, while the Puritans saw in them only superstition and 'Popery', and believed, quite wrongly, that Laud was trying to bring back the Roman Catholic religion. He lost no time in carrying out his plans. Bishops were urged to inspect their bishoprics, and to deal with any clergy who did not carry out the services properly. Clergymen who disobeyed were punished by the Court of High Commission, and laymen by the Star Chamber, which dealt out heavy punishments to people who spoke or wrote against the Church or the Court. The Puritans complained of persecution, and some even fled to America to avoid it, but they were just as intolerant themselves whenever they had the power to be.

To pay his expenses, Charles went on collecting money by forced loans, and in other ways which were strictly speaking legal, but often unjust. He revived the Norman forest laws, which had never been repealed, and anyone who had enclosed land which had once been part

SHERRIFFS.

CHARLES I WITH PRINCE RUPERT DEMANDS THE FIVE MEMBERS
AT THE BAR OF THE COMMONS

of a royal forest was fined. Under an old law of Edward III he forced people who owned a certain amount of land to become knights, and pay for the privilege. The most important of these devices was 'ship money'. Kings had always claimed the right to collect ships, or money instead, from the sea ports in time of danger. The navy had been neglected, and Charles wanted to make it strong enough to hold its own with the French and Dutch fleets, and to protect the coast against pirates. So in 1634 he demanded 'ship money' from the ports, and next year he began to collect it as a regular thing from the whole country. In 1637 John Hampden, one of the leaders of the last Parliament, refused to pay, because it was a tax not voted by Parliament, and he was put on his trial. It was a complicated case, on which the judges, who were now more independent than they had been in James I's time, disagreed. In the end, a majority of them decided that the King had the right to demand ship money in an emergency, and was the only person in a position to decide when an emergency arose; so Hampden had to pay his tax, and a fine as well. There was much indignation about it, but in spite of that Charles might have gone on ruling without Parliament for some time longer, if he and Laud had not been foolish enough to start a religious war with Scotland.

Ever since the days of John Knox, the Scots had been strongly Presbyterian, and James I, who realized this, had left their religion alone; but in 1638 Laud decided that the English Prayer Book and form of service were to be used in Scotland. The first attempt to enforce this led to a riot in Edinburgh, which soon became a national rebellion, for the Scots thought that the English service was Roman Catholic in all but name; thousands of them signed a National Covenant, swearing to resist 'the usurped authority of the Roman anti-Christ, and his tyrannous laws made against Christian liberty'. They quickly collected an efficient army, with many experienced officers who had fought as volunteers on the Protestant side in the German war. Charles raised what troops he could, but they were clearly no match for the Scots, and, without fighting a battle, he had to agree to the Treaty of Berwick, leaving the Scottish Parliament and Church Assembly to draw up the terms of a permanent agreement. The Scots kept their army together, but Charles's unpaid and mutinous troops were mostly disbanded.

The King's next move was to summon Wentworth, whom he now made Earl of Strafford, from Ireland. Strafford advised Charles to call another Parliament, for he saw that nothing could be done without a proper army, and only Parliament could raise the money to pay for one. He hoped that they would support the King against the Scots. If they did not he would deal with any trouble as firmly as he had done in Ireland. But when the 'Short Parliament' met in 1640, the Commons insisted that their grievances should be remedied before they voted any money, and Charles dissolved Parliament at once. Strafford urged him to imprison the leaders, impose taxes himself, and bring over the Irish army for use against the Scots—or against the Commons if necessary. If Charles had followed this advice quickly he might still have saved himself, but while he hesitated the Scots, who were in close touch with the leaders of the Commons, struck first, and invaded England. Charles had to agree that they should occupy part of northern England, and to promise to pay their expenses until a settlement was reached. This, as the Scots knew very well, meant that he would have to summon Parliament again, and in November 1640 the 'Long Parliament' met.

The leader of the Commons was John Pym, a single-minded, forceful man, and a strong Puritan, who aimed quite deliberately at making the Commons the real rulers of England in place of the King. The first step was to get rid of Strafford, for they did not feel safe until he was out of the way. The Commons demanded his impeachment on a charge of treason, and the Lords ordered his arrest. Impeachment was a form of trial used against a great officer of state, in which the House of Commons accused him of a crime, and the House of Lords tried him. It soon became clear that he could not be found guilty, so they fell back on an Act of Attainder, which was a special Act of Parliament sentencing him to death without any trial at all. The Lords, alarmed by rumours of a plot to overthrow Parliament by force, passed the Bill, but it could not become law without the King's consent. Charles had promised Strafford that 'not a hair of his head should be touched'; but the fierce Puritan mob of London raged outside the palace clamouring for his death, and Charles feared for the safety of the Queen and his children if he refused. After twenty-four hours of anxious hesitation, he gave way. Strafford was beheaded, dying very bravely. 'It was his misfortune', wrote his

'HUGE CROWDS WATCH THE EXECUTION OF THE EARL OF
STRAFFORD ON TOWER HILL'

friend Laud, 'that he served a mild and gracious Prince who knew not
how to be or how to be made great.'

Next, the members made their position even more secure by enacting
that the Parliament then sitting could not be dissolved without its own
consent. Then they swept away all the instruments of Charles's personal
Government—the Star Chamber, the Court of High Commission, ship
money, forest laws, and the rest—and completed the work by a law that
Parliament must in future meet at least every three years. Charles had
to agree to all this. So far the Commons had been united, but in August
1641 they began to discuss religion. The extreme Puritans, led by Pym,
Hampden, and his cousin, Oliver Cromwell, proposed what they called
the 'Root and Branch' Bill, to abolish bishops, bring the Church under
the control of Parliament, and reform the Prayer Book. A moderate
party, led by Lord Falkland and Sir Edward Hyde, opposed it. In this
way two parties grew up which became the 'Roundheads' and the
'Cavaliers'. They could not agree over the Root and Branch Bill, and
Parliament adjourned for six months.

They were recalled by a terrible disaster in Ireland. Now that Strafford was no longer there to keep order, the Irish Catholics rose against their English masters, and many Protestants were massacred. The Puritans suspected the Queen of stirring up the revolt, but the real question was how to crush it. They would have to raise an army to do so, yet they were afraid that, if they did, Charles might use it, not against the Irish, but against them. The only safe way seemed to be to take power out of his hands altogether. To justify doing this, Pym drew up the Grand Remonstrance, a long list of all Charles's tyrannous deeds, and a demand that he should choose as his ministers only people of whom Parliament approved. There was a furious debate over this, and in the end it was only passed by eleven votes, which showed how strong the Cavalier party had become. When Charles rejected it, Pym followed it up by a Militia Bill, by which Parliament, and not the King, was to have control of the army.

If this became law, Charles's power would be gone for good, and he gave orders that five leaders of the Commons, including Pym and Hampden, should be impeached. It was not really legal for the King to order an impeachment, and the Parliament hesitated to obey, so on 4 January 1642, Charles decided to act himself. He had collected at Whitehall a number of tough, hard-bitten officers, who were waiting to lead troops to Ireland, and, with 400 of these 'Cavaliers' at his back, he went to Westminster to make the arrests. But the Commons had been warned, and the five members had fled by boat to London. Charles entered the House, while the members stood in dead silence, and his escort, with swords and pistols, swarmed round the door, and asked the Speaker where the five members were. The Speaker refused to tell him, unless the Commons gave him leave. 'I see the birds have flown', said Charles, 'I do expect that you will send them to me as soon as they return hither', and he walked out, while the members raised angry cries of 'Privilege!'

After this threat to their safety, the Commons took refuge in London, where they met at the Guildhall, protected by the city's train-bands— or territorial soldiers. Charles left Whitehall a few days later, and went to York. Both he and the Parliament began to raise forces, and the Civil War had begun.

How to make a

BOAR PUDDING

11. Land and People

4. AT THE OUTBREAK OF THE CIVIL WAR

FROM the defeat of the Armada to the outbreak of the great Civil War England was a peaceful country to live in, and yet we know there were growing up such differences amongst the English people that they could not be settled without resorting to armed force. It is a period from which many letters and private papers have survived, so that it is possible to build up a picture of how the different ranks of people lived in the seventeenth century, what they thought about the issues of the Civil War, and how they were affected by it.

One of the fullest collections of family papers belongs to the Verneys of Claydon in the county of Buckinghamshire. Sir Edmund Verney studied with James I's eldest son, Henry, saw service in foreign wars, and became a member of the household of Prince Charles. When Charles

HEADPIECE. Title and embellishment from a late Tudor cookery book came to the throne he was made Knight Marshal 'to preserve order and prevent access to the court of improper persons', and was one of those, no doubt, who helped to convert the ill-disciplined Court of James I into the well-ordered and dignified circle of Charles. His office may have been profitable, but it also cost him a great deal to buy his Court clothes and keep up a house in the new piazza in Covent Garden, so that he tried to eke out his income as a landlord by investment, by taking shares in new trade ventures, and by the purchase of patents.

Without such additions to his rents a gentleman of the seventeenth century could not prosper. A father left the following advice to his son:

> It is impossible for a mere country gentleman ever to grow rich or to raise his house. He must have some other vocation with his inheritance, as to be a courtier, lawyer, merchant or other vocation. If he hath no other . . . let him get a ship and judiciously manage it, or buy some auditor's place or be vice-admiral in his county. By only following the plough he may keep his wind and be upright but he will never increase his future.

Sir John Oglander wrote this on 25 June 1632, aged forty-eight years.

A country gentleman's younger sons might take up a profession or go into trade. From the letters of the Oxinden family we find that while one son succeeded his father as the squire, another entered the Church, and the two younger ones were apprenticed to a cloth merchant and a mercer. Another possible opening for younger sons appeared in the seventeenth century. Sir Edmund Verney's younger boy, Thomas, got into trouble over a love affair and was sent to Virginia. An agent suggested that he took with him three servants and a cooper, as this type of workman was scarce. By way of equipment he was to bring 'a feather bed, a bolster, pillow, blanketts, a rugg and three payre of sheets, flour, fowling pieces, strong waters and grocery'. Thomas was back within a year and went to serve in the French army, but we know that many settled in the Colonies, preferring to suffer some hardship and keep the right to worship and think as they pleased.

Great care was taken in arranging marriages in landed families so that estates should not be impoverished by a hasty match. Sir Edmund's son, Sir Ralph, was married to a neighbouring heiress, Mary Blackall, when he was fifteen and she was thirteen. It turned out to be a very happy match, for she fought hard to save his estates during the Civil War and finally followed him into exile, where she died. One father expressed a hope in his will that his daughter would marry a cousin of the same name so that 'the lands and tenements of the Cullings shall, if it may be, remain and continue in the name of the Cullings'. As a matter of fact she married her guardian, Henry Oxinden, who considered himself a member of the gentry while she was a yeoman's daughter. He thought it necessary to defend the match to his family by saying that her father had his sports and pleasures like a gentleman and had educated his daughter at a school for gentlemen's daughters. He ended up defiantly by reminding his cousin that 'the wisest men had ever held virtue the best and truest nobility'. Dorothy Osborne was forbidden to marry her suitor, Sir William Temple, because he had been a Parliamentarian while her father had been governor of Guernsey for the King. She said that she was against love matches but enraged her brother by refusing the many suitors he brought home, and carried on a secret correspondence with Sir William which ended in their marriage, even after her beauty had been marred by the smallpox. Although single women of gentle birth were well treated in large households which had need of their services, they resorted to what seemed to them to be desperate measures to avoid spinsterhood. Elizabeth Verney ran away with a parson when she was thirty, against her brother's will. In a letter of apology she wrote: 'I confess this piece of indiscretion in me is enough to put me in despair of your pardon. . . . I trust in God I am not so lost as some think I am because I have married one who has the repute of an honest man and one as in time I may live comfortably with.'

When a marriage was made, the seventeenth-century gentlewoman found herself mistress of a largely self-supporting household. At Claydon the estate provided cows, sheep, and pigs for the table, as well as horses for cartage and travel. The diet was supplemented by pigeons and poultry, fish from the fishponds, and game either shot or brought down by the hawk. All kinds of workshops, a dairy, a blacksmith's, a carpenter's, adjoined the house, as well as chambers for the storage of roots and apples. Many of these matters were cared for by menservants, but the lady of the house frequently found herself in charge. She and her maids baked the bread and brewed the beer. She kept an elaborate recipe book containing exotic recipes such as for 'a swan roast with numerous sallets'. She was also expert at curing, preserving, distilling. Fruit wines and medicines had to be made at home: in the Oxinden letters we read of a gift of '5 or 6 ounces of verie good syrup of our owne making, of mayden heare and coltsfoote of which you shall use as you please: they are very effectual and cordial and pectoral'. In addition, wool and flax were spun at home, and both coarse and fine needlework, the latter often decked with elaborate embroidery, were the tasks of the female part of the household. Many examples of seventeenth-century embroidery, cut work, drawn work, and, most fashionable of all, stump work, where the pattern or picture is padded to make it stand out, have survived.

The tendency to increased comfort and luxury which we saw in the homes of the upper classes in Tudor times continued in the seventeenth century. The Verneys had leather carpets for dining- and drawing-rooms put into their house, 'with green wrought velvet furniture and stooles with nails guilt'. Although the clumsy farthingales of Elizabethan and Jacobean times disappeared, both men and women dressed elaborately, with long curled hair, silken shirts or breeches adorned with ribbons and softly falling lace. The King was a great patron of painters, and it became the fashion among the nobility to have a portrait painted by Van Dyck. The gentry followed suit with lesser painters. 'The picture is very ill-favoured', wrote one lady to the Verneys, 'and makes me quite out of favour with myself: the face is so big and fat that it pleaseth me not at all but truly I think 'tis like the original.'

The country gentry were not looked up to only as the rulers of large households or as landlords. Many of them held the office of Justice of the Peace, an unpaid position, but one of very great importance in Tudor and Stuart times. The Justice of the Peace presided at Quarter Sessions and had to deal with many of the smaller offences against the law. He had to see that the Statutes of the land were carried out. When we think of some of these, the Poor Law, the Statute of Artificers, the laws against Roman Catholics or against Puritans, we can see how much work fell on the J.P. and how much any government had to rely on his goodwill. If the Justice of the Peace did not wish to enforce a law, very often it was not enforced. This was how the Catholic gentry of the north escaped punishment in the reign of Elizabeth. Sometimes the Privy Council, or the Council of the North, or of Wales and the Marches, pressed the Justices to act when they were reluctant, for example, to find work for the poor, as they were supposed to do according to the 1601 Act. When the J.P.s were asked to do something really distasteful to them, such as the collection of ship money, they resisted, and it was on their resistance that Stuart policy foundered more than once.

Nevertheless, when it came to war most of the gentry, with their household servants and many of their tenants, followed the King. We can see how this came about in the case of Sir Edmund Verney. He was no admirer of Strafford: 'I know but few that are fond of his presence.' He knew that Laud's attempt to introduce the English Prayer Book together with bishops into Scotland had caused the Scottish Wars, and evidently agreed with an understanding moderate Scotsman: '. . . is confident that nothing will satisfy them but taking away all Bishops'. In his case loyalty and his official position were the deciding factors. 'I have eaten his bread and served him nearly thirty years and will not do so base a thing as to forsake him now.' He was killed at Edgehill and his son Edmund at Newbury. His eldest son, Ralph, however, had declared for the Parliament, but a year or two later he broke with them and went into exile because, as a staunch supporter of the Church of England, he would not sign the Solemn League and Covenant which promised the establishment of Presbyterianism in return for a Scottish army.

A pleasant picture of the King's supporters emerges from the Verney papers and other Cavalier letters, but the Royalist side does not appear in the same light to the Puritan yeomen, traders, and preachers, who formed the chief supporters of Parliament. To them the Royalists appeared to be an extravagant, lawless band clinging to out-dated privileges, living in idleness while others toiled, encouraging the King to defy the Commons and neglect the true interests of the nation. They were suspected of being Roman Catholics although, except for the northern gentry, most of them were staunch Anglicans. Their very appearance was regarded as frivolous by the soberly clad Parliamentarians; to show their opposition to the lace and curls of the Court, the

SHERRIFFS

The Marquess of Montrose. (campaigning in Scotland.)

The Universities of Oxford and Cambridge

The Anglo-Irish and the Catholics.

The Divine Right of Kings

NEWCASTLE
LEEDS HULL
OXFORD
LONDON

The Church of England

The Aristocracy and tenantry.

On the map, the White area represents support of the King. Leeds was held for Parliament.

On the map, the Black area represents support of Parliament. Oxford was held for the King.

The Navy

The City of London and the Merchant interest

Cromwell

The Presbyterian Kirk of Scotland

The Puritans and Dissenters

The House of Commons

The Yeomen Farmers

APPROXIMATE GROUPING OF ALLEGIANCES IN THE CIVIL WAR, 1642-46

Puritans wore plain linen only and 'few, whatsoever degree they were of wore their hair long enough to cover their ears, and the minister and many others cut it close round their heads with so many little peaks as was ridiculous to behold; from this custom of thus wearing their hair the name "Roundhead" became the scornful term given to the whole Parliament side'.

The traditional festivities of English life, the gay country weddings, the bough gatherings on May morning, the dances round the maypole, were all regarded as sinful by the Puritans and were suppressed during the period of the Commonwealth. Thrift and sobriety were the virtues they admired; hard work to secure the blessings of this life, and godliness to obtain those of the world to come was their creed. Yet to paint the King's opponents as long-faced, tight-fisted, and crop-eared knaves is no less untrue than their own picture of the Cavaliers as reckless, extravagant fops, and misses their greatness and the reasons for the success of their cause.

Not all the nobility and gentry followed the King. The first Parliamentary campaigns were probably planned at Broughton Castle, near Banbury, the seat of Lord Saye and Sele, while the Earls of Essex and Manchester were the first commanders of the Parliamentary army. The opposition to Charles in Parliament had been led by Pym and Hampden, who were country squires; Oliver Cromwell too could claim to belong to the same class, although he had sold his family estate near Huntingdon in order to lease more profitable land, and preferred to be a hard-working farmer, championing the rights of the common people of the Fens, rather than the traditional country squire.

These Parliamentary leaders among the gentry believed that it was not enough to send Laud and Strafford to the scaffold or suppress the Court of the Star Chamber. They held that the King's policy would never truly be changed until his army and his ministers were under Parliamentary control. It was this belief that led Oliver Cromwell to attach such importance to the Grand Remonstrance: '. . . if it had been rejected he would have sold all he had the next morning and never have seen England more.' They were Puritans, too, and believed that Laud's High Church policy linked England with the Roman Catholic Church and the despotic rulers of Europe. The yeomen farmers and freeholders shared the political and religious beliefs of this group, and in the districts, for example in the north, in Lancashire and Yorkshire, where the gentry were Royalist and sometimes Catholic, they were not afraid to show their independence. The diaries of a Yorkshire yeoman, Adam Eyre, have recently been brought to light. He served in the Parliamentary army and was a great reader. 'This day I rested at home and spent most of the day reading'; and another day: 'Had various thoughts by reason of the variety of men's opinions I find in reading.' It was this habit of thinking about political and religious issues that made Cromwell's 'plain russet-coated captains' so formidable and difficult to beat.

Parliament found some of its most valuable supporters in the merchants of the great cities and ports, who felt themselves threatened by Stuart policy. 'Many merchants here in England, finding less encouragement given to their profession than in other countries and seeing themselves not so well esteemed as their noble vocation demands. . .', Munn began in *England's Treasure by Foreign Trade*, written in 1630. A great deal of wealth had accumulated in the hands of the East India Company and other great trading concerns such as the Levant Company since their foundation in the days of Elizabeth. The Merchant Adventurers, the London company that had the monopoly of the export of English cloth, still struggled to defend its privileges against the 'interlopers', provincial merchants who wanted freedom to trade on their own accord. In 1643 they purchased the confirmation of their privileges from Parliament for £30,000. The City of London took a very important part in the Puritan cause. In a pamphlet written in 1646 a Presbyterian wrote: 'If the Lord had not helped us by the forces, arms and supplies of men and money from London, we had been utterly destroyed and laid waste.'

Throughout the country the end of the reign of Elizabeth and the period up to the beginning of the Civil War saw the establishment of new industries and the expansion of old. Thread-making, lace manufacture, silk weaving, engraving, the making of parchment, needles, and glass were introduced often by Protestants from the Netherlands and France. Their associates in England were usually of Puritan belief. Brass as well as iron wares of all kinds began to be manufactured in the Birmingham district, and fustian, a cloth made of linen and cotton,

SHERIFFS

Pliable   Ignorance   Mr Stand-Fast   Christian   Mr Worldly Wiseman

CHARACTERS IN 'PILGRIM'S PROGRESS'

appeared in Lancashire for the first time. The woollen cloth trade continued to increase and flourished not only in its old centres but in other districts which had taken up the 'New Draperies'. The production of coal increased fourteenfold between 1560 and 1690. All these resources tended to be at the service of Parliament rather than the King.

At first sight it appears that industry was organized on medieval lines. The Elizabethan Statute of Artificers 1562, which was strictly enforced by the Stuart Privy Council, insisted on a seven-year apprenticeship and commanded men to follow the trade for which they had been trained. In the corporate towns the gilds still flourished, and Stuart times saw many charters of incorporation granted to companies of craftsmen such as the silk-throwers, the soap-makers, or the glovers. These grants show partly the royal need of money but also the policy of the Stuart Privy Council, which was to support the small craftsman against the competition of great merchants. In the cloth trade the great clothiers, who bought up the wool crop and then put it out to be manufactured to various workmen to whom they paid a miserable wage, were becoming very powerful. In Yorkshire and Devonshire the cottage

workers bought their own wool from a neighbouring market and returned later to sell the finished cloth, while many small masters all over
the country worked with very little capital.

We know that some of the great clothiers and tin manufacturers were
Puritan in religion; but it is the craftsmen and small clothiers of whom
we hear as being most zealous for the Parliamentary cause, like the
Bradford men who brought their wool sacks to fortify the church tower
against the attacks of the Duke of Newcastle. It is not unusual to hear
of a 'godly, understanding apprentice', and the London apprentices
marched out in force to turn back the Royalist force that marched on
London in 1642. Indeed, it was complained that many apprentices
deserted their apprenticeship to enlist in the Parliamentary army, and
when the struggle was over refused to serve out their time. Richard
Baxter, a Puritan preacher, speaks of the enthusiasm of the workers of
the Black Country.

In this town of Dudley I lived in most comfort, amongst a poor tractable
people, lately famous for drunkenness but commonly more ready to hear
God's word with submission and reformation than most places where I had
come; so that ... the church was usually crowded within and at the windows,
as ever I saw any London congregation; partly through the great willingness
of the people and partly by the exceeding populousness of the country where
the woods and commons are planted with nailers, scythe-smiths and other
iron labourers like a continual village.

There are many instances of humble people, stonemasons, shoemakers,
shipwrights, who defied the Court of High Commission, refused to go
to a church that was becoming too ceremonious for them, and prayed
together for light and guidance. It was this kind of background that
later inspired the tinker John Bunyan to write the *Pilgrim's Progress* and,
however strange the beliefs or wild the language of the different sects,
we should realize that each hoped to avoid the Slough of Despond and
the wiles of Mr. Worldly Wiseman and reach the Heavenly City by its
own path.

Country gentleman and yeoman, great merchant and small trader,
independent worker and preacher, these were the men who backed the
Parliament's cause. It is not surprising that many differences appeared

amongst them directly the immediate business of fighting the Royalists was over. Many of the Independents in the army and elsewhere wanted to change the whole political and social character of the country. The party that wanted radical political change was called the 'Levellers' and those who tried to secure social equality the 'Diggers' or 'True Levellers'. The doctrines of the Levellers are to be seen in the Army debates at Putney in 1647. 'The poorest he that is in England has a life to lead as the greatest he', argued Colonel Rainsborough, putting up a case for a vote for every man to General Ireton. 'And therefore I think it's clear that every man that is to live under a government ought first by his own consent to put himself under that government.' Their views on law reform and the abolition of tithes were put very forcibly by the pamphleteer John Lilburne. The Levellers gave their support to Cromwell in his dissolution of the Rump but later became dissatisfied with his policy, and when their demands were ignored, rose in revolt. The last remnant of their forces was destroyed in Burford in 1649 by Sir Thomas Fairfax, and one of them left his name scratched on the font in Burford Church, 'Anthony Sedley, Prisoner'.

The Diggers gave a practical application of the belief in community of property when they began to dig up St. George's Hill in Surrey and to plant it with parsnips, carrots, and beans. Gerard Winstanley expresses their complaint 'that earth, that is within this Creation made a common stock house for all, is bought and sold and kept in the hands of a few'. He believed property to be the cause of wars: 'And wherefore are men so made to destroy one another . . . but only to uphold civil property . . . but when once the earth becomes a common treasury again as it must, then this enmity of all lands will cease.' He despised mere political freedom. 'If the common people have no more freedom in England but only to live among their elder brothers and work for them for hire, what freedom have they in England more than in Turkey or in France?' Winstanley provides the link between John Ball, who preached the Peasants' Revolt of the fourteenth century, and the Socialists of the nineteenth and twentieth centuries, but at the time he had very few followers, and was scorned even by the political Levellers.

This chapter has tried to show the diversity of social life and of ideas in seventeenth-century England. Although civil strife is a terrible thing, the study of the period leaves the impression of a people who had sincerity and high ideals, whose principles were honestly held and zealously defended. One can understand what Milton, who supported Parliament but hated its intolerance, meant when he pleaded for freedom of publication: 'Lords and Commons of England, consider what nation it is whereof ye are and whereof ye are the governors; a nation not slow and dull but of quick, ingenious and piercing spirit, acute to invent, subtle and sinewy to discourse, not beneath the reach of any point the highest human capacity can soar to.'

12. The Civil War

ENGLAND in 1642 was not a warlike country. Some of the King's spirited young courtiers, and some of the fiercest Puritans welcomed a fight, but there were very few like this. The great majority had no wish for war, and hardly grasped what it was all about. 'They care not what government they live under', wrote the Puritan Haselrig in disgust, 'so long as they may plough and go to market.' Most Englishmen knew nothing of politics, and, if they fought at all, it was either to save their homes from plunder, or out of loyalty to the local gentry, or simply because they were conscripted into one or other army, and could not help it. Only the more thoughtful people on both sides fought for a cause, and from a sense of duty. Some families were divided, the father perhaps fighting for the King, and the son for the Parliament. Sir William Waller and Sir Ralph Hopton, who commanded the Roundheads and the Cavaliers respectively in the west of England, were neighbours and close friends. 'Hostility itself cannot violate my friendship to you,' Waller wrote, 'the

HEADPIECE. Oliver Cromwell with the national banner of the Commonwealth. His own silver lion on a black field is placed at fesse point. (The portrait is taken from the Dunbar medal)

great God knoweth with what reluctance I go upon this service, and with what perfect hatred I look upon a war without an enemy. We are both upon the stage, and must act the parts that are assigned to us in this tragedy. Let us do it in the way of honour, without personal animosities.'

Because many on both sides felt the same, it was on the whole a merciful war. There was a good deal of plundering, but there were hardly any of the outrages and massacres which were a normal part of warfare on the Continent. Only in Ireland both sides fought desperately and without mercy. Many people saw no fighting at all, and for many others the war was nothing but a few local skirmishes. In the summer of 1642, while the majority were hesitating, whole districts were secured for Parliament or King by the prompt action of a few resolute men. This happened in Huntingdonshire and Cambridgeshire, where Oliver Cromwell, the M.P. for Huntingdon, quickly raised a troop of cavalry among his friends and their tenants, and used it first to prevent £20,000 worth of silver sent by Cambridge University from reaching the King, and then to round up the leading Royalists. After that, these counties became a Roundhead recruiting ground for the rest of the war. In other places the sides were evenly matched, and the war consisted of a series of sharp little battles between forces of a few hundred men. Sometimes the approach of one of the main armies under Rupert or Essex gave one or other side the advantage for the time being, but as soon as it moved away again the local war went on as before.

In 1642 neither side was ready for war, but the Roundheads were really in the better position, for they were strong in the south and east of England, and above all, in London. This was an enormous advantage, for London contained nearly a tenth of the population, and even more of the wealth, of the whole kingdom; it was the centre of trade, and Parliament could collect customs duties, and borrow money from the wealthy city merchants. London also had the only force of even partly trained infantry in the country, the train-bands. The navy, which had always hated Popery, supported Parliament, and so did the seaport towns of Hull, Plymouth, and Bristol. This made it difficult for Charles to get any help from abroad, and enabled the Roundheads to protect their trade and shipping. In a long war, they were bound to win. The

F

**ANCESTORS OF THE HOUSEHOLD CAVALRY AND THE
COLDSTREAM GUARDS**

A trooper and a matchlock man in the New Model Army, 1648

King was strongly supported in the north and west of England by great nobles like the Marquis of Newcastle, and by the universities. The landlords and their tenants made excellent cavalry, and the tough borderers from Northumberland who formed Newcastle's 'White-coat' regiment were probably the best infantry on either side. But Charles's great weakness was lack of money, for he had no regular income. The university colleges and loyal families handed over their silver and gold plate to be melted down; but when this was used up there was nothing more, for the rest of their wealth was mostly in livestock and land. As the war went on Charles found it more and more difficult to pay and equip his troops, and had to scatter them about in small garrisons, where they could live on the country. This weakened his main army, and gave the Cavaliers a bad reputation for looting which turned many people against them. The King's only hope lay in a quick victory, before his money ran out and the enemy had time to gather their strength.

A weakness of both armies was that the troops were very reluctant to move far away from their homes, and victory was likely to go to whichever side first managed to produce a force disciplined and mobile enough to fight in any part of the country. Regiments were raised by local gentlemen who received commissions from the King or Parliament. An infantry regiment consisted of musketeers and pikemen. The musket was a clumsy and uncertain weapon, which was usually fired from a forked rest stuck in the ground. It took a long time to load, so the musketeers needed pikemen to protect them. The pikemen had 16-foot pikes and swords and generally some form of armour, which made them heavy and slow moving. Elaborate drill was needed for musketeers and pikemen to work together properly, and only the very best could stand up to cavalry in open country. Cavalry were reckoned more valuable than infantry, and were paid three times as much, though they had to provide their own horses. They were armed with sabres and pistols and wore steel caps and breast-plates or thick leather buff coats. There were also more lightly equipped dragoons, who were really mounted infantry, and were used for patrol and outpost work. They had swords and carbines (a lighter form of musket) and usually fought on foot. At the beginning of the war there were no regular uniforms, which made it difficult to distinguish friend from foe (at Edgehill the

Roundheads wore orange scarves for this purpose), but later red became the standard colour for the New Model Army.

Charles had many capable officers, but he tried to run the war himself and he was too irresolute to be a good general. His nephew, Prince Rupert, the son of Charles's sister Elizabeth and the Elector Palatine, had fought in Germany, and was a brilliant cavalry leader, but he was only twenty-three and was too rash and inexperienced to control his men in battle. The chief Roundhead general at the beginning of the war was the Earl of Essex, who was sound, cautious, and respected rather than brilliant.

Fighting began in April 1642 when Charles tried to occupy the fortress of Hull, but he had not enough troops to take it. He went to Nottingham, where he set up his standard, but soon moved away to the Welsh border, where the Royalists were stronger. Here his army grew quickly and in October he was strong enough to advance towards London, but at Edgehill, near Warwick, he was met by a Roundhead army under Lord Essex. Rupert swept through the Roundhead cavalry, but his men scattered in pursuit instead of coming back to help in the fierce struggle between the infantry. Neither side could claim complete victory, but the advantage was with the King, for he was able to continue his marsh on London. He occupied Oxford, which became his headquarters for the rest of the war, and his advance guard under Rupert got as far as Turnham Green, within a few miles of London; but it was compelled to fall back, and the Cavaliers never got so near London again.

Meanwhile Royalist armies had been raised in the north by the Marquis of Newcastle, and in the west by Sir Ralph Hopton, and in 1643 Charles planned a combined advance on London—Newcastle from Yorkshire, Hopton from Devon, and himself from Oxford. The plan was a good one, but each of the three armies was held up by a Roundhead fortress, and dared not advance until it was taken. Newcastle besieged Hull, but could not take it, and his advance guard was checked by a force led by Oliver Cromwell. Hopton got as far as Wiltshire, where he beat the Roundheads under Waller at Roundway Down near Devizes, but he could go no farther till Plymouth was taken. Charles himself besieged Gloucester. Parliament sent their London army to relieve the town, which they succeeded in doing, but Charles blocked their way back at Newbury. Again neither side gained a clear victory, but Essex succeeded in getting his troops back to London.

By the end of 1643 the advantage still seemed to lie with the King, and Pym played his last card to secure victory. He made a treaty with the Scots, by which they were to send an army of 20,000 men to help the Roundheads. It seems strange that Scots were willing to fight against their Stuart king, but they were still resentful of the way Charles and Archbishop Laud had tried to force the English Prayer Book on Scotland, and in exchange for their help Pym promised a Presbyterian Church, on Scottish lines, in England. The Scottish alliance certainly helped to defeat the King, but later on it led to fatal quarrels amongst the victors themselves, for by no means all Roundheads were strict Presbyterians, and there were many, especially in the army, who thought a Presbyterian Church assembly just as tyrannous as the bishops had been.

Meanwhile, in eastern England a new kind of army was taking shape which was to make the Roundheads' victory certain. Oliver Cromwell had seen at Edgehill that the Roundhead cavalry were no match for Rupert's. 'Your troopers', he said to his cousin John Hampden, 'are mostly old decayed serving-men, and tapsters, and such kind of fellows: and their troopers are gentlemen's sons and men of quality. You must get men of a spirit that is like to go as far as gentlemen will go, or else I am sure you will be beaten still.' Towards the end of 1642, he returned to East Anglia to raise a cavalry regiment from 'such men as had the fear of God before them, and made some conscience of what they did.' Most of them were freeholders, yeomen farmers and their sons, and Cromwell chose the ablest of them as officers. 'I had rather a plain russet-coated captain', he said, 'who knows what he fights for, and loves what he knows, than that which you call a gentleman—and is nothing else.' Discipline was strict: 'No man swears, but he pays twelve pence, and if he is in drink he is set in the stocks or worse'; and the training and drill were so thorough that every man could be depended on to obey orders in any crisis. In this way the Roundhead cavalry became more than a match for the King's, and it soon had a chance to show its quality.

In 1644 the Scottish army invaded the north. Newcastle had to give up the siege of Hull, and was himself soon besieged in York. Rupert was sent with all the troops Charles could spare to relieve York. He went by way of Lancashire, turning aside to sack the Puritan town of Bolton, and to relieve Lathom Hall where Lady Derby and a brave little garrison had been holding out against the local Roundheads. Then he crossed the Pennines, avoided the troops sent to stop him, and on 1 July he joined Newcastle in York. The Scots and Roundheads fell back to Marston Moor, a few miles to the south-west, and Rupert, who had about the same number of cavalry, but only 11,000 infantry to their 24,000, followed them, determined to force a battle. On 2 July, at about 7 o'clock in the evening, when the Cavaliers had decided that no battle was likely that day and were cooking their supper, the Roundheads suddenly attacked. After three hours of hard fighting the Royalists were overwhelmed and scattered.

This battle lost the north for the King and was really the turning-point of the war, but Charles had some striking successes elsewhere. In Scotland, the Marquis of Montrose, a soldier as great as Cromwell himself, raised a Highland force and drew off part of the Scottish army to protect its own land. Meanwhile at Lostwithiel in Cornwall, the Royalists surrounded Essex's army and took prisoner practically the whole of his infantry, though Essex himself and some of his cavalry managed to get away. Many of the Parliament's generals had shown themselves to be incompetent or half-hearted, and seemed to be thinking more of making peace than of winning the war outright. 'If we beat the King ninety and nine times,' said Manchester, 'yet he is still King and so will his posterity be after him; but if the King beats us, then we shall all be hanged and our posterity made slaves.' To many who felt like this, it seemed better to come to terms. In December Parliament passed the 'Self Denying Ordinance' by which all members of either House were to resign their military commands. It was a drastic measure, but it was the only way to get rid of generals like Manchester and Essex. Cromwell, who had complained bitterly of Manchester's 'backwardness in all action', strongly supported it, although it meant he would lose his command too. At the same time it was decided to raise a 'New Model' Army, trained on the same lines as Cromwell's own troops, the 'Ironsides', to be commanded by Fairfax. Cromwell, of course, was too

PRINCE RUPERT INTRODUCES THE 'THUNDERBOLT' CHARGE
TO ENGLAND AT EDGEHILL
His famous dog, Boy, is shown

valuable to be spared and he was soon reappointed as commander of
the cavalry. Although many of the new soldiers were conscripts, they
were staunch and eager to fight, especially as they were well disciplined
and regularly paid. Fairfax and Cromwell firmly resisted the Parliament's wish to give promotion only to strict Presbyterians. They wanted
good soldiers, whatever their religion.

Charles lost his chance to attack the New Model Army while it was
forming, and by the summer of 1645 it was ready for action. The King
was in the Midlands with his main force, hesitating between marching
north to join Montrose, or south to protect Oxford, when Cromwell
and Fairfax met him at Naseby near Rugby. Cromwell was extra-
ordinarily confident. 'When I saw the enemy draw up and march in
gallant array towards us,' he afterwards said, 'I could not but smile out
to God in praise, in assurance of victory.' Once more his cavalry
decided the battle, and, as at Marston Moor, the King's infantry were
overwhelmed after a heroic struggle. Fairfax and Cromwell now turned

west to deal with the last Cavalier army, in Somerset, and this too was routed a few weeks later at Langport. The King's cause was lost. Montrose was defeated at Philiphaugh near the border. Scattered Cavalier garrisons were mopped up during the winter, and at last in June 1646 the surrender of Oxford brought the war to an end. Just before Oxford fell, Charles left the city, rode northward and surrendered to the Scots at Newark. A few months later the Scots in return for £400,000 to cover their war expenses, handed Charles over to the Parliament, and went home.

Although the surrender of the King left the Roundheads supreme in the country, Parliament did not make good use of its victory. It was a very different assembly from that which had met in 1640. Three-quarters of the Lords, and many of the Commons of the original Long Parliament had fought for the King, and of the remainder some had died like Pym, or been killed in battle, like John Hampden (who had fallen at Chalgrove near Oxford). So the Lords were a mere handful —several of them discredited generals like Manchester—and the Commons had lost their best leaders. Their first act was to impose crushing fines on all landowners who had fought for the King; many of these sold their land in order to pay, and others had their land confiscated outright. At the same time the Parliament fiercely attacked the Church of England. Laud was most unjustly beheaded, all bishoprics were abolished, the Prayer Book was forbidden, and 'Anglican' (or Church of England) clergymen were replaced by Presbyterians. Before the war even the Cavaliers had had little enthusiasm for bishops. 'Those who hated them', wrote Falkland, 'hated them worse than the devil, and those who loved them did not love them so well as their dinner.' But now all this was changed, and their common sufferings brought together the Cavalier landowners and the Anglican Church in a strong alliance with, unfortunately, a determination to be revenged on the Puritans.

In both Houses of Parliament the majority were strict Presbyterians, who wanted to enforce their own kind of church on the whole country, as indeed they had promised the Scots. But there were thousands of people who, though they might be described as Puritans, were certainly not Presbyterians. They were called Independents, and many believed that there should be no national church at all: every congregation, however small, should be independent and free to worship as it liked, and any member of it should be allowed to lead the prayers or preach, whether he was a clergyman or not. These various sects differed from each other in many ways, and believed in the principle of 'live and let live'—which, however, they did not apply to either Roman Catholics or Anglicans. They were particularly strong in the army, where they were often the most reliable soldiers, and they were furiously indignant when the Parliament tried to impose a strict Presbyterian Church on them. To make things even worse, Parliament meanly tried to disband the army without giving its officers and men the back pay which was owed to them. The troops refused to disband until they got their money and a guarantee that their religion would not be interfered with.

Cromwell, who was both a member of Parliament and an army commander, was in a difficult position. For a time he did all he could to prevent a quarrel between the Parliament and the army. But this soon became impossible, for the Parliament leaders planned to arm the London train-bands and the defeated Royalist troops, and disband the angry army by force. As soon as he heard of this plot, Cromwell knew he had to choose between the army and the Parliament. He threw in his lot with the army, and, as was his way, he struck first. He sent a force to Oxford to seize the artillery which the Parliament was planning to use against him, and ordered a troop of cavalry to bring Charles from Holmby House in Northamptonshire, where he had been lodged, to army headquarters at Newmarket. Charles was ready to discuss terms with either party, and hoped that, by playing one off against the other, he would get back all his old powers. As yet nobody had thought of getting rid of the King, and even Cromwell said 'No men could enjoy their lives and estates quietly without the King had his rights.' Soon afterwards the army marched to London, occupied the city, and forced Parliament to expel eleven of the members whom they most distrusted. Then they offered their terms to the King. The terms were very reasonable. All were to be allowed to worship as they liked except Roman Catholics—even bishops might be restored, though they were to have very little power. The King was to share his power with a Council, and govern by the advice of Parliament, which was to be elected every two years. If Charles had honestly accepted these terms, he would have saved himself and England from new disasters, but he still hoped to regain his full power. 'I shall see them glad ere long,' he said, 'to accept more equal terms: they cannot do without me.'

Charles in fact had a plan of his own. He knew that both the Scottish and the English Presbyterians hated the Independents, and he hoped, by making promises all round, none of which he intended to keep, to unite them, and all his other supporters, against Cromwell and the army. He was not strictly guarded, and he escaped to Carisbrooke Castle in the Isle of Wight, where he was visited by commissioners from the Scots, and his plans were soon complete. In 1648 Royalist risings broke out in South Wales, Kent, and Essex, while the northern Royalists seized Carlisle, and a Scottish army moved towards the border. The army leaders acted quickly. Cromwell went to South Wales, where he drove the enemy into Pembroke, but was faced with a difficult siege before he could capture the town. Fairfax scattered the Royalists in Kent, but some of them crossed the Thames and seized Colchester where they put up a desperate resistance, which kept him busy for two months. Meanwhile the Scots were advancing into Westmorland and Lancashire, a small force under Lambert falling back before them. As soon as Pembroke was taken, Cromwell set out on a three weeks march northwards, and joined forces with Lambert in Yorkshire. By 16 August he had crossed the Pennines and was near Preston, on the flank of the Scottish army which was straggling southwards. His plan was to strike behind them, cutting them off from their route back to Scotland. On 17 August he attacked their rear-guard at Preston, routed it, and turned south after the main body. A few days later, after a running fight, he caught and destroyed it near Warrington. Soon afterwards Fairfax captured Colchester, where the Royalist commanders, Lucas and Lisle, were court martialled and shot, and the prisoners were shipped like slaves to the West Indies.

The second civil war, as it is called, convinced the army leaders that there could be no peace as long as Charles was alive. They decided that it was impossible to trust him, and before they marched from London they had resolved 'if the Lord should bring them back in peace, to call that man of blood, Charles Stuart, to account for the blood he hath shed'. This would not be an easy matter, for Parliament still contained a majority of Presbyterians, who would never consent to the King's death. So in December a Colonel Pride, with a force of soldiers was sent down to Parliament House to arrest fifty of the members, and bar the way to nearly 100 more. This action, known as 'Pride's purge' was more violent and illegal than anything which Charles had ever done. It left little more than 100 members, mostly Independents, nicknamed 'the Rump', and they decided to try the King on a charge of making war on his subjects. When the few remaining Lords would not agree to this, the Rump declared that 'the people are, under God, the origin of all power' and carried on without them. Judges were appointed, but half of them refused to serve, for the court had no legal authority. One lawyer said 'No court can try the King, and no man can be tried by this court.' Charles made no defence: he simply denied that they had any right to try him. 'It is not my case alone,' he said, 'it is the freedom and liberty of the people of England. For if power (force) without law may alter the fundamental laws of the Kingdom, I do not know what subject may be assured of his life, or anything he can call his own.' The King was sentenced to death, and on 30 January 1649, he was executed. He met his death with the greatest dignity and courage: 'assuredly he plainly evidenced that it is not in the power of rebels to make a King who knows himself lose his majesty.' Cromwell, more than any other man, had been responsible for his death; for he had enormous influence, and he had come to believe that it was the will of God, and the only way England could be saved from more civil war. But it is very probable that nine out of every ten Englishmen hated the deed, and their hatred made it impossible for Cromwell ever to set up a government based on consent, and not on force.

13. Commonwealth and Protectorate

WHEN, on a bleak January morning in 1649, the executioner held the head of Charles I high up above the crowds in Whitehall, so that all men might see that the King was truly dead, a terrible groan broke from them. No doubt the first feeling of most people when they saw or first heard of the execution was one of horror, and probably the second was of great uncertainty about the future. The King was dead, that was certain enough, and so was the fact that it was the Puritans who had beaten him in the war, imprisoned him, tried him, and brought about his death. The Puritans, then, with Cromwell towering among them,

HEADPIECE. Robert Blake, Admiral and General of the Forces in England, 1657. From an engraving in the National Maritime Museum. In the background is shown the red naval ensign of the time

172

were the masters of the realm. But what would happen next? Would they remain masters and England be a republic, or would their enemies —and to judge by the groans there were plenty of them—manage to overthrow them and set Charles, Prince of Wales, on the throne? Would civil war break out again? And what would happen about religion? It was clearly an uncertain and dangerous time for everyone, particularly the new republic, or commonwealth, and the dangers lay not only in England, where angry Royalists abounded, but also farther afield. France, Holland, and Spain were hostile, the Scots at once proclaimed the Prince of Wales as King Charles II, and in Ireland the Earl of Ormonde held nearly the whole of the country in the name of the same uncrowned king. Even part of the navy, up to now so loyal to Parliament, deserted and put itself under the command of the versatile Prince Rupert, who took with astonishing ease to a new profession and became quite as skilful a sailor as he had been a soldier.

Of all these dangers the most pressing seemed to be in Ireland, which had been in constant disorder since 1641, and Cromwell was at once sent there to dispose of Ormonde and his supporters. He stayed in Ireland nine months but even in that short time he earned a lasting reputation for his cruelty. He seized the towns of Drogheda and Wexford and terrorized the Irish by his treatment of the garrisons after they had surrendered, especially at Drogheda, where by his personal order 2,000 people were slaughtered, or died in the burning buildings. This ruthless behaviour is oddly out of keeping with Cromwell's usual attitude. He was not a cruel person, nor in the habit of maltreating his defeated enemies. But he was desperately anxious to subdue Ireland quickly so as to be free to cope with other dangers, and he also seems to have thought of the Irish people as barbarous wretches whose hands were stained with much innocent blood. There is no excuse for him except that in this case he was thinking just as most men of his time thought, and acting accordingly. He left Ireland before the last starved remnants of the Royalist movement was destroyed—his son-in-law General Ireton finished off the process—but no mercy was shown to anyone, and Cromwell's letters written at the time are unpleasant to read.

He left Ireland because another danger was now pressing in Scotland.

The young Charles II, aged twenty, had landed there in May 1650 and was given a warm welcome. There were plenty of people ready to support him, but they were not at all easy to please and Charles had to walk very delicately in order to be sure of enough help from them. There were some who had already fought gallantly for his father under the Marquis of Montrose (many of these were Catholics) and there were others who had fought against him, and who were strict Presbyterians. The two groups hated each other, but the Presbyterians were the most numerous and Charles knew that their support was absolutely necessary if he was to be crowned. He therefore promised to belong to the Presbyterian Church and to set it up in England as soon as he was master there, and to betray the noble Montrose, whose influence and religious views were poison to the Presbyterian party. It was a strange position, for Montrose was captured and hanged by men fighting in the name of the very king for whom he had already poured out his personal wealth and happiness.

In 1650, after much negotiation and some deception by Charles, who was not attracted by the Presbyterians, he was crowned at Scone, and it was at this point that Cromwell marched north to deal with the situation. For a time it looked as if he might actually fail to do this, in spite of the fact that he had the pick of the New Model Army with him. He could not capture Edinburgh and he could not get enough food for his troops. By September they were half-starved, and he retreated from Edinburgh to the small coast town of Dunbar, where he hoped to get some supplies by sea, and where, if retreat was necessary, the road to England lay open behind him. Above the town the Scots, led by General David Leslie, waited in the hills ready to cut Cromwell off if he should move southward. But Leslie was not content to wait, and on 3 September he left the security of the hills and descended to the level ground to attack. Cromwell, however, attacked first and before the Scots were ready. 'Let God arise and let his enemies be scattered' was the word passed round among the Ironsides in the September morning before the light mists had streamed away. And then believing that God was indeed on their side they arose and broke the Scottish army. The next day, when Leslie had escaped and his men were scattered, Edinburgh was taken.

OLD EDINBURGH CASTLE

Although 10,000 prisoners were captured at Dunbar there was still strength in Scotland to raise another army for Charles, this time with a different plan of campaign—to invade England, in the belief that on the way south the English Cavaliers would rise in thousands and join the King. It was a bold plan because it risked leaving Cromwell behind in possession of Scotland so that retreat—if retreat should ever be necessary—would be practically impossible. However, in spite of this obvious danger Charles and his troops raced out of Scotland and made for the south and London, and Cromwell followed, ready to block their path if they retreated. He caught up with the King at Worcester, and on 3 September 1651, exactly a year after the Battle of Dunbar, the Ironsides for the last time demolished the Royalist army. Charles survived the battle, with its bitter hand-to-hand fighting in the narrow little streets of the town, and rode away to the west, closely hunted. He lived in acute peril for weeks until, like his great-nephew Charles Edward nearly a century later, he escaped to France. But Charles II, 'the black boy', as his nickname was to those who, for the next nine years, secretly drank his health, was to return in time, to be king, which his descendant never did.

The Battle of Worcester ended the fighting in the British Isles, but there were still many problems for the Puritans. One of them was to find a satisfactory government, for the Rump Parliament pleased nobody and was especially disliked by the army. The soldiers felt that it was they who had saved the country and so they should control the government. One party, the Levellers, wanted, as you have heard, to do away with all distinctions of birth or rank, and to have a Parliament freely elected by the whole people. Cromwell thought this kind of talk dangerous folly: to him the differences between classes were real and important, and he had no belief in the ability of the mob to govern. But he, too, was becoming very impatient with the Rump, although he himself was a member of it, for it seemed determined to keep itself in power for as long as possible. He did his best to induce the other members to resign so that a fresh start could be made, but the most he could get out of it was a scheme that a new Parliament should meet but that the old members should have the right to decide who should sit in it. It is not difficult to guess what would have happened. 'We should have fine work then', said Cromwell, 'with one Parliament stepping into the seat of another just left warm for them. I think this a pitiful remedy.' He persuaded some of the members to promise that they would go no farther with the scheme, but the next morning they again began to discuss it, and Cromwell was told. He hurried down to the House, ordering a party of soldiers to follow him and wait outside; then he took his usual seat, and listened to the debate. When the Speaker was about to ask the House to vote on the scheme, Cromwell rose to speak. He began mildly enough, but as he spoke his anger mounted, and the members sat in shocked silence while he accused them of injustice and dishonesty. 'It is not fit', he said at last, 'that you should sit as a Parliament any longer. You have sat long enough unless you had done more good. I say you are no Parliament. I will put an end to your sitting'; and he turned to call in the soldiers. The Speaker was pulled from his chair, and the troops drove the members out of doors. As Cromwell turned to go, his eye fell on the mace which is always carried before the Speaker as a sign of his authority. 'What shall we do with that bauble?' he said to one of the soldiers; 'Here, take it away.' Then he walked out and locked the doors. Even Charles I at his most impatient and obstinate would never have dared to behave in so high-handed a manner; you will remember that, when he went into the House to search for the five members in 1642 and failed to find them, he retired baffled. There was no attempt to pull the Speaker from his chair or drive out the members or take away the mace. Charles could not do any of these things, but Cromwell could, for the simple reason that he had enough armed soldiers behind him to enforce his will.

The dismissal of the Rump left Cromwell commander of the army and master of the country, yet he did not want power for himself. He earnestly wanted to find a kind of government which would give the country security and freedom, and which would allow men to worship God in their own way so long as their religion did not make them dangerous; and he was prepared to experiment till he found it. But none of his experiments produced this kind of government because, with enemies abroad and at home, there could be no security without a strong army; yet Englishmen came to dislike the army so much that the first act of any really free Parliament would have been to disband it. As for religious freedom, practically every sect demanded it for itself but was not willing to grant it to others. As Cromwell said, 'I am as much for government by consent as any man, but where will you find it?'

His first attempt was a Parliament chosen not by the whole country but by the Independent congregations and nicknamed the 'Barebone' Parliament, after one of its members, Praise God Barebone. It contained most godly men who discussed large plans to reform the Church and the law, which alarmed the more sensible members, and it soon dissolved itself, handing its power back to Cromwell. He then tried a scheme drawn up by the army leaders by which he became Lord Protector and governed with the help of a council and an elected Parliament: but as soon as the Parliament met, it tried to increase its own powers and to reduce the army, so Cromwell dissolved it. A Royalist rising in 1655 made him give up any idea of 'consent' for a time, and the country was divided up into districts governed by major-generals. These officers made themselves bitterly hated, for not content with suppressing the Cavaliers they took great pains to stop all 'ungodly' behaviour by anyone, such as cock-fighting, gambling, swearing, drinking, Sabbath-breaking—and even horse-racing, because it attracted crowds and might give the Royalists a chance to make trouble. This only lasted for a few months, but it did more than anything else to disgust people with the army and with Puritanism. Cromwell's next Parliament offered him the title of king, but after some hesitation he refused it and continued as Protector, only with greater powers. This Parliament lasted no longer than the others, and for the last years of his life Cromwell, with his army officers, ruled the country without one. He had found that security and consent did not go together, and the first was far more important than the second. His duty was to act, as he put it, 'as a good constable set to keep the peace of the parish': and while he lived the peace was kept, though he was detested both by the Royalists and by the republicans, who thought he had usurped too much power.

Whatever troubles he might have at home, Cromwell not only protected England from her enemies abroad but made her more powerful and respected in Europe than she had been since Elizabeth's time. This was chiefly because he had a strong navy. Both Charles I and the Rump must share the credit for this: Charles I had built up the navy (collecting ship money to pay for it) and the Rump had carried on and increased it to eighty ships. (The Rump did not collect ship money but used the confiscated wealth of the Cavaliers; even so, they ran up an enormous debt in the process.) Command of the fleet was given to Blake, who had been a colonel in the army and had hardly any experience of the sea, but who soon proved himself to be one of England's greatest admirals.

Under Blake's command the fleet soon showed its quality. First, Prince Rupert's squadron was driven across the Atlantic and dispersed, and the English colonies were secured for the Parliament. The next enemy to be dealt with was the Dutch. While England had been occupied with the Civil War, they had gone ahead in the race for overseas trade, and had become one of the richest nations in Europe. In 1651 the Rump tried to regain some of the trade and cut out the Dutch, by passing a Navigation Act to the effect that foreign goods could only be brought to England in English ships, or in ships of the country from which the goods came. When they followed this with a demand that all ships should salute the English flag in the Channel, the Dutch declared war. In the struggle which followed the battle fleets were very evenly matched, but Dutch merchant shipping suffered heavily, for it had to pass close to the English coast to reach Holland, and the Dutch fleet could not protect it. It was these losses in merchant shipping more than any defeat of their main fleet which forced the Dutch to make peace in 1654, for their whole livelihood depended on seaborne trade. Next year English ships appeared in the Mediterranean, when Blake attacked the Moslem pirates off North Africa, bombarded their stronghold at Tunis, and forced them to release their English prisoners.

It was, however, against Spain that England's naval strength was most clearly shown. Cromwell wanted to use his forces against the Roman Catholic powers, of which Spain was the chief, and thought that he would be able, like Elizabeth, to raid Spanish shipping and colonies without undertaking a full-scale war. 'The design', he said, 'will cost little more than the laying by of the ships, and that with the hope of great profit.' An expedition sent to the West Indies succeeded in capturing Jamaica, but Spain promptly declared war, and Blake's fleet was sent to blockade the Spanish coast. In 1656 the Spanish treasure fleet was intercepted, four of its ships sunk, and a fifth captured with a cargo of silver worth £600,000. Next year Blake won an even greater success. He caught a Spanish fleet of sixteen ships in harbour at the island of Teneriffe. He silenced the harbour batteries, sailed in, and burnt or sank all sixteen without losing a ship of his own. This battle was a blow from which Spanish naval power never completely recovered; but it was Blake's last victory, for he died in August 1657, on his way back to England.

The army, too, played a great part in building up England's security and reputation. Until the Spanish war all its fighting had been done in the British Isles, but its successes against the Cavaliers, the Irish, and the Scots had made a great impression abroad, and had made it possible, for the first time, to unite England, Scotland, and Ireland under one government. In 1658 the army appeared on the Continent, a force of 6,000 men being sent to help the French against the Spaniards. The English troops greatly distinguished themselves in the Battle of the Dunes, fought near Dunkirk, where they defeated a strong Spanish army and afterwards occupied the town.

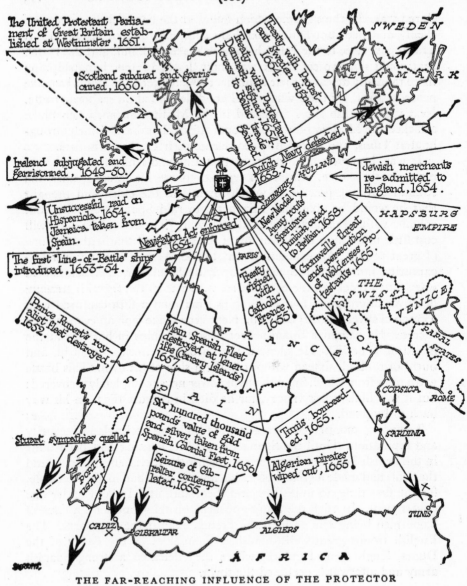

The United Protestant Parliament of Great Britain established at Westminster, 1651.

Scotland subdued and garrisoned, 1650.

Ireland subjugated and garrisoned, 1649-50.

Unsuccessful raid on Hispaniola, 1654. Jamaica taken from Spain.

The first "Line-of-Battle" ships introduced, 1653-54.

Navigation Act enforced 1654.

Prince Rupert's royalist fleet destroyed, 1652.

Main Spanish Fleet destroyed at Teneriffe (Canary Islands) 1657.

Six hundred thousand pounds value of gold and silver taken from Spanish Colonial Fleet, 1656.

Seizure of Gibraltar contemplated, 1655.

Stuart sympathies quelled

Treaty with Protestant Denmark signed, 1654. Access to Baltic trade gained.

Treaty with Protestant Sweden signed, 1654.

Dutch Navy defeated, 1653.

Jewish merchants re-admitted to England, 1654.

New Model Army routs Spaniards: Dunkirk ceded to Britain, 1658.

Cromwell's threat ends persecution of Waldenses Protestants, 1655.

Treaty signed with Catholic France 1655.

Tunis bombarded, 1655.

Algerian pirates wiped out, 1655.

SWEDEN

DENMARK

HOLLAND

DUNKIRK

PARIS

HAPSBURG EMPIRE

THE SWISS

SAVOY

VENICE

PAPAL STATES

CORSICA

ROME

SARDINIA

S P A I N

F R A N C E

PORTUGAL

CADIZ

GIBRALTAR

ALGIERS

TUNIS

A F R I C A

THE FAR-REACHING INFLUENCE OF THE PROTECTOR

In spite of these successes, the Spanish war was a mistake. It did not show the great profit Cromwell expected—in fact it burdened the country with a load of debt, and could only be kept going by very heavy taxes, which made the government more unpopular than ever. The war did little to help Protestants anywhere, but it did achieve two things. First, it made England respected as she had never been before. 'His greatness at home', wrote the Royalist historian, Clarendon, of Cromwell, 'was but a shadow of his glory abroad. It was hard to discover which feared him most, France, Spain, or the Low Countries, where his friendship was current at the value he put on it.' The other lasting result of Cromwell's wars was that the navy had several years of constant action during which the discipline of 'Oliver's Captains' and their successes did much to make it a professional service with strong traditions. Blake's victories provide a link between the age of Drake and the great naval wars of the eighteenth century.

By 1658, when he was at the height of his power, Cromwell's health was beginning to fail. He was weary in body and mind, and distracted with grief at the loss of his favourite daughter, who died that summer. Soon afterwards he fell ill with fever. His last Parliament had voted that he should have the power to name his successor, and he appointed his eldest son Richard. On 3 September, the anniversary of his victories at Dunbar and Worcester, he died. Many people, both of his own time and since, have described Cromwell as a cunning, ambitious man, ceaselessly scheming for more power and ready to commit any crime to get it, but there was far more to him than this. He had no long-distance plans for the future, but he was a practical man who tackled every problem as it arose on common-sense lines, often without seeing what the results would be. He did what he thought was his duty, and did not shirk responsibility. The secret of his strength was his religion, for every success seemed to him a sign that God was with him and an encouragement to go on; and in this way he justified even the execution of Charles I or the massacre at Drogheda. By nature he was a kindly man, and he granted more religious freedom than any other ruler of his time. He let the Jews come back to England for the first time since their expulsion by Edward I, he refused to persecute the Quakers, whom most people thought dangerous revolutionists, and he was on the whole merciful to his enemies. But he lived at a time when too much mercy was dangerous, and when he found that he could only keep the peace by interfering with freedom more than Charles I had ever done he did not hesitate to do it. When someone told him that nine out of every ten Englishmen were against him, he replied, 'What if I disarm the nine, and put a sword in the tenth man's hand? Will not that do the business?'

Cromwell's attempt to give England both security and freedom failed, and his settlement of Ireland was even less successful, for it left a small class of wealthy Protestant landowners holding down a large population of Catholic peasants—miserably poor, without any rights, and bitterly hating their English masters. But in spite of his failures Cromwell was one of the greatest figures of his time.

While he lived his system of government worked, but it depended on the Protector having absolute control over the army. Oliver Cromwell had been able to deal with his generals, but his son Richard, a simple country gentleman with no taste for war or politics, found it quite beyond him. There followed a period of confusion, while the generals quarrelled among themselves, and more and more people, disgusted with the rule of soldiers, began to think of restoring the King. At last, in 1660, General George Monck, who commanded the army of occupation in Scotland and who so far had kept out of politics, decided to bring the disorder to an end. He crossed the border with his army and moved towards London, meeting practically no resistance from the divided and leaderless troops in England. Once in London, Monck assembled a parliament, which sent a message to Charles II in France inviting him to return and claim his throne.

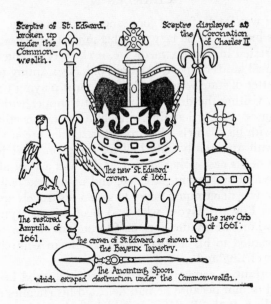

Sceptre of St. Edward, broken up under the Commonwealth.

Sceptre displayed at the Coronation of Charles II

The new "St. Edward" crown of 1661.

The restored Ampulla of 1661.

The new Orb of 1661.

The crown of St. Edward as shown in the Bayeux Tapestry.

The Anointing Spoon which escaped destruction under the Commonwealth.

14. Charles II

CHARLES II landed at Dover on 29 May 1660. It was his birthday and he was thirty years old, a tall, swarthy young man elegantly dressed and with long black curled hair, and certainly with nothing to show that a few months before he had had only one shirt to his back. For nine years he had been in exile in France or Holland living very much from hand to mouth, on the charity of his cousin Louis XIV and other relations, and the money which his faithful followers could scrape together. But that was little enough, since Cavaliers had been heavily fined by the Commonwealth government. Charles had known very little security in life for he was only twelve when the Civil War broke out and his life since then had been hard and often dangerous. It had made him believe that no man was honest except for his own advantage, so he neither expected honesty in others nor felt any need for it himself, as his actions

HEADPIECE. The new regalia, 1661, and some of the old

proved. He was fond of good food and good company, witty, and in some things inclined to be lazy; but his mind was active enough, and he was interested in science, medicine, architecture, and shipbuilding, and keen on all kinds of sport. Anxious officials wanting to consult him on some matter of state would find that he was playing tennis, walking in the park, visiting the dockyard, or having supper with Nell Gwynn or the Countess of Castlemaine, and at Council meetings he would sit playing with his spaniels—he brought a special breed with him from Holland—with apparently only half his mind on what was going on. Yet in spite of his easy-going ways Charles was a very able man. He had courage and had learnt patience, and he was exceedingly shrewd; moreover he was determined never to go on his travels again. His first minister was Edward Hyde, who had been his secretary during his exile, and whom he made Earl of Clarendon. Hyde was a typical Cavalier, devoted to his master, to the Anglican Church, and to the ancient laws of England.

It is important to remember that Charles returned because he had been invited to, not because he had defeated his enemies or turned out Cromwell. In fact the Parliament which invited him (known as the Convention) contained many men who had been Roundheads in the Civil War and had only recently become Royalists because they so much disliked the rule of the army. Charles II therefore came back on conditions which left him much less power than his father had. For example, while he was still in Holland, he had promised that there should be freedom of worship, and a general pardon for everyone who had fought for Parliament, apart from those who might be specially excepted. He promised also that he would agree to any arrangements Parliament might make about paying off the army and restoring land confiscated from Cavaliers by the rebels. Thus the settlement of the country was left chiefly to Parliament, not to the King. There were other restrictions too, for all the acts of the Long Parliament which Charles I had had to agree to still stood. The Courts of Star Chamber and High Commission were not restored, and the King had no right to raise taxes except by consent of Parliament.

The first job of the Convention Parliament was to raise money to pay off the army, and the soldiers who had held down England for so long went quietly back to civilian life, except for one or two regiments which Charles kept as his guards. The Act of Indemnity and Oblivion followed, a tremendous title which meant simply a pardon to all except the 'regicides'—the men who had actually signed the death warrant of Charles I. A dozen of these were executed, but Charles and Clarendon resisted proposals made by some members of Parliament that more people should be put to death. The restoration of their land to ex-Cavaliers was a difficult business. In the end those whose land had been actually confiscated got it back, but many more, who had had to sell land to pay fines and taxes under the Commonwealth, got nothing, and this left much ill feeling. Lastly the Convention settled the King's income, and fixed it at £1,200,000 a year. Some of the money came from the Crown lands, and the rest was to be raised from the customs duties, and an 'excise' tax on beer, cider, tea, and coffee. In fact these taxes brought in much less, and Charles's expenses were much more, than anyone expected, and although a very unpopular hearth or chimney tax was added in 1662, Charles never had enough money. He had big debts to pay off and he had to run the government. It is true that he was inclined to be extravagant, but no more so than his grandfather, and however careful he had been there still would not have been enough. All through his reign, Charles depended on extra grants from Parliament, which put the members in a very strong position, for they could refuse to vote the money unless the King did what they wanted.

In 1661 the Convention was dissolved, elections were held, and a new Parliament arrived at Westminster. It lasted till 1679 and was so strongly Royalist that it is known as the Cavalier Parliament. Its first task was to settle the religious question. The Anglican Church was restored, and the Cavaliers unhappily took the opportunity to avenge all they had suffered from the Puritans. All who would not join the Church were called 'Nonconformists', and the Cavaliers determined to break their power for good and all. In this spirit they passed the laws called, rather unfairly, the Clarendon Code—for certainly neither Clarendon nor Charles approved of them. They completely muzzled Nonconformists, who were forbidden to hold services, to teach their religion, to enter the universities, or to take any part in national or municipal government. Two thousand clergymen, who would not accept the whole of the official Prayer Book, were turned out of their posts. Charles II did not believe in persecution; he saw that these laws (passed, of course, in his name) broke the promise he had made, and he did his best to get them suspended. But Parliament was too strong for him, and he realized that in spite of the joy with which he had been received, and the enthusiasm of the Cavaliers, he was up against great difficulties. Two are clear already, religion and lack of money; the third was dealings with foreign powers—and they are all closely connected with each other. As far as his own religion went, Charles II was at heart a Roman Catholic, but he knew that he could not admit this, for Roman Catholics were feared and disliked in England, and he would have to be very careful about trying to help them. His brother, James, Duke of York, was more honest but much less clever. He was quite open about his religion, and attended mass in his private chapel. This made things much more difficult for Charles, for it inclined people to suspect that the whole Court was Roman Catholic, and to imagine Catholic plots whenever anything went wrong. It also made Parliament much less willing to grant Charles money.

The money shortage existed from the start, but it did not become really serious till 1664, when another war broke out with the Dutch. This was a war based on commercial and colonial rivalry. The first campaigns were to support the Royal African Company against the Dutch and to capture New Netherlands, their colony in America, but it continued with fiercely contested and very expensive naval battles. In spite of a grant by Parliament, Charles could not afford to equip the ships properly, or to pay the sailors, as he was expected to do, out of his income. The fleet, under James as Lord High Admiral, won one victory off Lowestoft, but after that things went badly and were made much worse by London's two great disasters, the Plague in 1665 and the Fire in 1666. There is a wonderful first-hand account of these in the diary of Samuel Pepys, a clever, industrious and cheerful little civil servant, who was Clerk of the Acts—or Secretary to the Navy Board—and who stuck to his post all through the Plague, carrying on the Navy Office almost single-handed, while everyone who could afford to do so fled into the country. London's trade was brought almost to a standstill, and the King's income from the customs fell off just when it was most

THE DUTCH REMOVE THE 'ROYAL CHARLES' FROM THE
MEDWAY, 1667

needed. Parliament refused to provide any more money. They had already voted nearly £2 millions for the war, and they insisted that it must have been wasted or stolen by the King's officials. This was partly true, for a great deal of dishonesty went on, but their refusal led to a shocking disaster.

The Admiralty, unable to keep the fleet at sea any longer, took a chance on the success of peace talks which had been started, and laid up the battle-fleet in the Medway, dismissing the sailors without their pay. The Dutch seized their opportunity and made a daring raid up the Thames. They broke through the boom which had been placed across Chatham Harbour, burned four battleships and towed away the flagship, the *Royal Charles*, as a prize in broad daylight. It was a fine piece of seamanship; Pepys wrote 'they did carry her down at a time both for tides and wind, when the best pilot in Chatham would not have undertaken it, heeling her on one side to make her draw little water; and so carried her away safe'. The English sailors, unpaid and mutinous, made no effort to stop them; in fact there were many Englishmen who had deserted the English service for lack of pay and were serving in Dutch ships, who shouted to their former shipmates 'We did heretofore fight for tickets: now we fight for dollars.' (The tickets were written promises of pay which were very seldom honoured.)

This final blow, coming on the top of the Plague and the Fire, plunged the country into rage and despair. Some thought it was God's judgement on the wickedness of the times; others put it down to treachery. 'People make nothing of talking treason in the streets openly', wrote Pepys, 'and say they are governed by Papists, and are betrayed by those about the king.' 'I do believe', adds Pepys gloomily, 'that it will cost blood to answer these miscarriages.' It did not in fact 'cost blood', but it brought about the fall of Clarendon, for when Parliament met it laid the blame on him. It was not really his fault, but he was Charles's chief minister, and he had many enemies among the nobles, who were jealous of him because his daughter had married the Duke of York, the heir to the throne. It may seem strange that Charles did nothing to help his faithful old servant, but he was himself tired of Clarendon's domineering ways, and he knew he was very unpopular. The Commons wanted to impeach him, but Charles prevented this by dismissing him

LE ROI SOLEIL, HIS MARK, FROM AN EFFIGY IN COLOURED WAX

from his post as Lord Chancellor, and banishing him. Clarendon lived in retirement in France, where he wrote a history of the Civil War.

Although he was ready to sacrifice Clarendon, Charles was thoroughly disgusted with Parliament's behaviour, and seeing clearly that he would never have any real power as long as he depended on them for money, he resolved to get it elsewhere. His thoughts turned naturally to his cousin Louis XIV of France. France had become by far the most powerful kingdom on the Continent, with a great army, and a Court which was the most brilliant and cultured in Europe. Louis, untroubled by Parliament, for no such thing now existed in France, had all the power in his own hands, and governed as he wished, with nobody to question what he did. Charles, hampered by a carping, critical Parliament, had always envied his cousin and longed to follow his example, and in 1670 he saw a chance to begin. Louis's greatest ambition was to extend France's borders to the Rhine; as you can see from a map this meant invading the Spanish Netherlands and part of Holland. He was anxious to get the help of the English fleet, so he offered Charles a large sum of money in exchange for his support. Since the fall of Clarendon,

Charles had ruled with the help of a small group of ministers known as the Cabal, and, in consultation with them, he made a treaty of alliance with France, which was signed at Dover in 1670. In it he agreed to fight the Dutch again, and—even the Cabal did not know this—to declare himself a Roman Catholic as soon as he could. Louis promised to send over French troops to help him if this led to any trouble with his subjects. The secret clause was to bring great trouble.

In 1672, with £166,000 from Louis XIV in his pocket, Charles prorogued Parliament. He then issued a Declaration of Indulgence, which set aside all the laws against both Roman Catholics and Nonconformists, for he did not dare to help one without the other. At the same time war was declared on the Dutch, and, protected by the English fleet, the French army invaded Holland. Charles knew that Parliament would not approve either of the Declaration of Indulgence or the war, but he hoped to get the war over quickly without consulting them, and to manage without them in future. His plans, however, were completely thrown out of gear by the Dutch, who held up the French army by opening the dykes and flooding the country, and defeated the English fleet in a battle at Southwold Bay off the Suffolk coast. In a year Charles had spent all the money Louis had given him. There was nothing for it but to call Parliament.

The members at once objected to the Declaration of Indulgence, for all the old hatred and fear of the Roman Catholics was as strong as ever, and even the Nonconformists, although they benefited from the Declaration, saw in it only a plot, like those of Elizabeth's time, to bring back the Catholic religion with foreign help. They were led by the Earl of Shaftesbury. He had been a member of the Cabal, and suspected that the King had tricked him over the Dover Treaty; he was a cunning and ambitious man, and a dangerous enemy. Charles had to give up his attempt at religious toleration, for he had no more money, and Parliament would not vote any. He was compelled to cancel the Declaration of Indulgence and make peace with the Dutch. He was back where he had been before his treaty with Louis, and, worse still, he had to agree to a Test Act, by which all Catholics in the government service were dismissed. This, of course, included James, who lost his post of Lord High Admiral. Nothing shows more clearly how Parliament had changed since Tudor times. Elizabeth's Church settlement had been the work of the Queen and Cecil, and when Parliament had tried to interfere with it they had been firmly warned off. Under Charles II, the Church settlement was the work of Parliament, and when the King tried to alter it he found Parliament too strong for him. He had the sense to see when he was beaten.

15. Land and People

5. RESTORATION ENGLAND

THIS day his Majesty, Charles II, came to London after a sad and long exile. This was also his birthday and with a triumph of above 20,000 horse and foot, brandishing their swords and shouting with inexpressible joy: the ways strewn with flowers, the bells ringing, the streets hung with tapestry, fountains running with wine . . . myriads of people flocking—so as they were seven hours passing the City even from two in the afternoon till nine at night.

So wrote John Evelyn in his diary for 29 May 1660 and no doubt he was right in believing that many people rejoiced at the end of the Puritan regulations of the Commonwealth, and especially of the uncertainties of the last few years. He had seen Oliver Cromwell pass on his last journey from Somerset House to be buried in Westminster Abbey, but in 1660

HEADPIECE. St. Paul's, 1666, and 'the horrid, bloody, malicious great flame' the Protector's body was dug up and hanged at Tyburn. Those who had been responsible for the execution of King Charles—the regicides —were brought to trial and although they protested that what they had done was in the name of the Parliament of England, they were executed. One of them, Major-General Harrison, was asked mockingly as he made his way to the scaffold, 'Where is your Good Old Cause?' 'Here it is', he said, as he clapped his hand on his heart, 'I am going to seal it with my blood', and he died as bravely as Charles I had done.

A year after the King's entry into London, Samuel Pepys saw his Coronation in Westminster Abbey. He managed to secure a seat on the great scaffold across the north end of the Abbey from which he saw the magnificent procession of the Dean and prebendaries of West-minster with the bishops in their gold copes, the nobility in their Parliament robes and the King in his robes, bareheaded, with his brother James, Duke of York, beside him and his crown and sceptre carried in front. Mr. Pepys could not see the ceremonies before the high altar but he heard the great shout when the crown was put on the King's head and saw the Lords put on their caps. 'And three times', wrote Pepys, 'the Garter King-of-Arms went to the three open places on the scaffold and proclaimed that if any could show any reason why Charles Stuart should not be King of England that he should come and speak.' This, as we know, is still done at the Coronation. Pepys went out before the end and found a place beside his wife in Westminster Hall where the King came to dine with all the ancient ceremonies. Then after much revelling 'did the day end with joy everywhere'.

Many of the crown jewels still used at modern coronation ceremonies, which can be seen at other times in the Wakefield Tower of the Tower of London, were made for Charles II, for most of the original regalia had been broken up after the execution of his father. This is true of the crown of Edward the Confessor with which the monarch is crowned, the sceptre, the orb, and the golden spurs. The ampulla, a vessel of pure gold in the form of an eagle which contains the sacred oil, and the anointing spoon, were renovated for him. It was in Charles II's reign that an attempt to steal the Crown Jewels was made by a certain Cap-tain Blood, but it failed. Blood was pardoned by the King and received back into polite society. Evelyn, who suspected him of being a spy, met

G

him at dinner and noted his 'villainous unmerciful look, a false countenance but very well spoken'.

The period that opened with such joy and ceremony did not proceed
very smoothly. In the years 1665–7 there occurred three terrible
disasters. The first was the great Plague, the last and perhaps the worst
of the outbreaks of bubonic plague that had ravaged England since the
Black Death of 1348. Pepys first saw the plague crosses on 7 June, 'I
did in Drury Lane see two or three houses marked with a red cross upon
the doors and "Lord have mercy upon us" writ there, being the first of
the kind that to my remembrance I ever saw.' Evelyn tells of the
mounting roll of deaths. 'July 16th. There died of plague in London
this week 1100', and in the week following 2,000. In September he
wrote, with some exaggeration, 'there perishing 10,000 poor creatures
weekly'. Both Pepys and Evelyn sent their wives into the country,
although Pepys as Clerk of the Acts of the Navy, and Evelyn, as Com-
missioner for the sick and wounded, had to stay in London most of
the time themselves. Everyone who had the means fled from London,
often carrying the plague with them. Few people realized that disease
was carried in clothes and the very poor would even pick up and use
the garments of the dead. 'In such plague we poor people have mickle
good' said a beggar. Compassion no doubt caused some to take a risk.
Pepys tells the story of a complaint made against a man who had rescued
the only child of a London saddler and had received him stark naked
from the hands of his father and brought him in fresh clothes to Greenwich. 'Whereupon hearing the story we did agree it [the child] should
be permitted to be received and kept in the town.' Although London
suffered most there are many records of the plague in the country too.

Even when it began to die down and Pepys could see the rare sight
of a nobleman's carriage in the street or the shops open, he was reminded of its terrible ravages by the numbers of new graves in the
churchyards. The precautions taken against the spread of the plague
usually consisted of burning some aromatic herbs or washing the hands
in rose vinegar, and the cures for it were often fantastic, such as putting
'a live pigeon cut in two parts' on the sores. These, of course, did no
good and when the disease died out it was chiefly through the driving
out of the black rats that carried plague fleas by brown rats which did

not, and through the sweeping away of plague-infested houses by the Fire.

The second disaster was the Great Fire of London, which seemed to men of property at the time a worse disaster than the Plague. The Pepys family were awakened about three in the morning on 2 September 1666 by their maid, Jane, who told them about the great fires she and the other maids could see. Thinking it was far enough away Mr. Pepys went back to bed and to sleep, but later in the day he found it had spread swiftly from the King's baker's shop in Pudding Lane where it had started, and was devouring the wooden houses of the city. Everyone was busy looking after his own property and removing goods to the waterside. According to the Lord Mayor, people resisted his attempts to pull down houses to prevent the fire from spreading. 'Lord what can I do? I am spent; people will not obey me', he cried in despair to Pepys. The horror of the fire was described by Evelyn. 'All the sky was of a fiery aspect like the top of a burning oven, and the light seen above forty miles round about for many nights. God grant mine eyes may never behold the like who now saw 10,000 houses all in one flame.' It was not until 5 September that the fire was brought under control and then only by blowing up houses in its path. Evelyn burned the soles of his shoes visiting the smoking ruins and lamented the fate of the city churches including St. Paul's, and the Halls of the great City Companies. He noted too, the dignity of the common people who had fled towards Highgate and Islington. They were stunned by their losses, yet did not ask for one penny of relief. The city itself was rebuilt in brick after the fire, but the slum districts lying outside the walls, St. Giles, Cripplegate, Whitechapel, Stepney, and Lambeth, were not burnt down and were not rebuilt, so that the Fire could not have been the sole reason for the disappearance of the Plague. One consequence the Fire certainly had, and that was to make Englishmen more interested in fire precautions. London was not the only town to suffer. Tiverton was burnt in 1598, Stratford in 1614, and later Warwick in 1697. At first leather tankards containing water, and brass syringes, were the only things recommended as safety measures, but in 1676 a Dutch engineer invented a fire engine with leather hosepipes and by the reign of Queen Anne each parish was supposed to have its own.

John of Winter's Grace, who fell at Bosworth, with his son, the first John Wintersgrace.

John Wintersgrace at his wedding in 1505.

In 1530, John and Mistress Wintersgrace welcome home their son, young John from an Embassy to the French Court

COSTUME CHRONICLE I

The third disaster, as it seemed to the people of the time, came from the War declared on the Dutch in 1664. Englishmen felt disgraced and humiliated when the Dutch raided the Thames Estuary, broke the boom of Chatham Harbour and towed off the eighty-gun *Royal Charles*. Evelyn wrote mournfully: 'How triumphantly the whole [Dutch] fleet lay within the very mouth of the Thames, all from the North Foreland, even to the buoy of the Nore, a dreadful spectacle as ever Englishman saw and a dishonour never to be wiped off'.

Disasters which seem to us now to be the results of war, insanitary and crowded conditions, and ignorance, seemed to many people at the time to be the judgement of God on evil living. Charles II had been welcomed for his gaiety and wit, but it soon became clear that he had learnt to be extravagant and coarse during his exile. His Court was noted for its wild gambling, and he relied for advice and friendship on men and women such as the Duke of Buckingham,

> stiff in opinions, always in the wrong
> Was everything by turns and nothing long

as Dryden described him, and Lady Castlemaine, who were despised by all decent people.

The Court led the move to get away from the austerity of the Commonwealth. In dress this led at first to the most extravagant fashions with a short loose coat, billowing shirt, skirt-like trousers, and endless ribbons and laces. About 1666 Charles and his courtiers dropped the French fashions and adopted 'the Persian mode' which Evelyn found very comely and useful. This may have been the origin of the long straight coat which was first worn at about this time. To begin with it hung straight from the shoulders becoming wider at the hem, but later it was shaped at the waist and with modifications became man's daily wear over a vest or waistcoat and breeches. Periwigs were also introduced from France and these came to stay although they changed their style. In the time of Charles they formed a curtain of curls round the head and shoulders but later on under James, William and Mary, and Anne, they were held back from the face but piled high on the head at either side of the parting. Pepys was proud of his first long skirted coat, but he was afraid that periwigs, during the Plague, might be made of the hair of infected persons. He solved the problem himself by having one made of his own hair. Although he often puts a comment on his wife's beauty in his diary he was reluctant to let her wear the new fashions and she had to plead to be allowed to put on her patches or her new fair wig. He did give her money to buy a new silk petticoat which would have been worn under her gown caught back by ribbons. Her neckline was low, so naturally he had to buy her a pearl necklace. Women's bodices were small-waisted and stiffened by whalebone. Later on the bodice was opened in front to show a stomacher or was laced across this and decorated with a row of ribbon bows called an échelle because it looked like a ladder. By the reign of Anne the skirt had become so wide and full at the back that it was arranged over a hoop, rather like the farthingale of Elizabeth's day. By this time too, women were wearing their head-dresses high and backed by an erection of wired lace, called a tower. To get a clear idea of the luxury of the period, you must remember that both men and women of the richer classes wore a profusion of lace and ribbons, and that both sexes used perfumes and other cosmetics.

Dressed in their gay clothes with perhaps the addition of a cloak, a beaver hat for the gentlemen, and a scarf and patches for the ladies, the gallants of the Court of Charles II would drive off by coach to Newmarket for the races, or go hunting the stag or fox in the park of some great gentleman, or over the fields of some neighbour's lands. Sometimes they would find their amusement at the theatre. Theatrical performances had been banned under Cromwell but now after the Restoration some of the old theatres began to open. The projecting stage of the Elizabethan theatre still existed but it was lit by footlights and candelabra. The arena was closed in; the young gallants had to sit in the pit instead of on the stage, and others had covered boxes round the walls. In the new theatres such as Drury Lane, there was a proscenium arch and a drop curtain. Evelyn saw *Hamlet* there and thought it rather crude, but nowadays we generally consider early Restoration dramas to be both crude and cheap. Later with plays like Congreve's *Way of the World* the theatre took on its true role of reflecting the society of the time. Here, for instance, we have the fop Witwoud who tries to hide the fact that he was once an apprentice, and his countrified half-brother, Sir

Wilfull, who shocks the company by the smell of his pipe and his heavy riding boots, but proves an honest fellow. Women first began to take part in plays at the Restoration but the type of plays they first appeared in did not add to their reputation.

Besides being the patrons of the theatre, Charles II and his courtiers certainly fostered the passion for building. Evelyn constantly writes of new 'palaces' being built by the King's ministers, such as Clarendon's town house in Albemarle Street or the great mansion at Petworth in Sussex. The King's contribution to architecture was that he was the patron of Sir Christopher Wren and made him Surveyor-General. Wren began his career as a mathematician and an astronomer. Evelyn refers to him as early as 1654 as a 'miracle of a youth' and a 'prodigious young scholar'. In 1664 he met him in Oxford examining planets through a telescope with Robert Boyle, and was borne off to see the new theatre that Wren was building for the Archbishop of Canterbury, to house the degree ceremonies of the University. This was the Sheldonian Theatre and its great ceiling unsupported by beams was Wren's first successful innovation. He designed other buildings in Oxford, such as Tom Tower and perhaps the Old Ashmolean Museum, but had his first great chance as Surveyor-General in London after the Fire. Both he and Evelyn submitted plans for the complete rebuilding of the city but funds would not run to such a scheme. However, Wren rebuilt St. Paul's and many of the city churches. His inspiration came from imperial Rome but his combination of columns, domes, and curious spires is peculiar to him. Some of the churches can still be seen today on the London skyline, although many were destroyed in the great fires of the Second World War.

Many of Wren's buildings such as Trinity College Library, Cambridge, and Petworth House, were decorated by a young man of Dutch extraction, named Grinling Gibbons. Evelyn tells the story of how he found the unknown sculptor carving in wood a copy of Tintoretto's crucifix, and how he marvelled at the fine detail and the wonderful skill of the carver. He took him to Court and showed his work to Charles II. The King was interested and sent the crucifix up to the Queen, the devout Catherine of Braganza. Evelyn was very disgusted, because Charles was put off buying a fine piece of work by the remarks of a foolish waiting woman, but this kind of thing must often have happened at Court. However, in Gibbons's case all was well because Wren took him under his patronage, and he carved for Wren and for other architects in his office, such as Nicholas Hawksmoor, who designed the rebuilding of Queen's College, Oxford.

Furniture fashions were also influenced by foreign taste. For the most part the early seventeenth century had seen the development of oak furniture of the rather heavy solid type, but now woods such as walnut, mahogany, cherry, and rosewood began to be used. Some of these were suitable for veneer, and marquetry or inlaying was practised, although never in England to the same extent as in France. Fine damasks, fringed and embroidered, were used for upholstery, and cane was very common for the seats and backs of chairs. A more complicated social life brought a demand for furniture with different uses, and one might find in a sitting room a day bed where the lady of fashion might recline, a writing desk or escritoire, where she might do her accounts or her husband write his diary, or small tables which would hold the china tea dishes. More cupboards, and such articles as dressing tables with handsome toilet articles began to grace the bedrooms. Some Chinese influence is to be found in tapestries, embroideries, and ornament towards the end of the period, and this is a sign of growing trade and contact with the East.

More comfort in the house might lead men to stay at home. Certainly Mr. Pepys liked to entertain his friends when once he had his house in Seething Lane decorated and arranged to his taste. His first dinner party there was a great success, except that it cost £5 and the fire smoked, to his intense mortification. At another time he thought it necessary to provide oysters, a dish of rabbits, lamb and a chine of beef all at one meal. In 1669 he mentions seven or eight dishes and a variety of wines. He liked his guests to admire his new furniture and especially his books. In 1666 he had new presses made for them and had the backs gilded to make them handsome. The gilded books in their fine mahogany glazed bookcases can still be seen in the Pepysian Library at Magdalene College, Cambridge, for he left his books to the college where he had been a student.

Lack of books, said the young clergyman of St. Martins-in-the-Fields,

IN THE COFFEE HOUSE IN 1680

led men to frequent the coffee houses. The rector gave this piece of information to Evelyn when he was telling him about his project for erecting a public library. Pepys used to go to drink chocolate at the coffee house, but the practice of drinking coffee had spread considerably since Evelyn first saw one Nathaniel Cornopios, a Greek, drink it in Oxford in 1637. People gathered informally at the coffee house to hear the news, listen to some scholar or wit, or do some business. You chose your coffee house according to your interests. If you were a classical scholar, the Grecian was your place of meeting. The poet Dryden held forth at Will's, the house of poets and critics. As the political parties grew up their members frequented different coffee houses. The Whigs favoured St. James, the Tories the Cocoa Tree Chocolate House. Lloyd's Coffee House, established in Queen Anne's day, eventually became a marine insurance centre.

One reason why men gathered at coffee houses was to hear a news-letter read aloud or perhaps a foreign newspaper, such as the *Haarlem Courier*, translated. In the time of Charles II there were no regular newspapers except the official *London Gazette*, but after the removal of the Censorship in 1695 more newspapers began to be published. The *Daily Courant*, said to be the first daily newspaper in the world, was published in 1702. Usually a paper would appear two or three times a week: it consisted of one sheet printed on two sides, and folded into four pages. News was given, sometimes without comment, sometimes with a Whig or Tory slant, and there was half a page of advertisement. This was in London. In the country until the reign of William and Mary, people had to rely on manuscript news-letters sent from London to a correspondent and passed round the neighbourhood. News of the Popish Plot and the Revolution of 1688 circulated in this way. By the reign of Anne newspapers were published in many provincial towns, and reviews and literary journals, such as Steele's *Tatler*, the *Spectator* by Steele and Addison, and Swift's *Examiner*, were widely read. Literary ideas and literary taste were formed in the coffee house and the club.

Science or natural philosophy, as it was called, was the leisure occupation of many gentlemen as well as the concern of the universities. Evelyn found the College of Physicians erecting a statue to William Harvey, the discoverer of the circulation of the blood, and went to a lecture given in his memory. He records the grant in 1662 of a Charter from Charles II to the Royal Society. This society of scientists and scholars had its origin during the Commonwealth or earlier, when little groups of learned men had met in London and Oxford to discuss their discoveries. Evelyn, Pepys, and Wren were all members and were interested, often from a practical point of view, in everything that went on. The specialization of today when one man is a biochemist, and another a nuclear physicist, did not exist. One evening, Evelyn records, they would go to look through the King's great telescope; another time he himself gave to the society his own 'Discourse on Forest Trees' meant to be of use to the navy, or Sir William Petty, an economist, considered the possibility of covering ships with lead. Pepys would take home the treatises of Robert Boyle, another member, to study. Boyle has been called the father of modern chemistry because he gave a more accurate classification of the elements than the familiar 'earth, air, fire, and water', and set down the relationship between the volume of a gas and its temperature and pressure (Boyle's Law, as it is still called). Another member, Hooke, left wonderful drawings of objects seen under early microscopes. Some of the best microscopes were made by Leeuwenhoek, a Dutchman, and the fact that he, with others, communicated his findings to the Royal Society, shows that the international character of scientific discovery was recognized. Greatest of all its members was Isaac Newton, who, building on the work of Galileo and Kepler, realized that the laws that govern moving bodies on the earth apply also to the stars in their courses. He delayed publication of his discoveries for twenty years because he was not satisfied with his calculations, but the *Principia*, when it was published in 1687, was dedicated to the Royal Society and bore its sign 'Let it be printed', with the name of Samuel Pepys, the year's president. Newton's views were accepted until our own day, when Einstein suggested laws coming perhaps nearer still to the truth.

The motto of the Royal Society, 'The words are the words of a master but we are not forced to swear by them. Instead we are borne to wherever our experiment leads us', shows us that the men of the Restoration period were beginning to think in rather different ways from the years of the Civil War and the Commonwealth when sincerity, enthusiasm, and intolerance were the keynotes. Ideas of toleration, coming partly from impatience with extremes (a Puritan was known as a 'Fanatick') and partly from a desire to see other people's point of view, began to appear, even though it is true that at the Restoration, by the Clarendon Code, severe restrictions had been laid on Nonconformists and that there was such a panic at the fear of a 'Popish Plot' in 1678 that the Catholic Duke of York was nearly excluded from the throne. Court circles were often cynical about religion and some of the political leaders used the people's religious fears for their own end, as Shaftesbury did at the time of the Popish Plot. Locke's *Letter concerning Toleration* appeared in 1689, and one of the results of the Revolution of 1688 was to grant toleration to all but Roman Catholics. This was acceptable not only because it was the alternative to a royal and Catholic despotism but because people were coming to believe that there was more than one way to salvation.

The growth of scientific ideas, literary styles, changes in taste and fashion, affected the town more than the country and only gradually filtered through from London to the provinces. What is the picture of provincial and country life from the Restoration to the end of the century? The power of the landed gentry, curbed by Cromwell and questioned altogether by some of his followers, was firmly re-established. The land question was settled by declaring that lands confiscated during the Commonwealth should be given back, but that the sale of lands should be recognized. Many of the Cavaliers complained that they had sold their lands to pay fines for supporting the King's cause, and murmured against the Act of Oblivion and Indemnity saying that the King had passed an act of oblivion for his friends and indemnity for his enemies. The Parliaments of the end of the seventeenth century were kind to landlords, for they restricted the import of cattle from Ireland and corn from abroad and gave a bounty on corn exported from England. The landlords had to pay a land tax which was made heavy by the costly foreign wars of William and Anne, but though the victims might grumble, they paid, for on the whole they were prosperous.

The way in which one noble house, the Bedford family, built up its fortunes has been described from their family accounts and papers. William, fifth Earl and first Duke of Bedford, had at first supported Parliament in its quarrels with the King, but changed to the King's side at the beginning of the Civil War. Some of his London property was confiscated, but during the Commonwealth he lived quietly at Woburn Abbey building up his estates. At the restoration he paid £43. 12s. 6d. for a Pardon for anything he might have done contrary to 'His Majesty during his Majesty's absence', and he carried the cap and coronet at the Coronation. His clothes, coach, and equipment cost well over £1,000. He paid 2s. to two labourers for spreading gravel on the street in front of his house in the Strand. For the next forty years he built up the family fortunes, adding to the family estates, investing in the draining of the fens, and collecting the rising rents of his property in Covent Garden. His sons were brought up by a tutor of Puritan sympathies. One of them, William Russell, was an early member of the Whig party, and, less cautious than his father, was beheaded for a plot against Charles II. The Duke arranged the marriage of his grandson to the granddaughter of Josiah Child, the most prominent member of the East India Company. It was by one or all of these methods, care and increase of estates, investment in city property and alliance with the banking and merchant families that the great landlords managed to grow stronger and richer. The connexion with trade explains their interest in the Navigation laws and such government committees as the committee on Trade and Plantations.

Not all the landlords were great and powerful, and we get from some writers a picture of the smaller country squire, talking only of dogs and horses or making some 'old family jests that fell to him with his estates'. Some might rise in the world through holding a Court office and some might sink through extravagance or careless management of their estates, but for the most part the country gentry continued to live quietly on their lands. As Justices of the Peace they administered the harsh game laws that had been passed by the Cavalier Parliament, which forbade even many freeholders to kill game on their own land. This was to preserve it for sport, and although shooting was driving out hawking it was just as disastrous for the yeoman or the farmer, who wanted to kill for the pot. An amiable and idealistic portrait of a country squire at the end of the century is given by Addison in his portrait of Sir Roger de Coverley. He is typical of his age in that he is a good churchman and persuades his tenants to worship in a more seemly fashion by providing each of them with a hassock and Prayer Book. The squire and the village parson ruled the village between them, and their alliance, which lasted through the eighteenth and nineteenth centuries, still survives in some places.

The two largest classes in England at the end of the seventeenth century, according to Gregory King, who made a list from the returns of those who paid the hearth tax, were the 'cottagers and paupers', and the 'labouring people and out servants'. These were particularly badly off where they had no land at all, not even a garden, or the right to graze a cow on the common fields. Then they were completely dependent on wages fixed by the Justice of the Peace, or on the Poor Law. By the Settlement Laws any landless man could be sent back to his own parish, and this was frequently done in case he should become chargeable to the poor rate. The staple diet of the poorer classes was bread and beer, though in the north they had a great variety of oatcakes and porridge. King says that most families, except the very poor, ate meat twice a week. These were the people, the very poor, who later suffered so greatly when in the eighteenth century they lost their remaining rights to land through enclosures and by sheer want were driven into the towns and factories.

Conditions of land and people were different in the many counties of England, but travel to see them was not easy. The town lady might step into her sedan chair, and the rising man would save up for a coach as did Mr. Pepys and his lady, but if one wanted to send goods to the provinces they had to go by barge on the rivers or more slowly by pack horses. Individual travellers had to go on horseback, and it was in this fashion that a notable woman, Miss Celia Fiennes, rode round England at the end of the seventeenth century and left us a picture of it. Miss Fiennes travelled for pleasure and for her health. She did not know of the benefits of sea air, but she thought that it was both fashionable and good for her to drink the waters at what she called 'the Spaws'. She found Tunbridge Wells very convenient and the people anxious to please the visitors. At Bath elaborate precautions were taken when the ladies entered the baths so that no portion of their anatomy was seen. They wore yellow calico bathing suits, had guides to lead them in the bath, and as they came out their maids had to fling over them night-gowns made of flannel. The water at the King's bath was not very pleasant, however, and smelt like egg water.

Celia Fiennes was the granddaughter of Lord Saye and Sele, who was one of the Puritan leaders in the Civil War, and was known as 'Old Subtelty' by his enemies. She naturally, therefore, took an interest in the Puritan cause and makes a note of all the dissenters' (or nonconformists') meetings that she found. Dissenters were numerous in the eastern counties; Colchester, Norwich, Bury St. Edmunds are spoken of as towns that are full of them. In the west country, at Cullompton, 'I was glad to see so many tho' they were of the meaner sort, for it is the poor that receive the gospel'. In the north, at Rochdale, she found a good large meeting-place, for 'religion doth better flourish than in those places where they have better advantage'. In Coventry, where she was struck by the flourishing character of the town, she made a joke about the supremacy of the dissenters. 'Of their magistrates and compaynes the majority of the heads are now in sober men's hands so it is esteemed a Fanatick town', but she approved of the mutual tolerance of the Presbyterians and Independents there, for though 'they may differ in small things, in the main they do agree and seem to love one another'. She herself was not so tolerant of the Quakers, whose meeting she described as 'in confusion and so incoherent that it very much moved my compassion and pitty to see their delusion and ignorance'. The Quakers had, in fact, grown in numbers, and they finally settled down to become a highly respected religious group. From this picture of the religious sects in the provinces we can supplement the town picture of tolerance or cynicism in religion, and the village obedience to Anglican squire and parson.

Although Celia Fiennes described in detail the historic buildings of the past that she visited, her own taste lay in new things. She liked the stone-and-brick façades of her own day, and such signs of improvement as the piped water of Norwich and Coventry. She describes the newly enclosed fields that she saw and the products of the newer industries such as the teapots of Staffordshire and the Manchester cotton tickings. Cloth-making was still the main industry, and she describes its usual domestic organization, how it was run by capitalist clothiers, who gave out the raw material to cottage workers at each stage, although sometimes workers might be collected in a small factory. She was surprised to find her supper cooking over a furze bush in Cornwall, for the forests were exhausted in that area and it was not easy to transport coal there. But she found coal being used from nearby cuttings in Wigan and Staffordshire, or brought from the coal areas of South Wales and the north to many adjacent districts. The impression she gives of its growing use is borne out by modern research, which shows that the production of coal increased fourteenfold from the middle of the sixteenth century to the end of the seventeenth century. It only increased twenty-three-fold in the nineteenth century. The workers in the mines and levels were regarded as less than human, and nowhere was there so great a barrier between master and man.

Eventually Celia Fiennes came to London and saw the coronation of Queen Anne, as Pepys had seen that of Charles II. She compared it with the coronation of William and Mary, who had both walked under the canopy because 'they were jointly set on the throne', while Anne had to summon her consort, George of Denmark, to dine with her in Westminster Hall.

The seventeenth century ended with the last Stuart monarch on the throne. The country, on the whole, was prosperous, its riches rooted in the land, but with a deep interest in foreign trade. Its craftsmen were skilful, its moneyed men were seeking new outlets, adventurous minds were preparing inventions. England was on the eve of those industrial changes which were to alter the face of the land, the life of the people, and the system of government so fundamentally that we are still working out the consequences.

16. Education

THE Renaissance was at work in many directions during the whole of the Tudor and Stuart periods, driving men to explore not only new lands but new realms of knowledge, new ways of worship, and new ideas of government; and naturally it had a powerful effect on education. Indeed, its beginnings had been called the New Learning by those scholars who rediscovered the fascination of the Greek language and of the knowledge and ideas unlocked for them when they had learnt it.

During the Middle Ages the education given to people, if they got any at all, had been a training specially suited to their class and to the life they would lead when they grew up. The sons of gentlemen were trained in chivalry and all that it involved, which meant much knowledge of and practice in the arts of fighting and hunting, and some in music

HEADPIECE. A horn-book of Stuart times with (right) a prayer in French written by Elizabeth I at the age of 12 and manners. For them reading and writing were not essential: it was far more desirable to be able to decipher heraldic bearings and understand coats of arms. Their sisters were trained in housekeeping and the management of servants, together with 'work', which always meant needlework, and accomplishments like singing and dancing. Those who were to earn their living as craftsmen or merchants were trained for seven years as apprentices in all the secrets and mystery of their trade and, because it was necessary to their job, they usually learnt to write and cast accounts. Others, who were to live a monastic life, went to schools for novices attached to a monastery or convent. But it is quite wrong to think of such schools as places where anyone who liked could go and receive an education. They were usually very small establishments and were supposed to be for novices only, though in special circumstances a few children might attend them who had no thought of taking the monastic vows. But even so such children were not likely to stay for long, for the education provided was not a general one; it was specially designed as a training for Holy Orders.

As time went on, and as the New Learning spread, and more and more books became available because of the printing-press, popular ideas about education began to change. The growing occupations of trade and law and statecraft demanded at the very least the ability to read, write, and keep accounts, and these professions were becoming more attractive and profitable. By the reign of Henry VIII it was no longer true, as it had been in the Middle Ages, that many of the high-born of the land despised learning. A father who could say 'I swear I would rather that my son should hang than study letters' was very much out of date. Justices of the Peace, though in their hearts they might care more for horses and hounds than books, at least had to be able to read the instructions that arrived so frequently from the Royal Council, and to draft the regulations and orders dealing with their multifarious duties. Thus the gentry were compelled to go to school.

A great variety of schools had grown up. They ranged from 'Seinte Maries College' at Winchester, founded by William of Wykeham as early as 1382 for '70 poor and needy scholars', to very much smaller schools which gave a little very simple instruction.

Two of the oldest schools in London were St. Anthony's in Thread-

needle Street, where Thomas More went as a small boy of seven, and
St. Paul's, which was refounded in 1509–12 by John Colet with the
special intention of spreading the New Learning, that is, the study of
purer Latin and of Greek, which had not been taught at all in medieval
schools. The first headmaster appointed by Dean Colet was William
Lily who, by order of Henry VIII, wrote a Latin grammar for use in
all grammar schools. The Paulines of Lily's day and all other schoolboys of the sixteenth century still concentrated on Latin, with Greek an
addition. They possessed very few books of their own, and because of
this they had to learn by heart not only the rules of grammar but long
passages of literature, which was very hard work. Master Lily did not
only write textbooks for his pupils, he gave them a great deal of advice
as well. 'Leave your bed betimes in the morning. Shake off soft sleep,
humbly go into the church and worship God. But first let your face be
washed and your hands, let your garments be clean and your hair
combed.' Boys, he said, must have a knife, quills, ink, paper, and books.
They were to write without blots and careless mistakes, and only in
their books, not on odd scraps of paper. School hours were very long,
usually from 6 a.m. till 5 p.m. with two breaks, for breakfast at 9
o'clock and dinner at noon.

The general upset of the Reformation had a bad effect on education
in England. Although there are today a considerable number of schools
called after Henry VIII or his son, many more were closed down than
were opened during their reigns. Probably neither of them intended
this, but the expense of government and, in Henry's case, of war, prevented them from being generous to education, and scores of schools
abruptly ceased to function. A good many of the grammar schools had
been reopened by the reign of Elizabeth I, often because some important
nobleman or wealthy merchant had promised to support a school out
of his own wealth if it were granted a charter to open. So, for grammar
schools, the setback was only a temporary one, and William Harrison
wrote at the end of Elizabeth's reign that there were few corporate towns 'now under the Queen's dominion that have not one
grammar school at the least'. These schools had a wide variety of
pupils, including children of yeomen, tradesmen, and merchants as well
as of the gentry. For there was as yet no strong feeling among the upper

classes that they must send their children to particular and select schools, although Winchester and Eton were already famous. Shrewsbury, founded in the reign of Edward VI, was very popular with the great families of Wales and the north. The Lord President of the Council of Wales sent his son there—young Philip Sidney—first giving him plenty of good advice. 'Be humble and obedient to your master, for unless you frame yourself to obey others, yea and feel in yourself what obedience is, you shall never be able to make others to obey you.'

All classes of people shared a common view of children, that 'a childe is a man in small letter'. They dressed them as immature adults, and believed that the sooner they acquired the knowledge and manners necessary for adult life the better. It was expected that for most of them education would be a painful process, and there was no attempt to make it pleasant, but it was accompanied with considerable severity and many beatings. Of course there were infant prodigies like Lucy Hutchinson, who attended closely to sermons at the age of four and then questioned her friends about the contents, and the much-loved son of John Evelyn the diarist, who could read English, French, and Latin at two and a half, knew all Aesop's fables and several propositions of Euclid at four, and died at the age of five. But these were exceptions.

Many children complained of the severity of their parents. Lady Jane Grey was afraid to speak in front of hers, and they reprimanded her sharply for every small fault. No doubt Sir Thomas More was thought ridiculously soft because he allowed his children to learn the alphabet by shooting arrows at the letters arranged round a butt, and never beat them at all except in fun and with peacocks' feathers. Jane's tutor, Roger Ascham, was far in advance of most teachers of the time, for he believed that people should be 'allured to attain good learning and not driven to it by beating', and he always dealt gently with Jane and with his other illustrious pupil, the Princess Elizabeth.

Long before children were old enough to go to school or to have a tutor—for many wealthy families preferred to educate their boys and girls at home—they had to learn to read. Almost as soon as a small creature could stagger about the house a horn-book was hung round his neck. This was a card on which was written the alphabet, a series of numbers, and the Lord's Prayer. It was mounted on a thin piece of wood shaped like a battledore, and covered with transparent horn to keep it clean and clear. It was quite light in weight and could be used for learning or at playtime for hitting a ball or a shuttlecock. The Lord's Prayer was usually finished off by a cross, and so the last line was known as the 'criss-cross row'. It was often copied by girls in their embroidery and can sometimes be seen in old samplers. From the hornbook the children could pass to proper books, though probably only a few possessed their own unless their parents were wealthy. The first Duke of Bedford gave a Bible, a Catechism, and a Book of Common Prayer to all his children as soon as they could read.

At home, while the children learnt their letters from the horn books they played with them as well, but at school no provision was made for organized games or sport, and it would have been unthinkable to find them included in the time-table as they are today. In fact the only instructions a sixteenth- or seventeenth-century schoolboy received about games was a list of those which he could *not* take part in. For although at Harrow the boys learnt archery and their parents had to supply bows, bowstrings, and a bracer, and in a few schools wrestling and leap-frog and the ancestors of fives and cricket were allowed, in most they were strictly forbidden. Schoolmasters did not concern themselves with games. When work was over they would simply say 'Go your ways and play, go', as Sir Hugh Evans did in *The Merry Wives of Windsor*, and probably think no more about it.

On the other hand, acting and speechmaking were considered important. At Westminster School plays were performed regularly—as they, of course, still are—and at Eton Master Nicholas Udall, head-master from about 1534 and the 'greatest beater' of his time, was very keen on theatricals and himself wrote plays for the boys to act. He was the author of *Ralph Roister Doister*, one of the first of English comedies, which became very popular with audiences far beyond the walls of his school. Latin orations, however, were more common than plays, and John Evelyn went to hear the boys of Westminster competing for scholarships to the universities by making speeches in Latin. He admired the speeches but did not think the boys would remember what they had learnt by heart for the occasion.

Girls were usually educated at home. They had their horn-books,

THE ROYAL GRAMMAR SCHOOL AT GUILDFORD ABOUT 1550

learnt to read and to write a little, and were trained by their mothers in housecraft and behaviour. Some went to petty schools where these existed, and some even to grammar schools such as Christ's Hospital. When Celia Fiennes was travelling round England at the end of the seventeenth century she noticed one or two girls' schools of good reputation. At Shrewsbury she wrote, 'Here is a very good schoole for young gentlewomen for learning work, behaviour, and musick'. By 'work', of course, she meant needlework. A few of these establishments reached a high standard, and Henry Purcell wrote his opera *Dido and Aeneas* for a girls' school in Hackney, but they were very few and only open to the daughters of the well-to-do.

Sometimes, but very rarely, girls received an education as good as their brothers, so that, like Margaret More in the sixteenth century, they even delighted the scholars who visited the house; and Dorothy Osborne in the seventeenth century could write most elegant and thoughtful letters. But most girls were skilled only in household affairs. Many, like Mistress Pepys, did not know how to occupy their leisure time, and at the end of the seventeenth century the lack of serious education for young ladies was blamed for their frivolity and their tendency to gamble away their fortune—if they had any.

Whether the sons of the upper classes were educated by tutors at home or at school, it was usual for their studies to be completed by a course at the university, by learning law at the Inns of Court, or by foreign travel. All through the period boys went to the university much earlier than they do today—fifteen was a very usual age—and they were closely looked after by their Tutors, who were usually Fellows of the college at which the young scholars were entered. The Tutor advised the young man as to his studies, read with him, and kept the parent in touch with his progress by correspondence. Sometimes these letters were complimentary, as when Robert Hogge of Corpus Christi College, Oxford, wrote to Richard Oxinden about his son Henry, 'the map and epitome of yourself, your hopeful sonne, who will be as well heir to your virtues as your possessions'. But sometimes they were not, for after a letter from the Tutor, Sir Edmund Verney wrote to his son 'Mun' to find out why he had cut some lectures, and added a list of the reasons why he should not do such a thing again. A Tutor's duties often included the management of his pupil's pocket-money and attendance upon him when he was sick.

In the Middle Ages poor scholars had been common in the universities, but in the sixteenth and seventeenth centuries there were far fewer of them, and it was said that 'there be none now but great men's sons in colleges and their fathers look not to have them preachers'. In fact, by the seventeenth century the university was looked on by some families as a road to advancement in many professions, and even if it did not lead directly to an official Court position it provided some of the training not only for the Church but for medicine, law, and for commerce, and certainly for a teaching or secretarial post in some great family. Yet poor men could easily obtain tuition in return for waiting at table or performing some other domestic task, especially in Scotland. The Provost of Queen's College, Oxford, wrote to Sir John Lowther telling him that his son, who was to be entered as a gentleman commoner, should not bring any servants with him to the University, for he could be waited on by a poor gownsman who would also help him with his studies. But Sir John himself already had in mind just such a poor scholar, probably a relation, to accompany his son to Oxford, and this arrangement which seems strange to us was accepted by the college authorities as quite usual.

Because the scholars were young, rules had to be made for their discipline, and this was an easier matter at Oxford or Cambridge than in continental universities, because it was usual in England to live in a college or hall of residence where rules could be more easily enforced. When Archbishop Laud was Chancellor of Oxford University, he made statutes for the whole body of undergraduates. He discouraged students from playing dice and cards, from frequenting houses where wine and tobacco were sold, or from hunting wild animals with hounds or ferrets. The hearty student, who played football and cudgel ball in the public streets, and the dandy who wore long curls, were equally condemned. Laud's proctors claimed the right not only to stop and question members of the University but also to search townsmen's houses and, as you can well imagine, this led to many disputes.

The Reformation brought about the end of the monastic houses at Oxford and Cambridge where monks had lodged for study. But new colleges such as St. John's, Cambridge, founded by the mother of Henry VII, Christ Church, begun by Wolsey and completed by Henry VIII, and the seventeenth-century foundations of Wadham and Pembroke in Oxford, rose all through the period. At the end of the reign of Elizabeth, Sir Thomas Bodley gave money to the University of Oxford to build the great library which is called after him. It was added as an extension to buildings given by Humphrey, Duke of Gloucester, at the end of the fifteenth century, which Sir Thomas had found in ruins with even the shelving taken away. Both the Bodleian Library and the Cambridge University Library have a copyright, which gives them the privilege of having a copy of every book that is printed in the kingdom. If you think of the number of new books they have to house each year today you will see that this is now a problem as well as a privilege. The colleges too began to build libraries of their own, such as the one built by Archbishop Laud in the beautiful Canterbury Quadrangle at St. John's College, Oxford, or the magnificent building designed by Wren for Trinity College, Cambridge.

SHERRIFFS

John Wintersgrace the First (I) proposes a loving-cup to Queen Elizabeth on her Coronation Day in 1559, to his son, John Wintersgrace the Second (II); his grandson, John the Third (III); his great-grandson, John the Fourth (IV) and to Mistress John the Third and her daughter Prue.

In 1588, John Wintersgrace the Third (III) takes leave of his grandson John the Fifth (V) before joining Drake's squadron in Plymouth Sound. His son John the Fourth (IV) is bound for the Army at Tilbury. Grandson John, who is enrolled in King Edward VI's new school at Christ's Hospital in the City, remains with his aunt and his tutor.

COSTUME CHRONICLE II

Both Oxford and Cambridge saw great changes in this period. In the sixteenth century both were torn with religious conflict. Latimer and Ridley were burnt in Oxford, while Cambridge was a breeding ground for advanced Puritans. In the Civil War, Oxford was the King's headquarters; Henrietta Maria had her Court in Merton quadrangle while Prince Rupert rode out on foraging expeditions from Magdalen tower. It was no wonder that the passion for Greek studies faded and the students began to assume the ways of the courtier.

If after going to Oxford or Cambridge a young man wished to become learned in the law, he became a student at one of the Inns of Court in London, for even if he had no thought of becoming a barrister, knowledge of the law was very useful for a future Justice of the Peace or in a family that might be involved in costly lawsuits, and probably as many men did this as went to the university. Sir Walter Raleigh liked to write himself down as a member of the Middle Temple, and Francis Bacon and the whole Cecil family were attached to Gray's Inn.

Foreign travel was another alternative, and sometimes boys were sent abroad after their university course and their law. Two of the sons of the Duke of Bedford were sent with their tutor to Saumur, a French university town, to learn the language. It is obvious from their letters that they were very bored there and urged their father to let them go to Italy. Eventually they were allowed to and then wrote home to say how much they preferred Venice to Rome, perhaps because they found a long awaited bill of exchange in Venice and were able to buy glass and lace to take back to their parents. Their travels were prolonged and their homecoming was actually much delayed because of Austrian wars with Turkey. Constant warfare and the disturbed condition of Europe was no doubt the reason why the Grand Tour did not become a regular part of a young gentleman's education until the eighteenth century. When it did it sometimes caused ill effects. The young men brought back expensive tastes and often were not content to settle down in the country to look after their estates. For instance, Edmund Verney returned to the family home at East Claydon in Buckinghamshire aged twenty-seven and wrote to a friend saying 'I hate rusticq matters'.

It should be remembered that for a long time after the Reformation schoolmasters had to be members of the Church of England. In

Elizabeth's reign the Archbishop of Canterbury ordered the clergy to inquire into the opinions of the schoolmasters in their parishes, to send in their names and to say whether any of them were 'known or suspected to be backward in the religion now established as the law of the land'. If Roman Catholics wanted their children educated in their own faith they had to send them abroad to Douai or St. Omer, thereby risking grave penalties. After the restoration of Charles II Protestant Nonconformists were forbidden to teach at all; if they were caught doing so they were fined £40. Yet somehow they managed to set up schools, one at Settle in Yorkshire, two or three in London, and others in Shropshire and Gloucestershire, and here, because they were necessarily outside the usual system, they could try out new subjects like natural science, and history, and geography, instead of concentrating entirely on classical studies and mathematics.

It is also important to remember that of all the books found in homes and places of learning the Bible remained the most common. In 1611 the Authorised Version had been published after years of hard work by some of the best scholars of the day, and its teaching and its beautiful language became part of the equipment for life of every man and woman. Not only was it written in the tongue which they daily used, but it became part of their personal belief and their hope, for most men's minds were less set on the present than ours are today. This was partly due, no doubt, to the fact that their expectation of life was short. The death-rate was high especially among children and young people —parents who wanted certain names handed on in the family gave them to several of their children—and this gave people a strong sense of the short and transitory nature of human life and made them think a good deal about the world to come. The Bible to them was indeed 'the most valuable thing that this world affords', in which they found wisdom, the royal law, the lively oracles of God and great comfort too in all their perplexities and troubles.

SHERRIFFS

17. The Struggle for Power, 1673–88

ALTHOUGH James, Duke of York, had been dismissed from his post under the Test Act, he was still the heir to the throne, for Charles had no legitimate son. This was a most alarming prospect for many people and particularly for Shaftesbury, who had made himself so odious to James that he could expect little mercy when he became king. His mind worked very like Northumberland's in the reign of Edward VI, but instead of persuading the King to alter the succession, he hoped to get Parliament to set aside James in favour of his sister Mary, or else the Duke of Monmouth—an illegitimate son of Charles II, who was very much under Shaftesbury's thumb.

Charles II, easygoing as he was over many things, could not tolerate this, and he took great pains to keep on good terms with Parliament. He made no more attempts to help the Roman Catholics, and he chose

HEADPIECE. The Rev. Titus Oates in 1678, from an unsigned portrait as his minister a staunch Anglican, the Earl of Danby. He had some anxious moments when some members, alarmed about French successes on the Continent, tried to persuade him to go to war with France; but he kept them quiet partly by bribing them with offices and pensions and partly by proroguing Parliament. For Louis so strongly disliked the possibility of England fighting for the Dutch instead of against them, that he paid out another £166,000, and Charles was in pocket again. Shaftesbury almost despaired of doing anything, but he began to build up a party called first the Country party, and later nicknamed the Whigs.

In 1678 Shaftesbury at last got his chance to make serious trouble for the King and his brother. There arrived in England a squat, bull-necked clergyman called Titus Oates, with a loud harsh voice, and narrow eyes deeply set in an enormous head. He had already changed his religion three times, ending up in a Jesuit College in Spain, from which he had been expelled for vice. He was in every way a most unpleasant man. Oates declared that he had found out details of a vast Roman Catholic plot to murder the King, place James on the throne, land a French army, and massacre all the leading Protestants. It sounds rather far-fetched but there was a grain of truth behind the story, for James, with his usual folly, had held a secret meeting of Jesuits in his rooms at Whitehall, and his secretary had been writing letters to the French Court; but when Charles questioned Oates he twice caught him lying, and the whole tale was so wildly exaggerated that little attention would have been paid to it if one or two curious things had not happened which seemed to bear it out. A well-known London magistrate to whom Oates told the story was mysteriously murdered, and it was taken for granted that the Catholics had killed him because he knew too much. Soon afterwards, on Oates's information, James's secretary was arrested, and letters were found which seemed to show that a plot existed. After this nobody dreamed of doubting the story, and the country was thrown into a panic. Men went about armed for fear of Popish murderers, and for a short time Oates was treated as the saviour of the country. He kept up his position by accusing more and more people of taking part in the plot. Scores of innocent people were arrested on his evidence, and many were executed without any attempt at a fair trial. Soon Danby himself was accused of being in the pay of France, and the Commons demanded his impeachment. Charles II was afraid that his own dealings with France would come out at the trial, so in order to prevent it taking place, he at last dissolved Parliament.

Shaftesbury and his supporters had done all they could to work up the panic about the 'Popish Plot', and had used it to unite the Anglicans and Nonconformists, who for a time forgot their own quarrels in their hatred and fear of the Catholics; so the Whig or Country party had a big majority in the newly elected House of Commons. They at once proposed an Exclusion Bill, to prevent James from coming to the throne. Charles dissolved Parliament before it could become law. He believed that if he bided his time the general excitement would die down. He was right, and when things were calmer the party which supported Charles began to grow. It was called at first the Court party, but later known as the Tories. Meanwhile Charles was so short of money that another Parliament had to be called. This time the Exclusion Bill passed the Commons but was narrowly defeated in the Lords, and it looked as if Charles would have to give way after all; but at this point Louis XIV again took a hand. He had been quite glad to see England in confusion and disorder, and had been able to go on with his plans in Europe without interference, but he did not want things to go too far, for if the Whigs got control, England might turn against him. In 1681 he made one more secret engagement with Charles, offering him enough money to make him independent of Parliament for the rest of his reign. The next time Parliament met (this time at Oxford, where Charles had summoned it so as to be away from Shaftesbury's supporters, the London mob), Charles, with Louis XIV's money behind him, promptly dissolved it.

By this time the effects of the Popish Plot were wearing off. People began to realize how they had been tricked and how near the Whigs had come to plunging them into another civil war. Once the fear of the Catholics had died down, the Anglicans recovered all their old dislike of the Nonconformists, and the Tory party grew steadily stronger. Charles soon felt that he was strong enough to attack Shaftesbury, who was arrested on a charge of treason; but he could only be tried in London, where he was still so popular that no jury would convict him, and

SHERRIFFS

The fifth John Wintersgrace Ⓥ with his wife; his two sons, John the Sixth Ⓥ and Henry and daughter Peg in the year of the Stuart Accession.

On February 2nd 1626
John Wintersgrace the Fifth attends
the Coronation of King Charles I ⓐ and in 1627 he goes to the Siege of La Rochelle ⓑ.

COSTUME CHRONICLE III

he was acquitted. In 1682 the Whig lord mayor, aldermen, and sheriffs were replaced by Tories, and even London ceased to be safe for the Whig leaders. They formed a desperate plot to murder Charles as he came back from Newmarket, and make Monmouth king. An ambush was planned, at a place called the Rye House, on the Newmarket road, but the plot was betrayed, and the conspirators were arrested. Shaftesbury had already fled abroad, where he died in 1682, while some of the other Whig leaders were executed.

For the last years of his reign, Charles had peace. The power of the Whigs was broken, apparently for good, and he had no need to summon another Parliament. His skill and shrewdness had not only saved the throne for James, but even made him quite popular in contrast to the Whigs. Loyalty to the King was again in fashion, and Tory parsons and squires proclaimed that it was a sin for a subject ever to resist the King, whatever he did. Charles did not enjoy his triumph for long, for he fell ill in 1685 and knew he had not long to live. Almost his last act was to send for a priest, and to be formally received into the Roman Catholic Church: twenty-four hours later he died.

Charles II had tried to do two things—to rule independently of Parliament, and to free the Roman Catholics. In the end he had achieved the first, but only by giving up the second. James II was less unscrupulous but also less intelligent, for he failed to learn from experience. Misled by the enthusiasm of the Tories when he came to the throne, he did not realize till it was too late that their hatred of the Roman Catholics was even stronger than their loyalty to him. They had welcomed his accession, because they hoped that his religion would be only a personal matter, and would not affect how he governed. As soon as he showed that he meant to make the country Catholic they turned against him. In fact it only took him three years to lose the throne which Charles II had so carefully saved for him.

James was a solemn, sincere, and earnest man, without any of Charles's shrewdness or good nature. He started with much in his favour. Parliament voted him a larger income then his brother, he could count on the support of Louis XIV if necessary, and he had inherited a useful army, which Charles had built up quietly during the last two years, and which gave James a permanent armed force such as no king had ever had

RECRUITS FOR 'KING' MONMOUTH

before. It was soon needed, for the Whig exiles made a last attempt to put Monmouth on the throne. Monmouth landed in Dorset, where he had always been popular, and where there were many Nonconformists to support him. He soon had an army of about 5,000 men, but most of them were poor countrymen, with no military training, and without proper weapons. James's army moved west to meet them, and a battle was fought at Sedgemoor, near Bridgwater, in July 1685. Monmouth's men fought very bravely but they stood no chance against regular troops, and they were soon routed. Monmouth himself escaped from the battle, but he was caught soon afterwards. James, who hated him, ignored his appeals for mercy, and had him beheaded. A fierce revenge was taken on the rebels. Many were executed at once on the orders of military courts, and others were imprisoned and tried by the Lord Chief Justice, Judge Jeffreys, who went down to the west on purpose to deal with them. Jeffreys sentenced more than 300 people to be hanged, and 900 more were shipped off as slaves to the West Indies. When he returned to London he was promoted to be Lord Chancellor.

The failure of the rebellion convinced James that he had nothing to fear, and encouraged him to go ahead more quickly with his plans, but he made it an excuse to raise the army to 30,000, and he concentrated more than half of them in a large camp on Hounslow Heath, near London, where they would be near at hand if they were needed. Some of the soldiers were Roman Catholics from Ireland, and James began to appoint Roman Catholic officers, in spite of the Test Act. He claimed that he had the right to dispense with—or set aside—the law in individual cases, and the judges backed him up. He went on to appoint Roman Catholics to the Council, to the Universities, and to offices of every kind. In 1686 he even revived the Court of High Commission, and used it to spread Roman Catholic teaching in the Church itself.

The Anglicans watched all this with dismay, and they soon received a terrible warning from events in France. Louis XIV had so far allowed a good deal of religious freedom to the Huguenots, who had long since ceased to be a danger, and were some of the most hard working and prosperous of his subjects, but in 1685 he deprived them of their rights and deliberately set out to convert them by force to the Catholic religion, or else wipe them out. Every form of torture and cruelty was used to make them change their faith. They were forbidden to leave the country, but some thousands made their escape to Britain, and the tales of what they had suffered revived all the old hatred and fear of the Roman Catholics. James saw that the Anglicans were beginning to turn against him and tried to win over the Nonconformists, as Charles II had done, by a Declaration of Indulgence; but they were not taken in, and both they and the Anglicans protested against it. When James gave orders that it was to be read out in all the churches, the Archbishop of Canterbury and six other bishops said that it was against their consciences to do so, and asked him to withdraw the order. James was furious at having his orders questioned, and ordered the bishops to be arrested on a charge of 'seditious libel'. The whole nation waited anxiously for the verdict, and when the Court found the bishops not guilty there were rejoicings all over the country, even among James's own troops on Hounslow Heath.

James had made himself hated, but people still hesitated to rebel. For one thing, at the age of fifty-five, he was not likely to live very long, and the heir to the throne was a Protestant. James had married twice, and his first wife, Clarendon's daughter, had borne him two daughters. They were both Protestant, and the elder one, Mary, had married William, Prince of Orange, the ruler of Holland, and the greatest enemy of Louis XIV. When his first wife died James married again; his second wife was a Roman Catholic, but so far she had had no children, so it seemed just a question of holding on until James died. But in 1688 the whole position was changed by the birth of a son, who would certainly be brought up as a Roman Catholic. England was faced with the prospect of a whole line of Catholic kings. This was the turning-point, and eight of the chief men of the kingdom, including both Whigs and Tories, sent a message to William and Mary inviting them to come over and claim the throne.

William had no wish to take over the thankless task of ruling England, but he had been working for some years to build up a Protestant alliance strong enough to check Louis XIV. He badly needed England's support, and this was his chance to make sure of getting it. He promised that he would allow religious freedom to all, Protestants and Catholics alike, but that he would enforce the Test Act and prevent Catholics from having any share in the government. He also insisted that he must be accompanied by a Dutch army, in case the English troops remained loyal to James. Even so, William could not leave Holland as long as it was threatened by the French. Louis XIV saw the danger James was running into and offered to attack Holland, so as to keep William at home; but James foolishly refused his help. After that, Louis left James to fend for himself; he probably thought that William's expedition would start a civil war which would keep both Holland and England harmless for some time to come, so the French army was sent not against Holland but into Germany, and William's expedition sailed.

William landed at Torbay on 5 November 1688. James's army was ordered to concentrate at Salisbury to resist him, but many of its commanders deserted to William, among them John Churchill, who had played an important part in the defeat of Monmouth, and who later became the Duke of Marlborough. Without their leaders, the English troops put up no resistance, and William advanced steadily towards London. James, who had been hesitating what to do, lost his nerve. He sent his wife and son out of the country, and soon afterwards he hurriedly fled to France. This made things much easier for William, for the Tory idea of loyalty to the King was so strong that if James had promised to give up his religious policy and stayed in England, the Tories would still have supported him. As it was, William could claim that James had abdicated by his flight, and that Mary was legally Queen of England.

In February 1689 Parliament met, and began to discuss the terms on which the country should be ruled. William, for his part, was content to leave the details to them, so long as he had full powers to use England's strength against Louis XIV. Neither side had any liking for the other, and the settlement they produced was simply a bargain. The Tories still clung to their loyalty to the King, and suggested that William and Mary should rule as regents for James II, or failing that, that Mary should be queen and William govern only in her name; but William firmly refused to become legally a subject to his own wife, and insisted on being king. In the end it was settled that William and Mary should rule jointly, and a number of acts were passed fixing the conditions under which they should reign.

All the recent disputes between the King and Parliament were decided in Parliament's favour. The King had no fixed income for life, but all taxes were voted for a year at a time, which of course meant that Parliament had to meet every year. At the same time, no Parliament could last for more than three years without a general election, so that no king in future should be able to imitate Charles II, and keep the same Parliament in power for eighteen years because it suited him. The power to set aside laws, which both Charles II and James II had claimed, was now abolished. Finally a Toleration Act was passed, which allowed freedom of worship to Protestant Nonconformists, but did not permit either them or the Catholics to hold any government post. The 'Glorious Revolution' as it is sometimes called, was a real turning-point in English history. William was made king not by inheritance, and still less by Divine Right, but by Act of Parliament; and from then onwards it was really Parliament, not the King, who governed England.

18. Scotland, Ireland, and Britain beyond the Seas

SCOTLAND

WHILE England was settling down to the firm rule of the Tudor kings, Scotland remained in turmoil and disorder, under the unlucky royal house of Stuart. Of the five Jameses who ruled Scotland from 1406 to 1542, all but one died by violence, and all but one inherited the throne as children, so that their reigns began with a regency. Conditions were like those in England during the Wars of the Roses. The barons made themselves practically independent, and they and their retainers carried on quarrels and feuds quite unchecked. Moreover, Scotland was very

HEADPIECE. John Knox, a composite drawing based on three contemporary portraits

229

poor. There were few towns and little trade, and many of the people lived near the edge of starvation, struggling with a cold wet climate, and stony infertile fields. But however disunited and poor the Scots might be, they had always, since the days of Edward I, been the enemies of England and the friends of France. Scotland had gained little from this alliance, for the English kings did all they could to weaken her, either by open war or by encouraging the Scottish barons against their king. Even when the two countries were officially at peace, each made raids across the border, robbing, burning, and driving off cattle.

Life, even in the more civilized parts of Scotland, was therefore hard; and it was harder still in the Highlands, which had no central government at all. The Highlanders lived in clans, each ruled by its own chief. All the members of the clan had the same surname, wore the same tartan and were kinsmen of each other. They regarded their chief not only as their ruler, but as the head of the family, and they were brought up to obey him, serve him, and die for him if necessary. Bitter feuds raged between the clans, and were carried on from one generation to another. It was chiefly this that prevented the Highlanders being more of a danger to the richer and more civilized Lowlands. But if ever the clansmen could be persuaded to forget their quarrels and unite, they would make a formidable army, for they were fit, hard, and fearless, and brought up to a life of hardship and danger.

James IV (who became King of Scotland in 1488, when his father 'happenit to be slain' in a baronial rising) and Henry VII of England both wanted to end the wars between their two countries. Peace was made by James marrying the Princess Margaret, Henry's daughter; but it did not last long. James IV was rash and impulsive, and when Henry VIII went to war with France in 1512, he went back to the old French alliance and invaded England. In 1513 the Scottish army was shattered by the English, under the Earl of Surrey, at Flodden. James IV himself was killed, together with many of his nobles. He was succeeded by his son James V, who was less than two years old.

For the next fifteen years, Scotland was again governed by regents, but in 1528 James V took charge himself. He married a French princess, Mary of Guise, a devout Roman Catholic whose relatives were very powerful at the French Court, and in this way the alliance between

Scotland and France became stronger than ever. It soon led to new quarrels with England, and in 1542 a Scottish army was surprised and defeated at Solway Moss. James was already a sick man when the battle was fought, and the news of it hastened his death. He lived just long enough to know that his daughter had been born, then 'he turned his back to his Lords, and his face unto the wall' and died.

James V's daughter, Mary, was thus Queen of Scotland almost from her birth, and her mother governed for her, supported by troops from France. Her task was difficult enough, but it was made harder still by the beginning of the Reformation in Scotland. The Scottish Church was in a far worse state than the English Church had been. Much of the best land belonged to bishoprics and monasteries, and men were appointed to church posts without any pretence that they were fit to hold them. A relative of James IV had been made Archbishop of St. Andrews at the age of thirteen, and many of the higher clergy were just like the other barons: an archbishop and two bishops had been killed fighting at Flodden. This kind of thing partly explains why the Protestant Reformation spread so quickly. But another important reason was that, as in England, many people became Protestant in the hope of spoiling the Church of its wealth. When the clergy sentenced some Protestants to be burnt to death as heretics, their friends retaliated by murdering the Archbishop, and a rebellion broke out, encouraged by the preacher John Knox, and led by the Protestant 'Lords of the Congregation'. We have already seen how Elizabeth helped the Protestants, and how the French were driven out of Scotland, and we have traced the tragic career of Mary Queen of Scots.

After Mary's flight to England, Scotland was governed by a regency on behalf of her son James VI, who was strictly brought up as a Protestant. There was still a Roman Catholic party among the barons, which supported Mary, but the Protestant lords managed to keep control. In 1585 they made a close alliance with England and from then onwards, although Elizabeth never said so publicly, it was understood that James should become King of England on her death. James realized how important it was for him to keep Elizabeth's friendship, and although he made a show of protesting when his mother was executed, and even uttered threats of war, he did not really mean anything serious—as

Elizabeth knew very well. When he was old enough to take over the government of Scotland himself, he did what he could to stop the quarrels of the barons, and improved the courts of justice. He also revived the custom of holding Parliaments, rather on the English model: but, as in England, most of the governing was done by the King and his Council. By 1603 when he became James I of England as well as James VI of Scotland, he had established his authority firmly, and hoped to gain control of the Church as well.

The Protestant Church, set up by Knox and his friends, was strictly Presbyterian, and governed itself through its own Church Assembly. James knew from his own experience how tyrannous and intolerant it was, and he did not feel that he would be really king until he had mastered it. He was a shrewd and persevering man, and he gradually worked the Assembly round to accepting bishops, appointed by the King, although they had much less power than the bishops in England, and James did not interfere with the plain and simple services which the Presbyterians liked. Charles I was not so wise as his father. James only wanted a Church governed by bishops ('Episcopacy' as it was called) because it strengthened the King's authority, but with Charles it was a matter of conscience. He thought Episcopacy was the only right form of Church government, and that it was his duty to enforce it. He angered the barons by trying to claim back for the Church the lands which had been taken from it, and in 1635, and again in 1637, he gave orders that the Scots should have the same kind of services as Archbishop Laud had already imposed on England.

Even in England, many people thought Laud's form of service too like that of the Roman Catholics, and in Presbyterian Scotland it was regarded as plain 'popery'. The first attempt to use the new service book caused a riot, and the Scots, led by the nobles, banded together to resist. A National Covenant was drawn up, which thousands of people signed, pledging themselves to resist any changes in religion not approved by their own Church Assembly. When the Assembly met, it refused to accept any changes in the service, and passed an Act abolishing bishops altogether; and the Scottish Parliament backed it up. These events led to the Bishops Wars, which forced Charles to summon the English Parliament, and this, in turn, led to the outbreak of the Civil

War. Just before the fighting began, Charles paid his last visit to Scotland and tried to win Scottish support. He agreed that the Scots should keep their Presbyterian Church, but they still did not trust him, and the only important noble who came over to his side was the young Earl of Montrose.

At first, as you know, Scotland took no part in the Civil War. The Scots were not interested in the King's quarrels with his English subjects, but they were very anxious to defend their religion, and they did not think that it would ever be really safe until England was Presbyterian too. So when, in 1643, Pym offered to set up a Presbyterian Church in England in exchange for Scottish help, they agreed to the Solemn League and Covenant, and sent an army to help the Roundheads. Scottish soldiers played an important part in winning the Battle of Marston Moor, in 1644; but while they were fighting in England the tables were suddenly turned in Scotland.

Charles I had made Montrose a Marquis, and his Lieutenant in Scotland, and Montrose now raised the royal standard in the Highlands. He was as good a general as Cromwell, and he had the knack of dealing with the Highlanders. He managed to unite a number of the clans, and a small force from Ireland, and with this army he set out to conquer Scotland for the King. Although he had no artillery, and hardly any cavalry, he very nearly succeeded. Most resistance could be expected from the Campbells, the strongest clan in Scotland. Their chief, the Earl of Argyll, was the greatest of the Scottish nobles, and a personal enemy of Montrose. The Campbells were bitterly hated by their neighbours who had many ancient wrongs to avenge. Early in 1645 Montrose led his troops into the Campbell country, burning and plundering, and utterly defeated Argyll at Inverlochy. Later he stormed Aberdeen and Dundee, defeated three Lowland forces which were sent against him, occupied Glasgow, and led his men almost to the English border. But he was too late to save Charles who, a month earlier, had been defeated at Naseby. The Scots were now able to use their main army against Montrose, and in September 1645 his forces were shattered at the Battle of Philiphaugh. Montrose himself escaped, but no mercy was shown to his followers, and many, including the women who had followed their husbands to the wars, were massacred.

The end of the war brought new problems for the Scots. They had only entered the Civil War because the English Parliament had promised to set up a Presbyterian Church in England. But Parliament was quite unable to keep its promise, for the real power now rested with Cromwell and the army, and they objected to a Presbyterian Church just as much as to bishops. As the Parliament failed them the Scots actually turned again to the King, and made a treaty called the 'Engagement' by which they agreed to restore him to the throne in exchange for his promise to give Presbyterianism a three years trial in England. This led to the second civil war, and the defeat of the Scots at Preston in 1648. The strictest Presbyterians, including Argyll, had never really approved of the Engagement, and after the battle Argyll made himself master of Scotland. He made peace with Cromwell, entertained him at Edinburgh, and agreed to prevent those who had fought for the King from holding any office in Scotland. But the execution of the King a few weeks later changed everything. It horrified the Scots, who immediately proclaimed Charles II king, but made it a condition that he must sign the Covenant. Charles II, who thought Presbyterianism no religion for a gentleman, wanted to avoid doing so if he could, and hesitated before finally agreeing. But an attempt by Montrose to make him king without conditions failed. Montrose was captured and executed by his old enemy Argyll, and Charles had to agree to Argyll's terms, and sign the Covenant. He landed in Scotland in the summer of 1650.

Charles II had the difficult task of combining Presbyterians, who had fought against his father, with Royalists who had fought for him, and they naturally distrusted each other. A month after Charles landed, Cromwell, who, on his return from Ireland, had hurried north to deal with this new Royalist threat, crossed the border. The Scots had to depend on the only army they had, a force from which all who had fought for the King were excluded—among them many of the best soldiers in the country. Cromwell failed in an attempt to take Edinburgh, and the Scots had an excellent chance of destroying his army. But they threw away their opportunity by risking a battle in unfavourable conditions, and Cromwell defeated their army at Dunbar. After this, even Argyll saw that the Scots could not win unless they forgot their differences and worked together. A new army was raised, this time including the ex-Royalists, and it was this force that Charles led into England, only to be pursued by Cromwell and destroyed at the Battle of Worcester—the 'crowning mercy' as Cromwell called it—in 1651.

After that, the Scots could do no more. In less than four years they had raised three large armies, and each in turn had been defeated by Cromwell. Scotland was occupied by English troops under General Monck, one of Cromwell's subordinates, and was governed by a committee of English officials and judges. On the whole, they did their work well, and Scotland, for the first time in many years, had a period of peace and good order. When Cromwell became Protector in 1653, the Scottish and English Parliaments were united, and Scotsmen enjoyed the same trading rights as Englishmen, so that the country became more prosperous. But the Scots hated the loss of their independence, and the taxes they had to pay to support the army. So when, after Cromwell's death, General Monck, who had himself become a Royalist, withdrew the army of occupation and used it to restore the King, Scotland also proclaimed Charles II.

The Scots were so glad to regain their independence and their king that at first they denied him nothing. The Scottish Parliament gave Charles all the powers his father had claimed. Charles had no intention of keeping his promise to safeguard the Presbyterian Church, and before long he again appointed Scottish bishops. Most Scotsmen were tired of religious strife, and accepted the new arrangement quietly, but some of the extreme Presbyterians, who were especially strong in the south-west, would not be satisfied with anything less than a completely Presbyterian Church. About 300 ministers resigned rather than submit to bishops, and their congregations would not accept the new ministers who replaced them. They refused to go to Church, and met in lonely places in the hills, where their banished clergy continued to hold services.

The government determined to suppress these men, who were called the Covenanters. Heavy fines were imposed for not going to Church, and troops were sent to collect them by force. The Covenanters were soon in open rebellion. They brutally murdered the Archbishop of St. Andrews, and raided Glasgow, but their forces were soon scattered by troops under the Duke of Monmouth at Bothwell Bridge in 1679. In spite of their defeat, the Covenanters went on resisting, and the accession of the Roman Catholic James II made things worse. Argyll, who had fled abroad at the Restoration, came back to Scotland in the hope of raising a Presbyterian rebellion, but he was captured and executed, and the Covenanters were persecuted more fiercely than ever.

In 1688 James fled from England, and the English crown was offered to William and Mary. The Scots also accepted William, on condition that Episcopacy was again abolished. William, who wanted all the support he could get, and had no strong feelings about bishops, agreed to their terms. After one brief attempt by the Catholic Highlanders to restore James II, Scotland settled down under the new king, and the Presbyterian ministers returned to their parishes. England and Scotland were again independent countries, and there was very little love between them; but the wisest men on both sides of the border were beginning to see that they had much to offer each other. By 1707 the majority on both sides were willing to sink their differences, and agree to the Act of Union, which made England and Scotland into the United Kingdom of Great Britain.

IRELAND

'The King of the Saxons, namely Richard, was slain in battle, and the son of the Welshman was made King. And there lived not of the race of the blood royal at that time but one young man, who came, on being exiled the year after, to Ireland. And in the beginning of harvest was fought the battle.' In these words an Irish historian, writing in 1485, described the Battle of Bosworth, the accession of Henry Tudor, and the rebellion of Lambert Simnel; and the detached way in which he writes about it all is a reminder how little England and Ireland had to do with each other at this time. To the Irish, the accession of the first Tudor was only a mildly interesting event in the history of a foreign country. Yet, when 'the Welshman's' granddaughter died Ireland was part of the English kingdom.

Ireland had never been conquered and settled, as England had been by the Normans. In the Middle Ages English kings called themselves Lords of Ireland, but they had held the island as vassals of the Pope, who claimed to be its overlord, and they had little real power there. In the twelfth and thirteenth centuries a number of English barons had been given leave to go over and take what land they could from 'the King's Irish enemies' as the Celtic Irish were called, and they had succeeded in conquering great estates for themselves in eastern, southern, and south-western Ireland. They had to do homage to the King of England for their lands, but they never took this very seriously, and many of them married Irish wives, and adopted Irish dress and customs. The most powerful of these barons (who may be called Anglo-Irish) were the FitzGeralds, Earls of Kildare, and the Butlers, Earls of Ormonde, who were practically independent rulers. The only part of Ireland which was really under the King's control was the district round Dublin, known as the Pale.

Beyond the Pale, and the estates of the Anglo-Irish barons, the country was inhabited by Celtic clans. Each had its chieftain, and, when one died, his successor was elected by the clansmen from his relations. It was not necessarily the eldest son who was chosen, as in England, but the best warrior; for the main duty of an Irish chief was to lead his clan in battle, and the clans were ceaselessly fighting each other. Thus for centuries the Celtic part of Ireland was in even greater confusion than England during the Wars of the Roses. An Englishman wrote in 1509

There be more than 60 countries called 'regions', inhabited by the King's Irish enemies, where reigneth more than 60 captains that liveth by the sword; and every captain maketh war and peace for himself, and obeyeth no other person, either English or Irish, except only such persons as may subdue him by the sword. Also there is more than 30 great captains of English noble folk [the Anglo-Irish] that followeth the same Irish order.

When the Tudors had made themselves masters of England, their first step was to break the power of the Anglo-Irish barons—especially the Earls of Kildare. By 1540 this had been done, partly by what Henry VIII called 'sober ways, politic drifts, and peaceable persuasions' and partly by force.

Henry VIII, when he no longer accepted the authority of the Pope, declared himself King of Ireland. The Celtic Irish chieftains were persuaded to surrender their lands and receive them back from Henry as their overlord; at the same time they promised not to keep private armies, and to adopt English law and customs. Many of them received lands from the Irish monasteries, which Henry VIII dissolved, and with them the title of Earl (for example Con O'Neill, the great Ulster chieftain whose ancestors had been High Kings of Ireland, became Earl of Tyrone).

For a time this seemed to succeed, but trouble soon began again. For one thing, English law treated men like the Earl of Tyrone as the actual owners of the land, which on the father's death, was inherited by his eldest son. But by ancient Irish custom the land belonged to the whole clan. The chief only had a life interest in it and when he died the clan chose his successor. Thus there were endless disputes about succession to the Irish earldoms which often led to civil war, and the country was soon as disturbed as ever. The other cause of trouble was religion. Neither the Anglo-Irish nor the Celtic Irish had objected to Henry's denial of the Pope, but it was different when Edward VI tried to make Ireland Protestant. There were very few Protestants in the country, and the Act of Uniformity could not be enforced. On the other hand, the French, who hoped to use the Irish against England, did what they could to encourage the Roman Catholics, and the accession of Mary Tudor encouraged them still further. Elizabeth I got an Irish Parliament to accept her Church settlement, but was quite unable to enforce it. A strong force of Jesuit missionaries from the continent of Europe worked hard in Ireland, and it remained a Roman Catholic country.

As the danger from Spain grew, it became more important than ever to keep Ireland under control, and Elizabeth's attempts to do this led to two serious rebellions both helped by Spain—one in Munster and one in Ulster led by the Earl of Tyrone. The Munster rebellion dragged on for four years because Elizabeth could not afford a strong enough army to deal with it properly, but by 1583, when almost the whole province had been laid waste, the fighting came to an end. Great areas of land were taken from the rebels, and sold cheaply to Englishmen who undertook to 'plant' it with English settlers. But the country had been so ruined by war that Englishmen were not at all keen to settle there. The 'undertakers', who wanted a quick profit, let the land instead to Irishmen, who promised to pay them high rents, but hated them bitterly as usurpers, and were always on the look-out for a chance to regain ownership of it themselves.

The Ulster rebellion broke out in 1598. Hugh O'Neill, the Earl of Tyrone, formed an alliance of Ulster chieftains, and succeeded in defeating the English Deputy or Governor. After this, the revolt spread quickly, and soon only the Earl of Ormonde's lands and the towns of the Pale remained in English hands. A new army was sent over under the Earl of Essex, but he found the situation quite beyond him, and this failure led to his downfall. Lord Mountjoy, who succeeded Essex, was a very able soldier, who avoided battles, but gradually wore O'Neill down by laying waste the land, and setting up garrisons at key points to cut off his supplies. In 1601 a strong force of Spanish troops managed to land in southern Ireland, but Mountjoy defeated them and their Irish allies at Kinsale. After this, the rebellion began to fail, although fighting dragged on till 1603, and O'Neill at last surrendered six days after Elizabeth's death.

The rebel leaders, the Earls of Tyrone and Tyrconnel, were not badly treated by James I. They were allowed to keep most of their land, but they lost their independence. They were so dissatisfied that in 1607 they left Ireland, taking with them many of their loyal followers. The flight of the earls gave James an opportunity to 'plant' Ulster, as Elizabeth had planted Munster, only he was able to do it more thoroughly. Most of those who had held land under the earls were deprived of it, and their places were taken by Puritans from England and the Lowlands of Scotland. The Catholic Irish were either driven out of Ulster, or got new masters of different race and religion whom they hated bitterly.

For the next twenty years, Ireland was neglected and misgoverned; but in 1633 Charles I, who was then trying to rule without a Parliament, and was very short of money, sent over Thomas Wentworth to restore order and, if possible, to raise some money from the country. For seven years Wentworth gave Ireland more efficient government than she had ever known before. He cleared the coast of pirates, who

SHERRIFFS

Roman numeral VII in circle

Roman numeral VII in circle

At the outbreak of Civil War in 1642 the sixth John Wintersgrace (VI), dressed in satin, lace and velvet decides for King Charles. Brother Henry, in linen and leather chooses Parliament. John the Seventh (VII), with his mother and sister Sukie, looks on.

Roman numeral VII in circle

Roman numeral VI in circle

Roman numeral VIII in circle

John Wintersgrace the Seventh (VII) with his family, is greeted in 1680 by his father, Old John (VI), in the Dutch Mode of his exile with King Charles II. His son and grandson (VIII) wear the new "frock" coat.

COSTUME CHRONICLE IV

had been using Ireland as a base from which to attack English shipping, and built up a strong army which was regularly paid. He saw that the laws were enforced, and he encouraged the linen trade. But his only object was to make Ireland useful to England, so he stopped the wool trade, which might have become a rival to England's, and he took every chance to replace Irish landowners by Englishmen: he planned indeed to plant Connaught like Munster and Ulster.

Wentworth did what he set out to do, which was to keep Ireland quiet and to raise money, but he made many enemies. As long as he was there, he held them in check, but as soon as he was recalled to England they seized their chance. All over the country the Irish rose in rebellion. The new settlement of Ulster was, for the time being, practically wiped out, and many of the settlers were killed. It was this revolt which, in 1641, finally brought to a head the quarrel between Charles I and his Parliament, and the Civil War broke out in the following year. Ireland was left to its own devices while Cavaliers and Roundheads fought each other in England, and it was not until seven years later, after the beheading of Charles I, that Cromwell was able to deal with the rebellion. He had a formidable task, for the Earl of Ormonde, a faithful royalist, had succeeded in uniting almost the whole of Ireland, Catholic as well as Protestant, against him.

In 1649 Cromwell landed with a strong army at Dublin, determined to crush the Irish rebellion once and for all. He was usually a merciful man, but he showed no mercy to the Irish, whom he thought treacherous savages. When his troops stormed Drogheda he 'forbade them to spare any that were in arms in the town. And I think', he wrote, 'that that night they put to the sword about 2,000 men. I am persuaded that this is a righteous judgement of God upon these barbarous wretches.' Cromwell himself only stayed in Ireland for a few months, but his generals, Ireton and Ludlow, carried on his work. The Irish rebels were crushed, but only after several years of merciless struggle. About a third of the population died in the fighting, or from famine and disease.

Nearly two-thirds of the land was taken from the Irish, and given to soldiers who had fought in the war, or to bankers who had lent the money to pay for it. Cromwell hoped that a big English population would settle in Ireland, and did all he could to encourage Englishmen to go there. The two countries were now united. M.P.s represented Ireland at Westminster, and all the restrictions on Irish trade were removed. But in spite of all this, Cromwell's plan failed. The discharged soldiers did not want to settle in a foreign country, ruined by war, and most of them promptly sold the land they were given and went home. Army officers and wealthy merchants bought the land—often very cheaply—and became the owners of great estates in Ireland. They did not live on their estates, but they needed men to work them, and, as there were no English available, they had to accept Irishmen. In this way Ireland became a country governed, and mostly owned, by English Protestants, but inhabited by Irish Catholics who were forbidden to practise their religion, and were compelled to pay high rents for the right to use the land which they considered their own, and which had been taken from them.

The restoration of Charles II made little difference to this state of affairs, for most of the Cromwellian landlords were allowed to keep their Irish estates, but it did end the union between the two countries. Ireland again had its own Parliament, but it only represented the Protestant landowners. The freedom of trade between England and Ireland was abolished, for fear that Irish merchants might become rivals to the English: even the export of cattle to England was forbidden for fear of its competing with English farming. The Roman Catholics had rather more peace under Charles II, who did not believe in persecution, but they had no real freedom. For this reason, Catholics supported James II when he was trying to restore the Roman Catholic Church in England: and when this led to the revolution of 1688, and James was driven out of England, it was to Ireland that he looked for help. The Irish Catholics rose to support him, but were again crushed, this time by William III at the Battle of the Boyne in 1690. At the beginning of the eighteenth century Ireland was ruled by a small number of wealthy Protestant landlords, while three-quarters of the population, desperately poor, and without rights or freedom struggled to make a living from small patches of land, for which they had to pay heavy rents, and which they lacked the tools or the skill to farm efficiently.

BRITAIN BEYOND THE SEAS

THE great pioneers of exploration and colonization in Tudor times were, as you know, not Englishmen but Spaniards and Portuguese or men who, like Columbus, worked for Spain or Portugal. The voyages of the Cabots were followed up only when the English, finding themselves blocked from the great prizes of the New World by Spain, and from an easy passage to the East by Portugal, began to devote their energies, first, to the attempt to find a north-west or north-east passage to India and Cathay, and then to the plunder of the Spanish treasure fleets. Colonization formed at first no part of the explorers' plans and when the idea of making settlements was first put forward, these were seen merely as stopping places on the way to the East, such as Goa on the west coast of India, or starting-points for the search for gold.

It was towards the end of the reign of Elizabeth that the first serious projects for colonial settlements were undertaken, for at this time English merchants were anxious to find new markets overseas for their goods. The two greatest enthusiasts were Sir Walter Raleigh and his half-brother Sir Humphrey Gilbert. In 1578 Gilbert received a patent from the Queen. This was an open letter telling all who might read it of the instructions she had given him, 'to inhabit and fortify any barbarous lands not actually in the possession of any Christian sovereign'. After a completely unsuccessful voyage in 1578, Gilbert set sail again in 1583, and formally took possession of Newfoundland in the name of the Queen and in the presence of fishermen of many nations. He then proceeded to explore the coast of Nova Scotia intending to plant a colony, but fogs and storms and faint-heartedness amongst the crews caused him to return. Not only was this project a failure but Gilbert himself, returning home in the little frigate *Squirrel*, was drowned. Raleigh now began to back expeditions to settle on the more southerly part of the North American coast. He did not himself accompany the colonists but raised funds and secured the patents, the ships, and the crews. In 1584 two small ships were sent by way of the Canaries and the West Indies to the coast of what is now called Carolina, but which the leaders took possession of in the name Virginia, a name that referred, in the reign of Elizabeth, to the whole coast from Cape Cod to Florida.

As the climate and vegetation seemed suitable for colonization and the Indian tribes friendly, Raleigh sent a larger expedition out in the next year under Sir Richard Grenville. A party landed on Roanoke Island and agreed to remain and explore the territory while Grenville returned home for further supplies. It seems clear that these men were not prepared in any way for the hard work of starting a pioneer settlement. They still hoped for quick returns by finding gold, and very unwisely they quarrelled with the Indians. Before Grenville could return they had either died of hardship or had accepted an offer made by Drake to take them home. After this Raleigh sent other groups of colonists, in 1587, for instance, a group of 150, but they never succeeded in establishing themselves partly because of their own unreal view of the situation, partly because, while the nation was at war with Spain, it was not easy to organize regular supplies to them by sea.

The colonists of the reign of James I did not easily abandon dreams of finding gold and the fabulous city of El Dorado, but they gradually learnt to make more provision for the practical difficulties of settlement. What were the problems that faced a pioneer? First there was the necessity of providing equipment, which Captain John Smith, one of the leaders of the first successful settlement in Virginia, estimated would cost £12 per head; this included clothes, tools, arms, household implements and some food such as meal, pease, oil, and vinegar. Then there was the hardship of the Atlantic crossing in a ship of perhaps 300 tons— the *Queen Mary* is about 80,000 tons—a crossing which took eight weeks or more. Those who survived the voyage had to face the danger of an unknown harbour, native peoples who might or might not be friendly, and the immediate necessity of finding shelter and growing food. Shelter was usually in the form of a log house, built in the first clearing of the virgin forest. It might have a bark roof and bark shutters for doors and windows. Food was either caught or grown from seed brought from home, or better still, from Indian corn seed, suitable to the climate. This was the background of the first settlements.

In 1606, two years after the signing of peace with Spain, a Royal Council of Virginia was formed to administer any settlements that might be founded, although a great deal of independence was given to the separate companies, such as the London Virginia Company or the Massachusetts Bay Company, who financed the expeditions under the general supervision of the Privy Council. Without the backing of the wealthy men who invested in these companies the colonies could not have been started, but of course such men did not do the pioneering work themselves. The Royal Virginian expedition set off in 1606 with orders to find a healthy spot by a navigable river. A navigable river they found, but their settlement upon it at Jamestown (1607) proved to be swampy and fever haunted, and in the first years the colonists went through the most terrible privations. It was only after their reluctant acceptance of very severe discipline, and the discovery that tobacco growing might bring prosperity even if the idea of finding gold disappeared that they began to make headway. They were helped too by more regular supplies from England than had been possible in the war-filled days of Elizabeth, and by the fact that their leaders were brave if ruthless men. Captain John Smith may have been telling a romantic story when he described his rescue from death in the nick of time by Pocahontas, the beautiful daughter of chief Powhatan, but by some means or other he managed to preserve reasonably good relations with the Indian tribes in the first years. By 1635 Virginia had 5,000 inhabitants and two years later the tobacco output was as much as 500,000 lb.

Virginia was not the only colony established in the southern region of the North American coast in the early Stuart period. Maryland, on the northern shores of Chesapeake Bay, was another, but unlike Virginia it was founded by the initiative of a single family, the Calverts, whose home was Kipling Hall on the borders of Yorkshire and County Durham. In the reign of James I George Calvert was a member of Parliament and a secretary of state, and James gave him the title of Lord Baltimore as a reward for his services. But because he was a Roman Catholic he resigned his position on the council and began to plan a colony in America where freedom of worship would be possible. He first established a small settlement in Newfoundland but the harsh climate soon drove the colonists home. In 1634 George Calvert's son, the second Lord Baltimore, made another attempt farther south, this time successfully. The colony was named Maryland after Queen Henrietta Maria and its chief town was called Baltimore after the founder. Maryland provided a refuge for Roman Catholics who in

England could not openly worship according to their beliefs. In this it resembled the Puritan settlements but was much more tolerant than they were, for from the first the Baltimores admitted and in fact welcomed people of religious beliefs differing from their own. Socially and economically it resembled its neighbour, Virginia, for its inhabitants took to the cultivation of tobacco on landed estates which were first worked by indentured servants and later by negro slaves imported from Africa. The first consignment of these negroes arrived in the colonies of the mainland in 1619.

Before the final establishment of Maryland, the first Puritan Colony appeared in New England. In 1608 a band of Puritan refugees had left England for Holland and made their temporary home in Amsterdam and Leyden. They found it difficult to earn a living in Holland, however, and finally made an agreement with the Virginia company to settle in the New World. They sailed from Delft to Southampton in a little ship called the *Speedwell*; there they were joined by others and in 1620 the whole band of the Pilgrim Fathers, as they came to be called, crossed the Atlantic in the *Mayflower*. Instead of landing in Virginia as they had intended, they were set ashore near Cape Cod at a point which they called Plymouth. 'Thus they arrived at Cape Cod', says the writer of *New England's Memorial*, 'and being brought safe to land, they fell upon their knees, and blessed the God of heaven, who had brought them over the vast and furious ocean, and delivered them from many perils and miseries.' Before they finally chose a place of settlement 'they sounded the harbour and found it fit for shipping and marched into the land, and found divers cornfields and little running brooks . . . at least it was the best they could find and the season and their present necessity made them glad to accept it'. On Christmas Day they began to build the first house for common use and storage, and some small cottages. Their sufferings in that hard American winter were terrible. Of the 100 people who landed, only fifty survived till the spring, but the Pilgrim Fathers were determined to survive or perish for the sake of the land in which they would be free to practise their own religion as they wished.

The Pilgrim Fathers were followed in 1630 by a richer and more powerful group of Puritans who founded the colony of Massachusetts.

This new colony became the largest on the coast and soon absorbed the pioneer settlement at Plymouth. Its government enforced a rigid observance of its own strict religious code and anyone who differed in any way from the majority had to go elsewhere. This intolerance led to new offshoots of the Massachusetts colony at Connecticut, New Haven, Rhode Island, and Maine. The number of Puritans who crossed the Atlantic increased all through the reign as Archbishop Laud attempted to get uniformity in the Church of England. Between 1630 and 1643 20,000 men, women, and children crossed to New England in 200 ships. They were content to become farmers, fishers, and merchant seamen for they had abandoned the Elizabethan dream of finding gold. Many citizens of the United States like to trace their descent from these first settlers who braved the hard pioneering conditions of New England to keep their political and religious freedom.

All the colonies established some kind of representative assembly resembling the English Parliament, although laws concerning their trade were settled in England, as we shall see. They also imported many of the traditions of English local government. The southern colonists were more aristocratic and tended to imitate the English country landlords, while the more democratic conditions of the English village and small town were mirrored in the New England township and court house. The two groups of colonists took different sides in the Civil war. The Southern colonists declared for the King and recognized Charles II after his father's execution, while the New Englanders on the whole supported the Commonwealth. But the issues became rather remote to the people beyond the Atlantic and there were already signs of the isolationism which has always been one side of American political life.

Maritime enterprise and colonial rivalry have often been the cause of wars in which England was involved. This was already so in the sixteenth and seventeenth centuries. It was one factor in the long rivalry of Elizabethan England and Spain; the story of which is told in Chapter 6. In the reigns of James I and Charles I the two countries were at peace, but Cromwell threw in his country's lot with France against Spain. The chief colonial gain was Jamaica; it was thought of, at the time, as an unimportant island, but it proved a source of great wealth when its sugar and coffee industries were developed. But already, in the time of the Commonwealth, English merchants and statesmen began to see that the rival to be feared by them was not Catholic Spain but Puritan Holland. The Dutch had become the great carriers of the world's trade, and this was resented by English traders both in war-time, when they might carry the goods of the enemy under a neutral flag, and in peace-time, when they might earn profits by carrying colonial goods, which, it was argued, should be carried in English ships. In 1651 Parliament passed a Navigation Act which forbade the import into England of goods from the Continent unless they were carried in English ships, or those of the country that produced the goods, and forbade the import of goods into England, Ireland, and the Colonies, from Asia, Africa, and America unless they came in English, Irish, or Colonial ships. In a way, the Act did not begin a new policy for it was usual for the government to take measures to encourage English shipping. All European statesmen in the seventeenth century believed that there was only a limited amount of trade and so if one country got more others got less. This was called the mercantilist theory of trade.

The Act of 1651 was the chief cause of the first Anglo-Dutch War which lasted from 1652-4. The naval engagements may be said to have ended in a draw, but the Dutch agreed to abide by the Navigation Act. Certain matters concerning the saluting of the English flag in the Channel and freedom for the Dutch to fish in the North Sea, were also agreed on. But the struggle was not settled by this peace and a further Navigation Act, passed in 1660, renewed the conflict. As far as colonial trade was concerned this was even more severe than the first, because, in addition to the clauses of the first act, it enumerated certain colonial goods which were to be imported only into England. These were the chief products of the colonies—sugar, tobacco, dye woods, cotton wool, indigo, and ginger. The view common in England at the time was expressed by a member of the East India Company, 'All colonies and plantations do endamage their mother Kingdom whereof the trades of such plantations are not confined to the said Mother Kingdom by good laws and severe execution of those laws.' It was a view with which the colonies did not always agree.

The Dutch too had established colonies on the east coast of North America, which lay between the two groups of English colonies—New England in the north and Virginia in the south. As the result of the second Dutch war they were all handed over to the English. New Amsterdam (renamed New York), New Jersey, and Delaware became English colonies. Further settlements, too, were started from England in the reign of Charles II. The Committee of Trade and Plantations on which sat powerful men such as Lord Shaftesbury, a member of the Cabal, supervised the colonies after the Restoration. Many of these statesmen sponsored the settlement of the two Carolinas, and tried to encourage men from Virginia to go there, for they now believed that England was being robbed of sturdy citizens by emigration. John Locke, a famous philosopher who was Shaftesbury's secretary, drew up a very complicated constitution for South Carolina, but the colonists abandoned it when they got safely across the Atlantic. Charles II himself made a grant of land to the Quaker, William Penn, who established a colony called Pennsylvania for people who belonged to the Society of Friends. Penn's chief contribution to the early history of colonization is that he made a pact not to harm the Indians and succeeded in persuading his colonists to live peacefully with them. There was, however, a gradual fading of Quaker influence with unfortunate results for the Indians. No one could claim that the natives of the North American continent did not suffer eventually from the coming of the white man, and this we should remember, however many stirring tales are told about the struggles of settlers with cunning redskin chiefs. By the end of the seventeenth century, the English were in complete control of the Atlantic seaboard from Cape Cod to north of the Florida peninsula. The challenge to their power was to come in the next century neither from Holland nor from Spain, but from the string of French forts that cut off the road to the interior.

Rivalry with the Dutch in the seventeenth century was not confined to the West, for the two countries disputed the succession to the Portuguese settlements in the Indian Ocean. The merchants of both countries had formed themselves into companies to trade with the East. The English East India Company was formed in 1600, and the Dutch finally formed a United East India Company in 1603. To the Dutch, the attempt to wrest the trade of the Spice Islands from Portugal was part of their struggle for national independence against Spain, which at the time, was also in control of Portugal. By 1609, they claimed ownership of most of the East Indian Islands, and had no intention of allowing the English to share the spoils with them. The struggle between the two countries ended when a band of English merchants were executed at Amboyna in 1623 and James I was not strong or wealthy enough to offer any resistance. The incident rankled so much in England that Cromwell exacted compensation for the relatives of these merchants at the end of the Anglo-Dutch War of 1654. The failure to secure a footing in the Spice Islands made the English East India Company more enthusiastic about trading with the Indian mainland. At first the merchants only invested money for one voyage at a time, but as the Indian trade grew more certain they made their Company into a true Joint Stock enterprise in which they invested money until they chose to sell their shares to someone else.

Great merchant ships of over 1,000 tons were built for the Eastern trade and these proud East Indiamen brought saltpetre, raw silk, pepper and other spices, tea, coffee, and porcelain from India or the Far East. Trading stations such as Surat and Madras and, as part of the dowry of Catherine of Braganza wife of Charles II, Bombay, were established on the coast of India. Ambassadors were sent to the court of the great Moghul Emperor, under whom at the time most of the ancient and varied civilizations of India were unified. For the moment, the East India Company did not interfere in the politics of India except to secure trading stations, but the fact that the Dutch secured the chief part of the trade with the Spice Islands and that the English turned to the mainland was to affect the history of the next two centuries, down even to our own day.

REFERENCE SECTION

THE KINGS OF ENGLAND

1485–1509	Henry VII	
1509–47	Henry VIII	
1547–9	Regency of Somerset	*TUDOR*
1549–53	Edward VI	
1553–8	Mary	
1558–1603	Elizabeth	
1603–25	James I	*STUART*
1625–49	Charles I	
1649–53	Commonwealth	
1653–60	Protectorate	
1660–85	Charles II	
1685–8	James II	*STUART*
1688–1702	William and Mary	
1702–14	Anne	

		Kings of England
500	Romans leave Britain and Anglo-Saxon invasions begin	
543	St. Benedict *d.*	
597	St. Augustine *d.*	1485 Henry VII
632	Mohammed *d.*	1509 Henry VIII
664	Synod of Whitby	
	Danish invasions begin	
800	Charlemagne, Emperor	
871	Alfred, king of Wessex	
978	Ethelred the Redeless	
1016	Canute the Dane	1547 Regency of Somerset
1066	William I	
1085	Domesday Survey	1549 Edward VI
1170	Murder of Becket	1553 Mary
1215	Magna Carta	
1272	Edward I	1558 Elizabeth
1327	Edward III	
1338	Hundred Years War begins	
1348	Black Death	
1381	Peasants' Revolt	
1415	Battle of Agincourt	
1455	Wars of the Roses begin	
		1603 James I

1500		
1600	**PERIOD**	
1688	**COVERED BY**	
	THIS BOOK	1625 Charles I

1707	Union with Scotland	1649 Commonwealth
1714	George I	1653 Protectorate
1775–83	American War of Independence	1660 Charles II
1789	French Revolution	
1792–1815	Napoleonic Wars	
1837	Victoria, Queen	
1851	Great Exhibition	
1885	First motor-car	
1914–18	World War I	1685 James II
	League of Nations	
1939–45	World War II	1688 William and Mary
	U.N.O.	1702 Anne

252

CHART

Important Events in British History	*Other Contemporary Events*
1476 Caxton printing in London 1485 Battle of Bosworth	1452 Birth of Leonardo da Vinci 1492 Columbus crosses the Atlantic
	1516 Erasmus's New Testament 1517 Luther's 95 Theses
1529–36 Reformation Parliament 1534 Act of Supremacy 1535 More and Fisher executed 1536–40 Dissolution of Monasteries	1527 Sack of Rome 1540 Jesuit Order founded
1549 First Prayer Book in English Act of Uniformity	
1554 Mary marries Philip of Spain	1556 Peace of Augsburg
1563 Thirty-nine Articles	1564 Birth of Shakespeare Death of Calvin
1569 Northern Rising 1570 Elizabeth excommunicated	1572 St. Bartholomew's Eve massacre 1577 Drake sails round the world
1587 Execution of Mary Queen of Scots 1588 Defeat of the Armada	1598 Edict of Nantes
1600 East India Company founded 1601 Poor Law	
1604 Hampton Court Conference 1605 Gunpowder Plot	1607 Virginia founded
1611 Authorized Version of the Bible)	1618 Thirty Years War begins
1620 Pilgrim Fathers 1628 Petition of Right	1627 Birth of Robert Boyle
1642 Civil War	1632 Birth of Christopher Wren
	1643–1715 Reign of Louis XIV 1648 Peace of Westphalia
1649 Execution of Charles I 1652 First Anglo-Dutch war	
1660 Restoration 1661–5 Clarendon Code 1662 Royal Society receives Charter 1665–6 Fire of London, and the Plague	
1670 Secret Treaty of Dover	1667 Milton's *Paradise Lost*
1673 Test Act 1678 Popish Plot 1685 Battle of Sedgemoor 1687 Declaration of Indulgence	1685 Revocation of the Edict of Nantes 1687 Newton's *Principia*
1688 Act of Settlement	1694 Bank of England founded

INDEX

References in *italic* are to illustrations

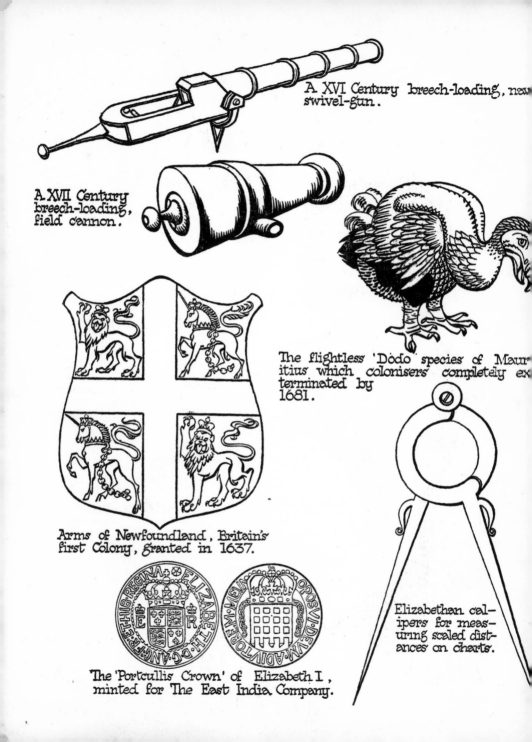

A XVI Century breech-loading, new swivel-gun.

A XVII Century breech-loading, field cannon.

The flightless 'Dodo' species of Mauritius which colonisers completely exterminated by 1681.

Arms of Newfoundland, Britain's first Colony, granted in 1637.

Elizabethan calipers for measuring scaled distances on charts.

The 'Portcullis Crown' of Elizabeth I, minted for The East India Company.